AUG. 3 0 1988

Dover Memorial Library
Gardner-Webb College
P. O. Box 836
Boiling Springs, N C 28017

D1112737

Edward Bond
Plays : Three

Bingo, The Fool, The Woman, Stone

This third selection from Edward Bond's dramatic work contains three full-length plays on Shakespearean themes, all first staged at major theatres in the 1970s, and one shorter play about oppression dating from the same period. Introducing the volumes are four pieces written by the author in the mid-1980s and appearing in print here for the first time.

Benedict Nightingale (*New Statesman*) on *Bingo* and its chief character, William Shakespeare: 'How is it (we're to ask) that a man whom we worship for his humanity could bear to live in a society we know to have been so cruel? How can we, his descendants, bear to live in a society directly derived from it? . . . It's a fascinating play . . .'

'In his superb new play, *The Fool*,' wrote John Lahr in *Plays and Players*, 'Bond attains a new theatrical maturity. Luring his audience into the robust and violent rural world of John Clare, the farm labourer turned poet, at the beginning of England's industrialisation in 1815, Bond creates a pageant of exploitation which demonstrates how imagination as well as manpower were victimised by the ruthless pursuit of profit.'

Martin Esslin (*Plays and Players*) on *The Woman*: 'It is not an easy play: it has to be pondered and thought about afterwards. But that very richness and density make it a great play. And it is the work of a real poet of the theatre: who thinks in entrances and exits, in ascents and descents of steps, in light raising to high intensity and fading, in the tension between groups of figures'.

EDWARD BOND was born and educated in London. His plays include *The Pope's Wedding* (Royal Court Theatre, 1962), *Saved* (Royal Court, 1965), *Early Morning* (Royal Court, 1968) for which he won the George Devine Award, *Narrow Road to the Deep North* (Belgrade Theatre, Coventry, 1968; Royal Court, 1969), *Black Mass* (Sharpeville Commemoration Evening, Lyceum Theatre, 1970), *Passion* (CND Rally, Alexandra Palace, 1971), *Lear* (Royal Court, 1971), *The Sea* (Royal Court, 1973), *Bingo* (Northcott, Exeter, 1973; Royal Court, 1974), *The Fool* (Royal Court, 1975), *The Bundle* (RSC Warehouse, 1978), *The Woman* (National Theatre, 1978), *The Worlds* (New Half Moon Theatre, London, 1981), *Restoration* (Royal Court, 1981), *Summer* (National Theatre, 1982), *Derek* (RSC Youth Festival, The Other Place, Stratford-upon-Avon, 1982), *The Cat* (produced in Germany as *The English Cat* by the Stuttgart Opera, 1983), *Human Cannon* published in 1985) and *The War Plays* (*Red Black and Ignorant, The Tin Can People* and *Great Peace*) which were staged as a trilogy by the RSC at the Barbican Pit in 1985.

EDWARD BOND
Plays : Three

Bingo
The Fool
The Woman
Stone

*with introductory material
by the author*

A Methuen Paperback

PR
6052
.05
A19
v.3

METHUEN'S WORLD DRAMATISTS

This collection first published in Great Britain as a paperback original in 1987 by
Methuen London Ltd., 11 New Fetter Lane, London EC4P 4EE and in the United
States of America by Methuen Inc., 29 West 35th Street, New York, NY 10001.

Printed and bound in Great Britain by
Richard Clay Ltd., Bungay, Suffolk

Bingo first published in 1974 by Eyre Methuen Ltd.
Reprinted in 1975 and 1979 by Eyre Methuen Ltd., and in 1984 by Methuen
London Ltd., and Methuen Inc.
Copyright © 1974 by Edward Bond
The Fool first published in 1976 by Eyre Methuen Ltd.
Reprinted in 1980 by Eyre Methuen Ltd., and in 1982 by Methuen London Ltd.
Copyright © 1976 by Edward Bond
The Woman first published in 1979 by Eyre Methuen Ltd.
Reprinted in 1980 with a new essay 'A Socialist Rhapsody'
Copyright © 1979, 1980 by Edward Bond
Stone first published in 1976 by Eyre Methuen Ltd.
Reset and revised edition published in 1981 by Eyre Methuen.
Copyright © 1976, 1981 by Edward Bond.
'The Little Grey Bonnet' copyright © 1911 by Chappell & Co. Ltd.
Reproduced by kind permission. Words and music by Lionel Monckton.
This collection and introduction © 1987 by Edward Bond

British Library Cataloguing in Publication Data

Bond, Edward
    Plays. —— (Methuen's world dramatists).
    3: Bingo, The fool, The woman, Stone
    I. Title
    822'.914   PRØ52.05

ISBN 0-413-33890-8

CAUTION

All rights whatsoever in these plays are strictly reserved and application for
performance etc., should be made to Margaret Ramsay Ltd., 14a Goodwin's Court,
St Martin's Lane, London WC2N 4LL. No performance may be given unless a
licence has been obtained.

This paperback is sold subject to the condition that it shall not, by way of trade or
otherwise, be lent, resold, hired out or otherwise circulated without the publisher's
prior consent in any form of binding or cover other than that in which it is published
and without a similar condition including this condition being imposed on the
subsequent purchaser.

Contents

Edward Bond
A Chronology

PLAY	First performance
The Pope's Wedding	9.12.1962
Saved	3.11.1965
A Chaste Maid in Cheapside (*adaptation*)	13.1.1966
The Three Sisters (*translation*)	18.4.1967
Early Morning	31.3.1968
Narrow Road to the Deep North	24.6.1968
Black Mass (*part of* Sharpeville Sequence)	22.3.1970
Passion	11.4.1971
Lear	29.9.1971
The Sea	22.5.1973
Bingo: Scenes of money and death	14.11.1973
Spring Awakening (*translation*)	28.5.1974
The Fool: Scenes of bread and love	18.11.1975
Stone	8.6.1976
We Come to the River	12.7.1976
The White Devil (*adaptation*)	12.7.1976
Grandma Faust (*part one of* A-A-America!)	25.10.1976
The Swing (*part two of* A-A-America!)	22.11.1976
The Bundle: New Narrow Road to the Deep North	13.1.1978
The Woman	10.8.1978
The Worlds	8.3.1979
Restoration	21.7.1981
Summer	27.1.1982
Derek	18.10.1982
After the Assassinations	1.3.1983
The Cat (*performed as* The English Cat)	2.6.1983
Human Cannon	(published 14.3.1985)
The War Plays	
Part I: Red Black and Ignorant	29.5.1985
Part II: The Tin Can People	29.5.1985
Part III: Great Peace	17.7.1985

Four Pieces

A Short Book for Troubled Times

Chapter 1   How Things Go Wrong

There is a danger that our government will go to war and that many people will be killed. What would cause this war? Obviously it would be caused by something going wrong.

There are two ways in which things go wrong.

The first way is this. Suppose you drive a car badly. There's an accident and you and others are killed. It isn't wrong to drive a car but it's wrong to drive it badly. That's the first sort of wrong. You put it right by learning to do something better – in this case, driving a car better.

This is the second way in which things go wrong. Suppose there's a tin with poison in it. You swallow the poison and die. There's no way in which you can learn to take poison 'better'! Take it with sugar or jam, you still die. If you want to live you mustn't take poison. That's the second way in which things go wrong. In this way, you can't put a thing right by doing it better.

Would the cause of a nuclear war belong to the first or second way in which things go wrong? Most people would say the first. There would be a war because we weren't kind or patient enough – or perhaps not angry and threatening enough! Or because we had too few bombs – or too many. Opinions about which would vary, but they'd agree it was like driving a car: do it right, get the mixture right, and you can go on doing it.

But really the cause of nuclear war would belong to the second sort of wrong. It would happen whether we're kinder or more aggressive, more patient or more impatient – surprisingly, in themselves these things make no difference. However you take the poison, smiling or frowning, you die.

This makes our situation very dangerous. We're doing something fundamentally wrong. If we don't stop doing it there'll be a nuclear war.

Clearly we should know what this thing is.

Chapter 2   How We Behave

First we need to understand something about ourselves.

We often think things go wrong because we behave badly. Instead of behaving as people ought, we behave (we're told) like animals – we're selfish and aggressive. War is seen as a final summing up of these bad things. Yet when war happens we don't call ourselves bad. It's only the enemy who are bad.

So we need to look closer at behaviour.

If I jump into a river and risk my life to save a child, I'm good. In war, airmen risk their lives to bomb cities and burn children to death. As both sides call their airmen heroes, what they do must be good. If a football hooligan with a bayonet ran wild among the enemy – that would be good, too. If I take money from your pocket without your permission, that's bad. But if I own a business which does well because others work for me, yet for every pound I give them I give myself 200 pounds – then I'm showing enterprise, which again is good. If I show equal enterprise and rob a bank, that's bad – although in earlier times, when owning a bank was called 'usury' it was regarded as very bad!

Of course I don't deny the important differences between these ways of behaving. Some of them defend society and others attack it. And I don't want to be robbed or beaten up. But the point to grasp is this: in all these examples 'human nature' remains the same. What decides if an action is good or bad is what society – rightly or wrongly – thinks about it.

So where does society get its ideas?

Chapter 3   The Real Question

Instead of asking about 'human nature' we need to ask about the 'nature of society'.

Obviously the ideas a society likes are those which allow it to go on existing. That's one reason why a society says it needs laws and justice, and why it divides people into criminals and judges, prisoners and police, voters and leaders.

But we may also ask 'Is society itself just?' This is a very old question and all societies have asked it or something very like it. Doing so could almost be regarded as the foundation of civilisation.

Yet when we look at all earlier societies we find that although some were better than others, none had the slightest claim to be called just – not the slightest! This is a disturbing thought. It makes us ask why our society should be any better? And whether it's right to destroy the human race for its sake?

In fact our society is very unjust. Think of the enormous injustices in the ways in which we distribute money, jobs, education, houses, status, power, cultural privileges – the full list would be very long.

What's more, if there's going to be injustice in any one of these things, *there must be injustice in all of them*! Otherwise the isolated injustice would stick out like a sore thumb, and no one could tolerate it. Injustices, like thieves, stick together.

Many people deny that these injustices exist. But when pressed they always end by defending them. That is important, because it's not only the critics of society who say that society is unjust – the ruling class say it. Indeed they insist on it! Only they call the injustices 'inequalities', and say that they are made necessary by the badness and weakness of human nature, and that without these inequalities society couldn't be properly run. The ruling class defends its privileges because it thinks that without it there would be chaos. Well that argument can be examined. I think the ruling class causes chaos by the way it rules.

An unjust society can't make sound judgements about people,

ideas, behaviour or anything else. You might as well expect a
burglar to break into your house in order to leave you his jewels!

Chapter 4   Know Yourself

There's an old piece of advice which says 'know yourself'. It's
meant to remind us that even when we're happy we may be
heading for trouble!

To 'know yourself' you must 'know your society'. Otherwise
you can't know the meaning of what you and other people do – or
where your actions are taking you.

The problem is that it's impossible for an unjust society to
'know itself'. Injustice distorts every scrap of knowledge and piece
of information it lays hands on. It has to do this to hide its own
traces – even from itself. It distorts the nature of the light by
which it sees things.

This has far-reaching consequences.

Chapter 5   Private and Public

We don't hold most of our ideas in a cold and abstract way. Most
of them are deeply mixed in with our emotions and passions. No
doubt they have to be.

Ideas are rather like clothes. Often someone else makes our
clothes and we choose them off the peg. But we become attached
to them and they're almost like another skin. The same is true of
our ideas. In fact 'authority' sometimes complains of what we
wear just as it complains of what we think!

Our ideas are mixed up with the way we meet our basic needs –
needs such as eating and getting money to live, relations with
neighbours and family, friendships and loving. Your job is a
'public thing', but think of how it effects your 'private life' – or
how the lack of a job effects it.

The private and public, and the ways we think and feel, are all so mixed up in us that they can't be separated. They're not as close as a cup and saucer, but as the cup and the mouth drinking from it.

Chapter 6   Who Owns You?

So our private and public selves are closely mixed. Yet we think we own and control our private self in a way we don't own and control our public self. We say thought is free. But freedom of thought is the most difficult freedom to get.

We may know what we want for ourselves. But our society also wants certain things from us, and these things must effect not only our public self but also our private self. They must even help to form our feelings.

But if society is unjust, it means that when it puts pressure on us to live – to behave, think and feel – in ways which are good for it, then that pressure must be unjust. It's unjust because it isn't meant to be of equal benefit to everyone in society, but to protect the power and privileges of those who own and rule it.

Remember that this pressure penetrates even our private, inner self. Some of the ways it does this are obvious, but some are hidden even from those they effect.

We should ask whether we're even right to call our feelings our own! Of course, we're the ones who have them. But perhaps they don't really express our own needs, but are more like something striking us from outside – in the way lightning does, say.

Or is it as if sometimes the rulers and owners could manipulate even our emotions, as if inside we were a puppet worked by strings? If that's so then sometimes it will happen that we think we're expressing our strongest, deepest personal feelings – when really we're being no more than someone else's dummy. That's one of the terrible consequences of social injustice. Our loudest shouts and gentlest whispers may be spoken by someone else.

I look at photos of ordinary soldiers marching to the front to die in the First World War. They are happily singing – but I wonder whose feelings they're expressing.

And I wonder whose feelings people are expressing when they vote for nuclear weapons. Would they go to the victims of these weapons – the innocent children and their families, all of whom would be burned – and with their own hands burn them to death with a blow torch? Would you? – all of them? If not, yet still you vote for nuclear weapons, then you are not expressing your own feelings when you make your vote, even though you call it democratic.

It isn't easy to 'know yourself', or to be yourself.

Chapter 7   What Are You Doing?

We've seen that when we try to act for the common good we may in fact be acting for the private interests of the rulers and owners. The results of our acts may be twisted.

Surely this denies us one of our most important ways of expressing our humanity: helping others? In an unjust society even kindness and generosity lose their meaning. Often they make us passive, unconscious supporters of injustice.

Let's look at a simple example. I'm sick and my neighbour helps me. He has the pleasure of being kind – and I get better. I thank him. But what if he is a racist or a warmonger? His kindness to me was real, and because I shared it with him he can claim that racism and kindness may go together. This isn't a trivial example. In the last war many extreme Nazis were also very kind. Being kind was important to them because it allowed them to believe that although they were Nazis they were also humane and civilised.

This contradiction still puzzles many people. But the explanation is simple: people shouldn't be judged by their feelings or emotions but by their ideas. Anything else is dangerous.

Let's look at a sadder example. In war we praise an airman for burning children to death. When he comes home and kisses his own children he's praised for being a good father. But how can he then live with his own thoughts and feelings – he must repress them. But if he does that, how can he know himself! Surely his life cannot make any sense? He has lost his humanity.

The tragedy is that an unjust society doesn't support itself by using only the worst in people – it uses the best in them! That's why it's so degrading.

When we try to fulfil ourselves by acting selflessly to help others, we deny our humanity by serving violence and fear. So our lives become meaningless and foolish. This creates conflicts in us. Soon what began as unease turns into confusion and tension and ends intolerance and anger. The compromises by which we try to live become the corruptions by which we die.

This is the way in which injustice trivialises society and makes it barbarous.

Chapter 8   500 Miles an Hour

We've seen how society destroys our inner well-being and causes contradictions and conflicts in our lives. But perhaps this injustice might still be acceptable – if, that is, it was needed to run society efficiently. So let's look at that.

One of the ways we differ from animals is that to live we need many machines. Is our technology dangerous? No, used with foresight it's a great benefit. It solves many ancient problems, and sets us free to live in new, happier ways. In fact it forces us to live in them. That's the trouble – because that brings us into new conflicts with the ruling class.

If I ride a bike and by mistake steer it at a brick wall – well, the wall's on the far side of the road and I have time to correct my steering so that I don't hit it. But what if I'm in a machine travelling at 500 miles an hour? I make the same mistake (my actions and my 'human nature' don't change) but there is a different result: I'm dead.

Our technology is so powerful that we should think of the whole of society as being in a machine travelling at 500 miles an hour. What happens when the rulers steer it at a brick wall? We're all dead. That's why we can't live in the way our parents did. If we make their mistakes we shall not survive. We have to change the way we live and that means changing our society. But to do that we must change the ruling and owning class. Otherwise they won't let us change anything.

Unfortunately democracy isn't a way of making this change easily. Our democracy is designed to protect the power of the ruling class to go on ruling. This is called maintaining law and order. When the ruling class see themselves losing their power and privileges, they try to force society to go on living in the old ways. For example, they tell us to behave like people in the last century. But at the same time they want us to use the new technology – otherwise the owners' profits would be smaller. Yet it is this technology which makes the old ways impossible. And so our society is trapped.

What's more, when the rulers try to force the old ways onto us they even use modern technology to do it! Yes, the very technology which forces people to need greater democracy, is used to prevent it! It would be a farce if it wasn't so serious.

Today we see a new form of social life struggling to be free. It can only be satisfied by real democracy. But instead, all the old injustices are heaped over it. Most people are still asked to regard themselves as – and behave as – second-class citizens. And as the conflict between the old and the new worsens, more and more people are called parasites, misfits, antisocials – and finally animals.

The most valuable thing about people – their sense of shared human dignity and worth – is turned to frustration and anger. One person is set against another, and each one is divided against himself or herself.

These are the crimes committed in the name of law and order and peace.

Chapter 9   The Strange Rulers

Who are these strange rulers? They are the class who provide the top officials of government and other institutions, the managers of the media, the private owners of newspapers and of the shops, offices and factories in which the rest of us work. These people either belong to the ruling class or support and spread its ideas – if they didn't they'd be sacked.

There are no working-class judges, generals, newspaper proprietors or media pundits. Instead the working class provides the ordinary soldiers, the newspaper vendors, the jurors and TV clowns.

And as the rulers own the means of controlling many of the ideas and attitudes that form public opinion – so very often they control the way 'free' citizens vote, and the decisions 'free' jurors hand up to judges.

Of course it can happen that a newspaper-delivery-boy ends up owning a string of newspapers. That is one of the romances told in hell! Such an owner may even boast that his newspapers speak with the voice of the people and not the rulers: but really they only speak with the people's accent. And after all, even the rulers need some opposition to convince themselves that society is free. But that sort of opposition doesn't go far. No newspaper owner – whatever his origins – consults his printers on editorial policy. Or his delivery boys. If he did, he'd risk the security of the system which enables him to get his newspapers and keep them.

Suppose the printers met together and voted to run their owners' newspapers? In our society, that seems a joke! But why? Or why doesn't the owner give one of his papers to the tenants of a council tower-block? There aren't any organisational barriers that would stop them editing it. If this seems another joke, then what you're laughing at is the idea of democracy. Which is odd, as you're armed with nuclear weapons to defend it! Instead, you allow one man to own a newspaper and directly or indirectly dictate evey word printed in it. Now that's really funny! If you don't think so, perhaps your ideas have been formed by the newspaper owner – so that you believe it's democracy and not money that rules!

Really the matter is simple: there can be no democracy when the rich own the newspapers read by ordinary people in the street. Or when a few may buy the labour of many, as if they were harnessing horses to the plough.

Chapter 10   Napoleon and Teapots

Yet the ruling class who have so much power are their own most dangerous enemy! They may not always deceive us, but they almost always deceive themselves. Far more than others, they're unable to 'know themselves'.

They stick to their opinions with fatal passion. They believe they are the defenders of civilisation, and that without them there'd be chaos.

A crook knows he's a crook. But the rulers and owners pass their lives disguised even to themselves. They are polite and clean, speak in cultured tones, use words and ideas adroitly, and know how to run institutions and discipline people till they believe discipline is good for them. It isn't – it depends on what the discipline's for. In our time discipline has caused far more chaos, suffering and death than all the crimes of common hooligans and street thugs.

Owners don't need to shout on picket lines, they can defend their interests sitting quietly at boardroom tables. The War Minister (who calls himself the Defence Minister) claims the right to massacre millions of innocents to protect the system which gives his class its great privileges – but he doesn't call himself the Minister of Human Butchery.

The Prime Minister doesn't brandish a broken bottle and say 'We're going to war to defend injustice, and when you common people have died for us we'll go on raking in our loot'! If rulers said that there wouldn't be any need for words such as patriotism and honour.

The ruling class never (well, rarely) look like hooligans but they cause the greatest hooliganism of all – war.

Freedom must be difficult to define, since people with opposing views claim to defend it! But injustices are plain to see. I've listed some of them. And there can be no confusion when we say that an unjust society cannot defend freedom – because without justice there is no freedom. Or real democracy. Or any of the things which would make society truly civilised.

If our rulers were just they wouldn't tolerate one of the injustices heaped under their nose. Instead, they *parade* them before us with all the insolence of a class who think they're born to rule – or with the pathetic self-delusion of madmen who think they are Napoleon or a teapot!

Chapter 11 Chains in the Head

But you might say 'The people are free to vote against their rulers, they're happy, they cheer the President or the Princess of Wales, they have jobs, or the dole and TV . . . .'

We know from the past that many people were happy as they drove at 500 miles an hour into the brick wall. The drivers told them they were going in another direction.

The trouble is that the ruling class is often able to control public opinion. It's an elementary skill open to any unjust government. It selects and distributes information. And it manages the jobs, wages, handouts, bribes and dingdongs that go to the co-operative, law-abiding citizen.

I repeat my simple example: there is no democracy in a country where the newspapers are owned by the rich and read by the poor. Its a vicious hypocrisy to pretend otherwise.

But far more important than this, the ruling class forms and directs the whole of culture – entwining the good with the bad, and ranging from what's considered to be good manners to what's considered to be high art. And culture is in many ways the mirror in which people learn to be what they are.

At the beginning of the last paragraph I said 'forms and directs' – and not 'manipulates' – because in this context there is no difference. The ruling class deceives itself, always entwining the good with the bad. So that in their society justice must serve injustice and truth must serve lies.

Once slaves wore chains on their feet. They saw them and knew they were slaves. In modern democracy the chains aren't easy to see. Governing is now so complex and subtle that usually the chains *have* to be in the mind.

Modern democracy is the means which enables the rulers and owners to make people enslave themselves. In this form of slavery the body is free and the mind is in chains. Often when the mouth is opened you hear the chains clink.

Chapter 12   War

The ruling class are so fanatical in their self-delusion that they even claim to be carrying out god's will.

The US President doesn't say his enemies are mistaken. A mistake can be corrected (it belongs to the first sort of wrong). The President says his enemies are evil. Evil can't be corrected (it belongs to the second sort of wrong). It's the force of darkness, always seeking for ways to destroy you! That's why it can never be trusted – or even tolerated. It's your moral duty to fight it to the death!

In such an atmosphere, wherever it looks the ruling class sees moral weakness, disorder and decay, and enemy infiltration. The rulers can't even trust their own people. When the people ask for the greater freedom and democracy they need to live and work in their changing world – to use the new technology – the ruling class sees them as friends of their enemies. So they arm the police with more dangerous weapons. And policing methods delevoped to repress freedom fighters in colonies are used against the people at home.

So the crisis mounts. Danger increases. Soon the rulers are in a state of political hysteria.

And these are the people we arm with nuclear weapons . . .?

Chapter 13   The Law of Societies

Let's go back again to the two sorts of wrong. In the first sort we could see what was wrong and put it right. In the second sort the tin held poison. But it isn't labelled. If you don't 'know yourself and your society', you can't know what's in the tin. You may think it's freedom and democracy – when it's slavery and war.

Injustice is always a great threat to the human mind. When society itself is unjust, then it damages many things: ideas, feelings, emotions, relationships, work, technology, law, all the ways we see, treat and deal with one another – all are tainted. And so step by step we go toward nuclear war. We can no longer live with injustice.

It's strange but true: human beings are made in such a way that they can't have their own comfort and security at the cost of other people's. This isn't because injustice troubles their conscience. It's even more true when they deny injustice or are unaware of it.

Unjust societies must destroy themselves. This law comes into effect whenever people and machines are joined together into a society. If the relations between people are unjust (that is, if they are based on classes), then that injustice must distort the working of reason in society. Society is then unable to 'know itself'. Then when things go wrong, it can't understand the causes of the wrong. When technology makes changes in social organisation necessary, society can't provide them. Instead it becomes repressive, and this can lead only to the confusion and conflict I've described.

The essential thing about the second sort of wrong isn't that it may be hidden. It's that when you know what it is, you have to make fundamental changes. We can't create peace by getting rid of the worst social abuses and learning to live with the rest. The law of societies is firm: an unjust society is out of control and will either destroy its people – or they must create a new society.

We have to replace injustice with justice. Otherwise nothing can go right, and no matter what we do to try to get rid of nuclear weapons we shall fail. And that failure means that the nuclear weapons must be used.

Chapter 14   Peace

In this book I haven't dealt with the forces of justice. The book is small – and those forces are great.

Today we have the means to get rid of poverty and many diseases, and the superstition and ignorance that often go with them. People have always struggled for justice. Now the struggle could be won. We can only recover and strengthen our humanity, make our ideas sane, and give kindness and generosity their true meaning, by taking part in that struggle.

A last word of warning. Of course changing society isn't easy. We live in it while we change it. That's like changing the food on your plate while you eat it – or the style of your clothes while you're getting dressed. No wonder even the thought of such changes frightens and angers some people. They'd rather suffer injustice. Or even be tempted to climb up with the rulers. But it won't work, there is no escape. The law of societies can't be changed: an unjust society leads to war – and no one can win that any longer.

It's easier to fight injustice than live with it. Of course, a just society wouldn't be perfect. Things would still go wrong. But we'd be spared the great disasters such as nuclear war. And our children would thank us.

Tennis

The radio. A newsman (knighted) interviewing a man (rich) who had just bought a newspaper (famous).

The newsman (who was called 'Sir') asked the new owner (the millionaire) about press freedom. On buying the newspaper the new owner (rich even by millionaires' standards) had sacked the old editor and appointed a new one. The newsman (with the title) asked the owner (with the money) whether the editor (with the job) would be free to express his own views (which were democratic) in the newspaper (which was free).

The new owner (for a moment taking his mind off his money) said the new editor was a man with his own mind (liberally educated) and would be free to express it – so that it would be all right for us to spend our pennies (devalued) buying his newspaper (and making him even richer).

I looked in the *Radio Times*. Was I perhaps listening to a comedy show? No, the newsman (honoured by the Queen) was seriously being assured by the new owner (honoured by his bank manager) that the freedom of the press was safe in his hands (always scrupulously washed) – and no doubt in homes (cosy) throughout the land heads nodded in relief.

I wondered why the BBC (a respectable institution – presumably) should put out such squalid garbage, or why next day it didn't announce that it had sacked the newsman (dubbed in that medieval ceremony which looks so well on TV) on the grounds that he was obviously incapable of reporting events even of the nursery with any adult insight into their meaning. And why the newspaper (which was free) wasn't immediately taken out of the hands of its new owner, without compensation (he was so rich any likely compensation would be peanuts to him) on the grounds that as he must presume his potential readers to be as stupid as himself he was not fit to be in control of a newspaper?

Look at it this way. If I'm going to run a football team, I choose footballers to play in it. Have you ever been to a football match in which at a critical moment a player suddenly produced a tennis ball and racket and knocked up a game of tennis with the opposing goalie? I have not (although I admit my experience may be more restricted than yours). All the same, I think it safe to say that owners of football teams hire players to play football for them rather than tennis – or roller skaters or go-go dancers.

The same goes for newspaper owners. They buy dogs (trained in the best academies) to bark when their master appears, as naturally as they bark at the moon (while it floats, serenely unseeing and benignly impartial, over the sordid flux of this sorry world) or come to heel as if that were the highest expression of canine independence. This is no inconvenience to dogs, because they love their masters. Their masters furnish them with bowls of dog-food.

Perhaps next day the new editor (who didn't get as much out of the newspaper as the owner – but who didn't starve, either) would be interviewed by the newsman (who was only a Sir, but might one day be so highly spoken of in the newspaper that the Queen would be obliged to make him the first media peer) and asked: 'The new owner (affectionately known to Fleet Street as The Baron) gave you as editor (please don't bark till I've finished my question) the right to hire and fire. When you hire a journalist he knows that you may also fire him. So how can he be free to express his opinions? If he writes what you don't like, you'll sack him'.

The new editor (who'd been promised a salary increase if he survives his first week) might then tell the newsman (whose wife by the by is now a Lady) that his journalists are independently minded people who are free to write what they wish. Just as they were free to say what they wished in their interview (conducted as far as we know without laughter) with the editor (who banks at the same bank as the owner) before he gave them the job of protecting freedom by praising it in the newspaper (which is free) . . . .

A Talk

For thirty years a woman earned her living in a factory. She worked a set of levers. Her machine produced a stream of little metal shapes. She was asked what they were for. Once she'd known but now she'd forgotten. Yet she spent her life making them. We spend our life 'being our self'. We're sure that we are our 'self', only mad people doubt it. But we may not know what our 'self' is. This is the problem I want to talk about.

One reason why we claim to be our 'self' is that we experience our own emotions. They're often strong. Sometimes we compare them to powerful natural forces, such as fire and water. We can even say, paradoxically, 'I was so angry I wasn't myself!' or 'I was so much in love I didn't behave like myself at all!' These experiences are taken to show how strong the 'self' is, since 'I' can't even control my 'self'. My self seems stronger than my mind or my ordinary behaviour. It's as if my 'emotional self' were a deeper part of me, more fundamental.

But there's a problem. Water and fire behave in ways set by natural laws. They can't break these laws. If I turn a cup upside down the water falls out. If the cup is ten times bigger that doesn't increase its gravity enough to significantly hold the water back. If I set fire to a house or cornfield or can of petrol, they're all equally consumed by fire. Natural laws are never broken. When sets of natural laws conflict (as when I pour water on fire) what happens is still decided by natural laws. (For our present purposes we can ignore the puzzles of quantum physics.)

In some ways our emotions seem like natural forces. But our behaviour never obeys natural laws. That's important, and until you understand what it means you can't understand people. Emotions work in response to a stimulus – something that excites or calms them. Stimuli are learned, or to be more exact 'acquired'. What decides whether you feel an emotion, whether you 'experience yourself' in that way, are the stimuli that provoke it. So the stimulus-responses you acquire and the way you acquire them make you what you are. They decide how you 'experience yourself', and how the strongest, most basic part of your 'self' works.

Of course, you experience your *own* emotion. But if the stimuli come from outside, then they impose themselves on you as much as a car or rain does when it hits you. A puppet's strings act as stimuli that make direct contact with the puppet's limbs. With us, the stimuli (of which we are conscious) act first on our emotions, feelings or thoughts – and then as a result of this we may move our limbs. Or we might look at it another way and say: a door might think it was opening itself, but we know it's the pressure on the handle that opens it.

Unlike the puppet or the door, you can refuse to respond to certain stimuli and may seek certain stimuli. But your reasons for doing so may often themselves be traced back to stronger stimuli. That is the joker in the democratic pack. It means – as I often point out – that when dramatists create characters they are dealing with politico-psychologies. We will look at this again when we deal with values.

People disagree about how stimuli are acquired, and whether or not we're born with 'built in' responses which force us to respond to certain things in set ways. Of course 'built in responses' control the things we don't usually need to be aware of – as for instance with most of our breathing.

We should be clear about the differences between inborn and acquired responses. We learn to drive on one side of the road. Then we can drive on this side as automatically as we breathe. If by mistake we drive on the wrong side and a car comes towards us – then certain stimulus-responses work in us. Without thinking we feel fear and drive over to the other side. Or we may well react even before we're afraid – but our reaction will still be based on earlier lessons in fear. Babies aren't born with 'stimuli' which tell them when it's right to be afraid. They're born with physical structures which enable them to feel fear, but they have to learn what to be afraid of. They learn the 'right' stimuli, or of course the 'wrong' ones. So although the possibility of feeling emotions is inborn in us, when and how we feel an emotion depends on our experience and understanding.

In parenthesis I should say that I know I've just talked as if emotions and sensitivity were the same thing. I only wish to go into things as far as I need in order to make my points. In the end the distinction wouldn't effect what I have to say. But perhaps I should say that in general it's wrong to equate inborn responses with emotions. A baby has an inborn ability to ingest and digest food. But turning a mechanism – or even sensation – of hunger into its desire for food, must be acquired. I'm not concerned with the cultural teaching involved in eating (which is no doubt as fraught as toilet training!) but a stage of development before that. This stage has to do with a very early knowlege of the world. I think this means that what we can loosely call an instinctual life can't exist without being expressed as ideas. Perhaps this is in some ways analogous to 'imprinting' in ducks – the drive has no objective characteristic till it's imprinted, and then the ducks may be imprinted with a dog or laboratory assistant. With humans, it's as if the child has to acquire the world before it could acquire its instincts - as if it found its instincts as a miner finds ore in rock. This places images and metaphors and ideas very close to the foundation of the human self. But I don't wish to deal with these questions now. I shall refer to them only as they occur from time to time in my argument.

We can see how emotions and ideas become closely connected and often influence each other. We like to think that our ideas are our own. But the foundations of our self are created by responses to stimuli from outside. And as we shall see, these same stimuli must create our ideas.

We think of knowledge as 'facts'. But it's also 'points of view'. Some facts are 'true' – for instance, the number of people in this room is a true fact. But other facts are more like pieces of sculpture – there are different 'points of view' to them. What you see depends on how you look. The stimuli we learn give us our points of view. That's why appeals to reason are often wasted. We see 'reason' differently.

We've touched on an important question, and I'll return to it later when I talk about value. For the moment, notice how many of our 'points of view' are accidents of the time and place in which we're born. Strangely enough, these are often the points of view we hold most strongly (we shall see why later). You could have been born at a time when it seemed a fact that you should kill your enemies in front of your idol; we're more civilized and tend to kill them in the comfort of their own homes. It still happens that if you're born in one country you'll be a Hindu and in another a Buddhist. Or if you're born in one house you might be a Christian, and in another an atheist. What we don't so easily admit is that where we're born in society – *our class* – must in the same way also control many of 'our' points of view.

How do whole societies arrive at their points of view? Societies differ in many ways, but all of them agree on many of the basic patterns of stimulus-responses their children need to acquire. Anyway, merely growing up in the world teaches children many of them. All children learn that if they want to live in the world they mustn't keep falling over and cutting their knees. Children build up an understanding of the way the world works. This means they acquire a set of stimulus-responses. All societies – rich or poor, black or white – agree that children shouldn't keep falling over or putting their hand in the fire. We call these 'natural' stimulus-responses.

But a society isn't a natural thing, like a tree. It's more like something made from a tree, say a table. Societies are made by people living and working together. So societies need another set of stimulus-responses, ones which are 'made by people'. These are 'conventional' stimulus-responses. It's not a natural law but a convention to drive on one side of the road rather than another. Each society creates its own 'conventional stimuli'.

Of course many societies have some coventional stimuli in common. When this happens, it's because people in those societies obtain their living in similar ways. Two societies that use ships will share certain conventional stimuli but one may be a society of fishers and another of pirates. If so, then some of their conventional stimuli won't be shared. Each society's conventional stimuli control the way the society works (maintains and sustains its living), as well as who owns the tools and buildings and land and water which are used during this work. And the owners of these things, in practice, own and rule the rest of society. All a society's conventional stimuli together can be called its 'culture'. So to live in the world you need to learn 'natural' stimuli, and to live in society with other people you need to learn the appropriate 'cultural' stimuli.

Cultural stimuli concern the way people get their living. So they concern basic things, matters of life and death. If you want to survive in society, and prosper in it, you must respond 'correctly' to its cultural stimuli. That's why cultural stimuli often involve strong emotions. It means, for example, that something of no 'natural' importance (such as a particular way of dressing) may have great 'cultural' importance. And it explains our question why, although its often an accident whether we're a Hindu or Christian, we may still hold our beliefs with great force.

Cultural stimuli don't merely tell you how to behave in society. They also tell you your place in it. This place decides the sort of person you are. Now that seems to contradict your sense of free will, of being able to choose. In fact it only limits your choices. A prisoner is free to wish to escape or not to escape. If he wishes to escape, he is *forced* to do certain things. The prisoner's freedom to choose is different to the freedom to choose of someone who's never been a prisoner. In the same way, our class position imposes limitations on us, as well as giving us opportunities.

Leaves and apples grow on the same tree. Because the tree is a natural object and not a cultural one (the distinction between wild and cultivated trees is irrelevant), the apple doesn't have to be taught to be an apple and not a leaf. But people are born the same, and society teaches them to be an 'apple' or a 'leaf'. Or to be more exact, each of us is born into a class, and we learn the cultural stimuli that belong to our class and that can't be separated from it.

We learn cultural stimuli in one of two ways (or a mixture of the two). Firstly, through direct experience. If you live in a decayed inner city you learn certain cultural stimuli with every breath you take. If you live on a private estate you learn different cultural stimuli. No one need teach you many of them. You learn them from your situation. This isn't the same as learning *natural* stimuli – though even in natural stimuli there are cultural elements. For instance, the cut on your knee differs if you get it on a parking lot or a lawn – and so does treatment for the cut.

The second way of learning cultural stimuli is more formal. It's the teaching you get in established situations in institutions, schools, training centres, churches, factories, encounters with police and with other authorities, and so on. All these places and encounters are strongly influenced by class. In a private school you learn to walk more slowly than you do in a state school, and you're taught that 'leaders' walk with authority.

Cultural stimuli give you your class 'stamp'. In a class society there are different 'stamps'. Sometimes it's as if people who look very much the same and who live only a few miles apart are nevertheless in different worlds – as in a way they are! Lower class people are physically shorter and live shorter lives than upper class people. This is solely because the poorer people eat poorer food and live in poorer houses, and so on. An interesting sign of class 'stamping' is that until very recently working-class people – even in theatres where they made up most of the audience – were only shown in plays either as comic figures, or sentimental servants sacrificing themselves for their masters and mistresses.

Some people wish to deny much of this, because it's obviously cruel to divide people in this way. They say everyone's free to change their class through their own efforts. That's like people on shore telling shipwreck victims they're free to learn to swim! If we're not free to choose our cultural stimuli, how are we free to choose to kick our way over the backs of the drowning – assuming that doing so was good for society? Cultural stimuli give us the only patterns on which we can base our 'self'. Someone born blind can learn to play the piano but not to paint. In the same way, class divisions impose their restrictions.

But none of this touches the real point – which is, why are people divided into classes in the first place? Being able to change your class doesn't make up for that injustice. The answer is, that class divisions decide who owns society. And when the upper class owns the society in which the lower classes live, there's a real sense in which it can be said that they own the lower classes – because they own many of the cultural processes (especially, but not only, the second, more institutionalised way of learning cultural stimuli) by which the 'self' is formed.

An unjust society denies the importance of cultural stimuli. Instead, it believes that our behaviour largely depends on natural stimuli. You're born lazy or industrious or good or wicked. It's on such grounds that the ruling class bases its right to rule. I'm arguing that these beliefs are wrong.

Of course even people in the same class don't acquire exactly the same stimulus-responses. Class divides people only into broad groups. But personal qualities (inborn or developed) can't overcome the bad social effects of this division. There is a Bible story that claims that a poor woman's pennies donated to charity are worth as much as a rich woman's donations of pounds. In a sense this is true. Both women may be equally contented with their own charity. But if we think of society instead of the self, the situation changes. How did the women acquire their money? And what, for instance, if the poor woman is kinder than the rich woman (not unknown!). If the poor woman had more money, she'd give more than the rich woman does. The social power of kindness would then be greater. But this point is trivial compared to the greed, destitution and aggression fostered by injustice and sanctioned by charity.

In order to live in society, we need patterns of cultural stimuli and responses. All animals (including human beings) are born with many natural responses 'built in'. The decisive thing built into human beings is our openness, our ability to think and feel, which forces us to acquire patterns of stimulus-responses. If cultural stimuli were 'built in', then culture couldn't change. But it changes all the time.

Building nests is 'built in' to birds, but humans learn to weave baskets and so they can choose to weave different baskets. You can identify different cultures by their baskets, as you can identify different species of birds by their nests.

Nature evolves slowly, cultures change quickly. Cultural change is called history. Because classes are not natural but cultural they must be changed with the same historical speed as other parts of culture – though probably no faster.

Both cultural and natural stimuli work in complex ways. Just as natural laws often 'clash' (such a clash is the description of any natural event), so too do our stimuli. In time we learn ways of behaving. The host of our stimulus-responses forms a pattern. This pattern is derived from our experience of things and events, and our expectation of what the consequences of our own actions will be. This creates our personality, our character. And then we act in ways which are characteristic of us. This 'character' is also what we know and experience as our 'self'. We become responsible for its actions. And this gives us the scope of our free will.

But that doesn't mean we're free to do what we like, regardless of our class stamp – any more than we can break natural laws by jumping 100 metres. With training we can jump further. And we know when one person jumps further than another because we agree on what a metre is, and so we can measure the jumps, even when they differ by only small amounts. A metre is defined according to the realm of natural laws. But where cultural stimuli are concerned, we can't easily measure even the simplest things! This is because we measure cultural things by 'value', and value (as all cultural things) changes.

Suppose ten years ago I bought a kilo of apples and paid 10p for them. Today I buy another kilo of apples. I get the same amount of apples because a kilo, like a metre, doesn't change. But instead of 10p I now have to pay 50p for them. Why? Because the 'value' of money has changed. Whenever we measure or judge behaviour, we use values – cultural and not natural measures. This has an enormous effect on your life. It goes a long way to deciding what happens to you.

Culture fixes values, and that's why values change. Is it wrong to kill? Yes if you murder your neighbour. No if you kill your government's enemy – that is, the enemy of your ruling class (and you may end up being their corpse by proxy). The act of killing doesn't change, but its 'value' does. The 'value' of killing has changed dramatically through history – so that the past always seems to us a scandal. In a just society it would always be wrong to kill. I can only think of suicide and euthanasia as exceptions. Presumably, that is killing yourself out of hatred and others out of love.

Now there's an extraordinary thing about values. Your values depend on your class position. They do so in many ways. And even you yourself are judged, evaluated, on your class position. For instance, the upper class are 'genteel', though they often behave like thugs. And the lower class are 'rough', though presumably not all of them are thugs?

Although values depend on class positions, not each class holds firmly to its own set of values. If it did, society couldn't agree on anything and would not be able to work. So the essential values have to belong to one class, and obviously that will be the upper class. What's right and wrong is decided from their point of view. They are the only class that have the power – through force and influence, the control of work and wages and so on – to impose their values on others. That's why class society is always unjust. Its values have to be twisted. It is an unavoidable consequence of any society divided into classes that the higher class *must* impose their 'points of view', their 'values', on the lower classes. Otherwise the way society is owned couldn't be combined with the work people must do to gain their living. Then society would fall apart. It's as simple as that – and a lot of effort is needed to confuse the issue.

Once cultural stimuli have been fixed, it's hard to change them. As we've seen, they're attached to strong, life-and-death emotions. They also control ideas. This last point is difficult but important, so we should try to understand it.

A 'stimulus' is really an idea. What makes it so is that it relies on an interpretation of the world. It gives the world a meaning. Look again at the example of the car. We learn that when a car approaches us at speed, it's dangerous to be on the wrong side of the road. We've learned what a car is, and what it'll do to us if it hits us. We have the 'right' ideas about the car, and these stimulate our responses. As we've seen, we're formed by our responses to stimuli. So we must be formed by our responses to ideas.

Ideas control our emotions as responses to stimuli. This is a surprise! Usually it's put exactly the other way round. We're told our emotions easily swamp, override ideas – that the animal in us struggles to bring down the human being. Yet this is biologically untrue. Human beings are creatures of ideas. That is the only way specifically human biology can work. Ideas must release and govern our emotions. We are never the victim of our emotions, but we are often the victim of our ideas. That is a necessary consequence of the biological functioning and structure of our brains.

This is often obscured. One reason for this is the sheer complexity of our minds. Another is the force of our emotions. At the beginning, I said emotions seem sometimes to take us over. This is because of the rough-and-ready way we acquire cultural stimuli. We acquire many of them when we're children, when our ideas are elementary. That's why emotions and ideas can never add up in the way that 2 and 2 always make 4. Emotional life is of a different sort. It has to do with the maturing of judgement and understanding, the receiving of wounds and the giving of blows. As long as there are people, they will have to go through these stages of reaching maturity. It will give them both pain and joy. Hume saw reason as the slave of passions. He was right to see they were bound together. But he misstated the question of slavery. The relationship is the way in which slowly and with difficulty reason leads us to freedom. And at least this means we're not by

nature bound to be 'brutish beasts' always needing to be tamed
and controlled by the ruling class for the good of society.

Ideas live in us. They're not cold abstractions. They work with
our emotional responses. Emotions can't be released except by
ideas. This doesn't mean that ideas can easily control emotions.
Cultural stimuli, we've seen, are hard to change. But it's our ideas
that bind us to ourselves and make us what we are.

Now we can understand why ideas may be given aesthetic form
and movement, and why we respond to the metaphors of poets
and other writers – and what Blake meant (or should have meant,
even if he didn't) when he said that a tear was an intellectual thing.
All human beings search for the meaning of their lives, because
ideas lie at the centre of their existence.

In the example of the car, our ideas about the car were 'right',
and so we had the right cultural stimuli. We often acquire
incorrect ideas and join them with stimuli, which are then
'wrong'. When this happens to people we may be able to see it,
and then we say they behave strangely. For example, some people
are characteristically stimulated to set buildings on fire. We know
that arsonists are dangerous. But in an unjust society we will learn
many wrong stimulus-responses. Unfortunately, we may not
always see that they are dangerous, or degrading, because we're
part of society and may share its values. But whenever that
happens, and when as a result we behave inhumanly, that isn't
because dark, animal emotions are taking us over. Its because our
ideas and our teaching are wrong.

We can't get rid of our emotions and replace them with ideas.
Any attempt to do that would be inhuman. Creating the 'self'
always involves joy and pain. But we could achieve a safer, wise
relationship between emotion and ideas, and natural and cultural
stimuli. That would be possible in a just society, for reasons that
are clear – its organisation and culture would be rational and not
based on false interpretations of human nature. It would not need
to distort ideas, and so debase emotion. Till then, paradoxically,
the tensions created in us and society by injustice are often,

consciously or not, among the forces that work to create justice. The logic of history makes sense of human paradoxes.

Good and evil become questions of 'value' and 'points of view', as we've seen. I'll return to this later, but now I want to stress that 'wrong' learning doesn't come from natural stimuli, but cultural ones. A just society would not need to disguise its own processes. Instead it would help people to understand the host of stimuli which form them. They would be able to answer the question 'Who am I?' with true understanding. And so instead of being imprisoned in class rigidities, their characters would be based on that freedom which is open to human beings.

If you say 'The arsonist is born with an obsession with fire', I have to say you could never prove this, and so you could never know it. Even if it were true, it wouldn't explain why someone became an arsonist. Why didn't the obsession produce a foundry worker, or an expert at dousing fires in oil wells or forests? Or why not a fire-eater? Such things are decided by cultural stimuli. Houses don't exist in nature, you can't have an 'inborn' drive to burn them down. You can only have 'inborn drives' about natural things. Perhaps you want to say 'The arsonist is just plain wicked?' I shall return to wickedness later.

If so much depends on 'points of view' and 'changing values', how can we ever decide which cultural stimuli are good? Perhaps those that make people happy? But perhaps the arsonist is happy burning buildings? People can even be happy (we're told) destroying each other!

To learn what's good for us, you have to ask 'What's the good or best possible society?' The answer's simple. The best society is the just society. A just society wouldn't have to use cultural stimuli to force one class to serve the interests of another, with all the disasters that follow. But though it's easy to say justice, it's difficult to get it.

To make society more just you have to change the relationships between people. But people are already members of a society, with fixed 'points of view' and in fixed places. How can they see the world differently enough to be able to change it? Isn't it like an egg saying it doesn't want to be laid by a hen? And wouldn't society come to a standstill?

Two points. Firstly, we shall see that while it resists justice, an unjust society creates the forces that work for justice. In fact, that's been a basic mechanism of history. And secondly, it costs more waste, despair and in the end destruction, to try to keep an unjust society running, than it does to make it more just. That's a consequence of the nature of human biology, and of the way in which it requires us to maintain our existence in the world. In any unjust society, relationships between people must be irrational. Because of this even our best emotions may be misused by destructive cultural stimuli. It's not surprising that such societies must collapse.

In an effort to maintain itself, an unjust society often says people should stay 'in their places'. If they did, society would come to a standstill. We'd still be serfs working with wooden ploughs and worshipping stone idols. When the way we maintain our lives changes, the cultural stimuli which form us also change. And as they're the pattern on which our 'self' is based, so we ourselves change. Driving a tractor changes the whole of society. With a tractor you need petrol, oil wells, tankers, more roads, more laws, different forms of ownership, new ways of raising large sums of money (banks and stock exchanges), more shops, bigger cities, different relations in the home, and so on and so on . . . We can't stay in our old place, because the old place has gone.

We can see how technology changes our world. It also changes people. A serf couldn't leave his village without his owner's permission. Imagine asking permission from the lord of the manor every time you went out in your car! If the serf left without permission, he might be publicly flogged or even hanged. Imagine his 'point of view' towards authority – more reverential than yours!

Stimuli that effected the serf in one way, must effect you differently. You are different. Your responses are different. You see yourself and experience yourself differently. For instance, in our attitude to authority. Would you willingly watch someone being hanged for travelling without their owner's permission? What attitudes do people who live in inner cities have to police? Does the ruling class accept that those attitudes must change, just as inner city geography and life have changed? That's only possible if what the police are doing is allowed to change. What are they doing? Enforcing class relationships that belong between the serf and his owner, to the society of the wooden plough. So there are city riots. That's not because people are more wicked, but because they no longer use wooden ploughs, and so can no longer live in the society that petrol and tractors have made unjust.

It's often said that the more circumstances change, the more people stay the same. This is misleading. Presumably our feelings of happiness and anger are much the same as they were for our ancestors, in fact as they were since our species developed the subtleties of living with the bicameral brain. But, I repeat, what causes these feelings is very different, and so must be the behaviour they produce. We can't behave as we did in the past, that's the point. In fact, it's because our emotions and natural stimulus-responses remain much the same, that our behaviour changes so radically! Our behaviour is cultural. Hanging, for the serf, would have been as painful for him as it would be for us, otherwise he wouldn't have been threatened with it. Yet the threat of hanging which forced him to submit, would force us to rebel. What makes the difference is the car. Technology changes those who use it.

Of course, not all things change. Most ages and societies have treated children in ways which have much in common. Natural stimulus-responses have no great need to change, but cultural-stimuli have. Would a mother nowadays let her 6-year-old daughter drag heavy loads all day in a mine, till her body was deformed? There'd be a public outcry. So we're kinder? Well, every week UK parents kill at least three of their children – perhaps they wouldn't if they could usefully put them out to work? So we're crueller? But we don't watch people being eaten by lions in an arena, or burn old ladies because they have warts. So we're kinder? Yet we allow our rulers to prepare to kill millions of innocent people to protect – what?: a society that's so civilised it's prepared to kill millions of innocent people! And these are people who would certainly choose to live without our culture rather than die for it – people whose rulers, we say, have denied them their democratic freedom! Then is it just that our own rulers are more wicked?

No, it is just that the technology of our society has changed more than our culture. Culture is the way society's run and owned, and we're trying to run and own it in old ways. So in our society it becomes more difficult to be human. That's all.

We have the means of getting rid of many of the tragedies that caused misery in the past. But an unjust society returns the tragedy – and multiplies it a hundredfold.

As technology changes society, we ought to be able to become more human. We know more about medicine and can be of more help to the sick. We grow more food, and no one need starve. Yet more people starve than ever before. That is solely because our lives are unjust. The irrational hysteria that always results from class society, goads us into building 'weapons mountains'. For every pound we spend to feed the starving, we spend thousands on weapons. You may have given money to famine relief. Then you're kind? But you allow your government to spend thousands of millions of pounds on preparing to blow people to bits. You give a few shillings to put food in one child's belly, and millions to rip another child's belly open. Both children are equally innocent. Is that kindness?

Perhaps you give your pound to the starving like the rich woman: with the sanctimonious assurance that her action is as moral as the poor woman's? But the rich woman's wealth comes from multinational companies. These create poverty by conspiring with the rulers of the poor to trade in expensive technology and harmful consumer goods – and then in the weapons their own search for markets and natural resources make necessary. Once trade went under the protection of the Bible: now it goes under the protection of the gun. Or perhaps you give your pound like the poor woman: in the false belief that then it will be safe – and moral – to let the rich woman go on profiteering in starvation, war and charity? Really kindness would be doing all you could to stop your government making weapons. Of course, some people wouldn't call that kindness at all. Well as I said, it depends on your point of view. You see how difficult it is to be kind in an unjust society! In the end crime doesn't pay even for the judge.

You may be a law-abiding citizen, but – like the arsonist – you may be seeking your happiness in dangerous ways. Yet society will approve of all you do, because an unjust society twists values. And if its unjust culture forms your ideas and responses, then your 'self' isn't really yours at all. You become a living embodiment of injustice: in effect a social corpse, animated, if at all, only by the frantic energies of destructiveness. That isn't a natural but a cultural state. And it's the reason why sometimes, when people think they're expressing their highest humanity they're doing what no human being should ever do.

If enough of us go on doing such things, we'll be blown to pieces. Society can only survive by becoming more just, because that's the only way it can understand its own workings, and so know what's happening to it and correct its faults. But an unjust society isn't even interested in doing that. In the end, it would rather 'heroically' go down in flames, like Hitler in his bunker.

Technology is a force for justice because it forces people to become more responsible for their own lives. Their owners' culture becomes less and less use to them, till it's like a chain round their legs. But although the ruling class misuse technology in many ways, simply to use it they must allow concessions to its users. That's how the first, imperfect forms of democracy are created. And as technology goes on changing society, so democracy has to change. At first it's a way of controlling – and even manipulating – people. In time, it can become the way in which they are free.

That's why the woman, who after thirty years no longer knew

what her machine made, probably understood her life better than
the machine's owner understood his. His culture belongs to the
past, but her daily life prepares her for a more just and democratic
culture – and helps to create it.

What is culture's basic function? As so much is not 'inborn' in us,
we need patterns of what it means to be human. In a way it's like a
car owner's manual. But as our lives are complex and full of
change, we need more than a set of rigid instructions. That's one
use we have for art. Art derives from the basic relationship that we
looked at, between ideas and emotions. It can create images (in
pictures, stories. movement, sound, objects – from any natural
stimulus that can be made a cultural stimulus) which say: 'A just
human being behaves in such and such a way, and is such and
such a person'.

   Even when art celebrates and imposes the domination of one
class over another, it does so from the point of view of justice.
Politically, the struggle for justice is inherent in the use of reason
within society. But in some ways reason is like technology – which
created Mephistopheles and made him the tempter of humankind.
Technology makes bombs as well as bread. Nevertheless, the
pressures it creates in society are basically a force for justice – the
medicine flows from the wound. Art has often been owned and
used by the ruling classes, but even then its basic disciplines
override, in the same way as they do with technology, the misuses
to which they may be put. It's as if the disciplines themselves
implied the rationality of the human species.
   We will create images – patterns of humanity, mirrors in which
the creators fashion and change themselves – as long as there are
people and societies. If society were just, we would be more like
our ideal images. And of course these images are not abstractions,
they take historical forms. It's true that the movement towards
our ideals seems inherent in our use of reason – and that there is a
rational interpretation of the world. We may understand ourselves
and our society. We need not give confusion the glamour of
mystery. But it's as if the scaffolding of the world stood to one

side, and the world was built up, piece by piece, next to it. Or – to use another image – the bones stood up before humankind, and the flesh grows on them – in the way that grass may grow over rocks, in a propitious world.

At any rate, so far as our ideals and visions are concerned, we come closer to being like them by struggling to create justice. Justice means allowing people to become human.

Piano

A child with six fingers on one hand. He went to the Piano Teacher and said 'I shall be able to play the piano better than other people. Teach me'.

The Piano Teacher explained that an extra finger is not an advantage in playing the piano. Piano keys are laid out, and piano music is written, to be played by ten fingers.

The child went away disappointed.

Now there was a country in which people were born with four fingers on one hand. There pianos were built and piano music was written to be played by nine fingers. One day disaster struck. A child was born with ten fingers. But the child was brave and when it was older it said to the Piano Teacher 'At least I'll be able to play the piano better than others'. You know what the Piano Teacher said. And he was right. At that time and in that country pianos were best played with nine fingers.

But then something even worse happened. More children were born with ten fingers! This was a catastrophy. The Glove Makers said their industry faced ruin – glove factories were 'tooled up' to make nine-finger pairs of gloves. Typewriter sales slumped. Parents were in despair because children had yet another finger to put in things. The army had an internal revolt over which finger should squeeze the trigger. The Nine-Finger Traditionalist won and when the leaders of the Ten Finger Mutineers were stood in front of the firing squad the traditional finger was used. In this unhappy time only the manufacturers of rings and soap were pleased.

The Piano Teachers assembled to seek for ways to protect the Art of Piano Playing. After all, they couldn't put up prices, make more goods or argue over which finger to use.

They called in a Philosopher.

The Philosopher withdrew to live on a scant diet in the mountains. After six months he returned to the Piano Teachers and said 'Your problem is serious. Do not despair. Civilisation has overcome dangers almost as dangerous as this one. Remember the great 'Tea Drinking Problem'! The natives may grow your tea bush for you, and harvest and dry and shred the leaves. Your cook may boil the water and draw the infusion. Your maid may serve it on the silver tray. But the fatal moment can no longer be delayed – and you must drink the tea! To do this you must lift the cup. But this is work! How can polite, well-brought-up people be made to work? In their own drawing-rooms! Before the servants! Well, as you'd expect from the Guardians of Civilisation – they found the solution. To show that what they were doing was not really work, that it couldn't be classed (except by the uncharitable, whom we may ignore) as common labour, that it didn't disturb their inner calm in the slightest – as they raised the cup to their lips they crooked their little finger. On such things as the crooking of little fingers the whole of Civilisation rests. This leads me to suggest that as your pupils practice at their piano, they might crook their superfluous finger.'

As he spoke the Philosopher was sitting at a piano. He finished with a demonstration flourish, crooking one finger and running the rest over the keys. The President of the Piano Teachers was so cross he banged the piano lid on the Philosopher's hands and his crooked finger broke. The Philosopher howled. The howling of Philosophers is the ugliest sound in all history.

More and more children with ten fingers were born in this unfortunate country. In the end, almost all the children were born thus deformed. And then – as the nation stood on the brink – the President of the Piano Teachers saved it! He said 'You may dig with ten fingers, comb your hair with ten fingers, stir your pudding with ten fingers. Such mechanical tasks can with effort be adapted to the new conditions. But Piano Playing is an Art. It requires deep understanding – the sensitive touch of the feathers in the Angels' wings – the discipline of the boots of Warriors who march on the floor of the Abyss'. (He'd become President of the

Piano Teachers because of his poetical interpretations of even the obscurist pieces.) 'Play the piano with ten fingers? That you cannot and never will be able to! Does this mean that future generations will be denied the joy of expressing their souls at the piano? – for we must still believe that under their hideous deformity, the young are still much like us – still moved by the Vision of Beauty which their extra finger seems to push forever beyond their reach! How shall we save our culture? Simple! Cut off the extra fingers! Forever after when they hear a piano played our children will thank us.'

So that's what they did. Shortly after birth the extra finger is chopped off in a pretty little ceremony before the family and close friends. There is a cake. An official prays and then raises his nine fingers in blessing over the newly mutilated infant.

Now in Nine-Finger-Land they keep to the solid old ways that always worked in the past. Unfortunately, no matter how carefully its done, or how devoutly the official prays, cutting off one finger seems to cripple the rest. As the child grows the whole hand twists into a clump of claws. It becomes difficult to hold things. Working with tools and machines is clumsy. Children flinch when patted or stroked by the deformed hands. There are marital difficulties – but public mention of this is forbidden as Ten-Fingerism. There's a lot of arthritis about. Naturally, people are on edge – and when they try to relieve their feelings by clouting someone, they do not always remember to use their good hand – and so their sufferings are increased. Indeed the good hand is altogether a problem for the government – since selfish people may compare their mutilated hand unfavourably with it. The government is now laying plans for the good life without hands.

There are some parents who don't like to see the knife cutting into their child's flesh. They refuse to register their children for defingering. This has caused a public outcry. Factions! A crazy nonconformist went so far as to build a piano keyboard for ten fingers! A Bishop said 'The sight of little children clasping ten fingers in prayer is so obviously offensive in the eyes of the Lord that soon the Beast-With-Eleven-Fingers will come amongst us!'

Civil war is raging. The outcome is uncertain but the government fights a hard battle. The Nine-Finger Doctrine is still taught and children may yet be able to live the Nine-Finger-Way-of-Life . . .

The Nine-Finger Piano Teachers had a point. They knew how their pianos were made and what music was written for them, and people had to learn to play with things as they are. But there comes a time when things change. Pianos are made for fingers not fingers for pianos. No doubt nine fingers make beautiful sounds. But we may hope that sounds made by ten fingers may be just as beautiful. And so may the sounds made by eleven.

'A Talk' was first given to a group of students. The other three pieces were written for New Midland Dance Company to be used in connection with their production of the author's 'Burns: a piece for dancers and musicians'.

Bingo

Scenes of Money and Death

Introduction

Shakespeare had two daughters. Susanna is buried near him under stone in the chancel of the parish church, Judith was buried under grass outside in the churchyard and her grave is lost. Perhaps that sums up the difference between them. Shakespeare's opinions about them aren't known, but it seemed to me that his daughters' lives might have reflected those opinions: Susanna social, well-married and affluent, and Judith obscure, over-shadowed by her sister, married late to the unsuccessful publican of The Cage and deserted in her old age. Perhaps being brought up under Shakespeare's incisive perception and judgement shaped the whole of their lives.

Judith is the only daughter in the play. I gave the more comforting and strengthening role that I think Susanna played in his life to an old woman servant. I did this for my own dramatic convenience. The old woman's son is a victim of Shakespeare's business world. By making her close to Shakespeare I had a bridge between the two elements of the play, but I kept what I think is the true psychological situation: one woman (Susanna, or in the play the old woman) was close to him, and another (Judith, and probably also his wife) was estranged.

I've done something similar with my account of the enclosure which involved Shakespeare. Combe represents several men, and the undertaking signed in the second scene by Combe and Shakespeare was in fact between Shakespeare and a representative of the enclosers called Replingham (though Combe confirmed it later). Shakespeare's last binge was with Jonson and Drayton. Only Jonson is shown in the play. I've also altered some dates. For example, Shakespeare's theatre was burned down in 1613 not 1616. I made all these changes for dramatic convenience. To

recreate in an audience the impact scattered events had on someone's life you often have to concentrate them. I mention all this
because I want to protect the play from petty criticism. It is based
on the material historical facts so far as they're known, and on
psychological truth so far as I know it. The consequences that
follow in the play follow from the facts, they're not polemical
inventions. Of course, I can't insist that my description of Shakespeare's death is true. I'm like a man who looks down from a
bridge at the place where an accident has happened. The road is
wet, there's a skid mark, the car's wrecked, and a dead man lies by
the road in a pool of blood. I can only put the various things
together and say what probably happened. Orthodox critics
usually assume that Shakespeare would have driven a car so well
that he'd never have an accident. My account rather flatters
Shakespeare. If he didn't end in the way shown in the play, then
he was a reactionary blimp or some other fool. The only more
charitable account is that he was unaware or senile. But I admit
that I'm not really interested in Shakespeare's true biography in
the way a historian might be. Part of the play is about the relationship between any writer and his society.

*

Shakespeare created Lear, who is the most radical of all social
critics. But Lear's insight is expressed as madness or hysteria.
Why? I suppose partly because that was the only coherent way it
could have been expressed at that time. Partly also because if you
understand so much about suffering and violence, the partiality
of authority, and the final innocence of all defenceless things, *and
yet* live in a time when you can do nothing about it – then you feel
the suffering you describe, and your writing mimics that suffering.
When you write on that level you must tell the truth. A lie makes
you the hangman's assistant. It betrays the victim and this is
intolerable – because you are mimicking the victim, and the most
important thing you know is the innocence you share with him.
So if you lie the world stops being sane, there is no justice to

condemn suffering, and no difference between guilt and innocence – and only the mad know how to live with so much despair. Art is always sane. It always insists on the truth, and tries to express the justice and order that are necessary to sanity but are usually destroyed by society. All imagination is political. It has the urgency of passion, the force of appetite, the self-authenticity of pain or happiness – imagination is a desire that *makes* an artist create. The truths of imagination are strictly determined and necessary. They aren't 'revealed' to artists, they have to work and train and learn so that they become skilled at discovering them. But every artist often feels that what he's created is 'right' and he's not free to alter it. It's life that in comparison seems arbitrary and random – because society is usually based on injustice or expediency but art is the expression of moral sanity. Philistinism is so shocking because it assumes that, on the contrary, creative imagination is arbitrary and random, a self-satisfying game, mere fantasy – instead of being vital to human development. And of course, what artists most frequently lack is enough of this creative imagination. Or perhaps they only play it down because they're told art is for the rich and intellectual, that science is work but art only luxury or play. Perhaps also because many people do in fact 'exist' without art. Well, they've only had to do so in modern industrial societies and that's one reason why these societies are stagnant and inhuman. And there are also artists who shut themselves up in private fantasies. What they create has to be interpreted by an extra-artistic language. Their verbal or graphic images have no force, it's as if a spectator had to look up every word or sign in a dictionary. But imagination isn't random fantasy. The artist's imagination connects him to his audience's world just as much as his knowledge does. Because Jane Austen's imagination was weaker than her knowledge she could avoid writing about the Napoleonic wars – except perhaps as one cause of her general fear of poverty. But as she needed to express the objective truth about her characters – that is her need for moral sanity – this deepened her creative imagination. In *Persuasion*

she'd already started to write about the experience of poverty and
not just her fear of it, and if she'd lived longer she might well have
written about war. Writers who don't develop in this way become
shut up in private fantasies, experiments in style, unrewarding
obscurities – they become trivial and reactionary.

Shakespeare's plays show this need for sanity and its political
expression, justice. But how did he live? His behaviour as a
property-owner made him closer to Goneril than Lear. He supported and benefited from the Goneril-society – with its prisons,
workhouses, whipping, starvation, mutilation, pulpit-hysteria and
all the rest of it.

An example of this is his role in the Welcombe enclosure. A
large part of his income came from rents (or tithes) paid on common fields at Welcombe near Stratford. Some important landowners wanted to enclose these fields – for the reasons given in the
play – and there was a risk that the enclosure would affect
Shakespeare's rents. He could side either with the landowners or
with the poor who would lose their land and livelihood. He sided
with the landowners. They gave him a guarantee against loss –
and this is not a neutral document because it implies that should the
people fighting the enclosers come to him for help he would refuse
it. Well, the town did write to him for help and he did nothing.
The struggle is quite well documented and there's no record of
opposition from Shakespeare. He may have doubted that the
enclosers would succeed, but at best this means he sat at home
with his guarantee while others made the resistance that was the
only way to stop them. They were stopped for a time. The fields
were not finally enclosed till 1775.

Lear divided up his land at the beginning of the play, when he
was arbitrary and unjust – not when he was shouting out his
truths on the open common.

*

The subtitle is 'Scenes of money and death'. We live in a closed
society where you need money to live. You earn it, borrow it, or

steal it. Criminals, and hermits or drop-outs, depend on others who earn money – there's no greenwood to escape into any more, it's been cut down. We have no natural rights, only rights granted and protected by money. Money provides food, shelter, security, education, entertainment, the ground we walk on, the air we breathe, the bed we lie in. People come to think of these things as products of money, not of the earth or human relationships, and finally as the way of getting more money to get more things. Money has its own laws and conventions, and when you live by money you must live by these. To get money you must behave like money. I don't mean only that money creates certain attitudes or traits in people, it *forces* certain behaviour on them. Charity seems an argument against this, but in fact it proves it. If you have a lot of money you might give some of it to the poor, or some pictures to the nation. But you won't give all you have because then you'd have no reserve, no one would work for you for wages and so you couldn't collect more money. Your actions aren't finally controlled by human generosity (at best they're only prompted by that) but by your selfish need. The money you keep back isn't morally neutral – like enough clothes or food – because you use it to influence the lives of other people who are also trapped by money. We're wrong when we assume we're free to use money in human ways. When livelihood and dignity depend on money, human values are replaced by money values. Certainly that's what's happened in our commercial, technological society. Money destroys the effect of human values in our society because consumer demand can't grow fast enough to maintain profits and full employment while human values are effective. A consumer society depends on its members being avaricious, ostentatious, gluttonous, envious, wasteful, selfish and inhuman. Officially we teach morality but if we all became 'good' the economy would collapse. Affluent people can't afford ten commandments.

Money is an important social tool. It's the means of exchange and of accumulating the surplus necessary to create modern industry. But we've reached a point where money isn't used to remove poverty but to create and satisfy artificial needs so that consumption will maintain profits and industrial activity. Keynes said that to maintain effective demand in an economy it would be better to pay men for 'digging holes in the ground' rather than that they should be unemployed, but he added ironically that he presumed a 'sensible community' would find something more socially useful for them to do. Well, a lot of the trash we produce for civilized consumption is far more silly and dangerous than holes in the ground. And that's only concerned with keeping society running – the far more important and difficult work of making it more civilized is mostly ignored. We think we live in an age of science, but it's also an age of alchemy: we try to turn gold into human values.

*

It seems that sometimes people can be made to behave badly with frightening ease and rapidity, but it only seems so. Their awareness of human values doesn't simply vanish. People have faults and, as in all evolving species, weaknesses – but human values are the most enduring things we have, stronger than our rational minds. We have the need and right to protect ourselves and our families, and in a crisis we help those we know, not strangers – but it isn't easy for us to do this at others' expense or to make others suffer. It's difficult for human beings to be unkind, and unpleasant to be arrogant. There's always a reason for aggression, and the only effective weapon against it is to remove the cause. Fear is a lack of understanding, and the only way to remove it is by reason and reassurance. Even the hate that comes from fear and aggression begins as a passion for justice. That isn't a paradox. Why did Shylock ask for his enemy's flesh? Because his own had been spat on.

There are two main sorts of political aggression. The first is the aggression of the weak against the strong, the hungry against the over-fed. That's easy to understand. The strong are unjust, and to survive and get elementary rights many people are forced to act aggressively. The second aggression is of the strong against the weak. How can an American drop bombs on peasants in a jungle if, as I said, a sense of human values is part of his nature? It takes a lot of effort, years of false education and lies, indignity, shabby poverty, economic insecurity – or the insecurity of dishonest privilege – before men will do that. The ruling morality teaches them they are violent, dirty and destructive, that the only decent course open to civilized man is to act as his own gaoler, and that men in jungles are even worse because they're as savage as animals *and* as cunning as men – history proves it. So he drops bombs because he believes that if the peasant ever rowed a canoe across the Pacific and drove an ox cart over America till he came to his garden, he'd steal his vegetables and rape his grandmother – history proves it. And history like the Bible will prove anything.

An old fascist (or an old miser) is always bitter and cynical. Not because his conscience troubles him! – but because he lives in conflict with his fundamental sense of human values. Men can only be content when they live in peace and shared respect with other men. It seems odd to say these things in a century of fascism and brutality, but the world is unhappy and violent not because we're cursed with original sin *or* original aggression, but because it it is unjust. The world is not absurd, it is finally a place for men to be sane and rational in.

Of course demands for justice sometimes conflict. But the reason these conflicts are hard to resolve is that the 'judge' is often more guilty than the other parties. Most established social orders are not means of defending justice but of defending social injustice. That's why compromises inside a nation or between nations are difficult to get, and why law-and-order societies are morally responsible for the terrorism and crime they provoke.

*

I wrote *Bingo* because I think the contradictions in Shakespeare's life are similar to the contradictions in us. He was a 'corrupt seer' and we are a 'barbarous civilization'. Because of that our society could destroy itself. We believe in certain values but our society only works by destroying them, so that our daily lives are a denial of our hopes. That makes our world absurd and often it makes our own species hateful to us. Morality is reduced to surface details and trivialities. Is it so easy to live like that? Or aren't we surrounded by frustration and bitterness, cynicism and inefficiency, and an inner feeling of weakness that comes from knowing we waste our energy on things that finally can't satisfy us? That's true of all parts of our society, from the theatre of the absurd to the broken windows of a youth club. It's not so odd, then, to say that people are only happy when their lives are based on human values. *If* we survive we have only two possible futures. Firstly, as technological ants engineered from birth to fit into a rigid society. Or secondly, as people who live consistently by the values that are part of their nature.

*

You can't do much by deciding to be happier, saner or wiser. That partly depends on society, and you can only change your life by changing society and the role you have to play in it. If, for example, society encourages greed and yet is based on the poverty of other societies, you can understand that without any 'enlightenment'. What sort of society do we want? The earlier, simpler culture related closely to the land has gone, and not enough people remember its skills well enough to teach them – and anyway those skills were too simple to support the huge masses of people who've grown up in an industrial culture with a highly technological relationship to the environment. So we have to make sense of our technological culture and divorce it from rampant commercialism. A factory isn't bad in itself. It depends how many other factories there are, what they make and how they're organized. Finally the only way to answer these questions is for the people who work in the factories to answer them.

Some people still think workers are apes who'd swing round in trees all day if someone else didn't give them orders. They ask, how on earth could workers organize this mess? But the question is, how can we get out of the mess? That's why it's the *lack* of democracy that's so inefficient. Our problems can't be solved by more information, more control, more social engineering, more compulsion, more rewards, more expertise. Experts can only reshuffle the elements of the mess or add more elements. The faults of technology are probably political as much as technological, but what always happens is this: a mess isn't solved by removing its cause but by adding a new apparatus to contain or redistribute the mess, and then a new apparatus to deal with the new apparatus. (Transport is a perfect example of what happens.) There is no structural logic, no way of getting organizational simplicity, no real evolutionary discipline. Technology is a way of solving problems, but the *total technological culture* will break down from time to time, perhaps even more often than other cultures do, because there's no structural integration between its parts, and various technologies are always in conflict. There is chaos because machines and technology are given priority over people. The only way to get a workable simplicity is for people themselves to decide how they want to live and work and what sort of communities they want to be in. Then people will not be subordinated to more and more machines.

Politicians have talked about democracy for three hundred years and now people have come to expect it. The myth has gone out of state and authority, the social structure of authority doesn't impress or intimidate any more. You see, if someone's authority ultimately derives from god, *that* impresses. But an expert doesn't have that sort of moral charisma. There's no reason why *he* shouldn't work for *you*. Well, if no one believes in god any more how can he run the world efficiently? Most people no longer believe that if god's son came down to earth again he'd be better advised to send him to Eton. Most working people no longer believe there are other people who know better than they do how they should live and work. That doesn't mean that everything they will do is practical common sense; the essential thing about acting responsibly is to have responsibility. Then you learn from experience, you learn what you don't know and what education you need. And the time to take responsibility is when the people who've already got it can't make it work – and that's our situation now. Our problems won't vanish and we won't step straight into a rational society. But rational processes will be brought back into society and problems can be solved instead of being compounded. We have to choose a new purpose for society, a new culture. There *is* a counter-culture ready and it's been developing for hundreds of years: it is democracy.

1974

Bibliographical Note
Most biographies of Shakespeare barely mention the Welcombe enclosure, but all the documents and a full commentary are given in *William Shakespeare* by E. K. Chambers (2 vols).

For

Jane Howell

Bingo was first presented at the Northcott Theatre, Devon on 14 November 1973 with the following cast:

SHAKESPEARE	Bob Peck
OLD MAN	Paul Jesson
SON	David Howey
WILLIAM COMBE	David Roper
BEN JONSON	Rhys McConnochie
JEROME	Derek Fuke
WALLY	Martin Duncan
FIRST OLD WOMAN	Joanna Tope
JUDITH	Sue Cox
YOUNG WOMAN	Yvonne Edgell
JOAN	Margot Leicester
SECOND OLD WOMAN	Margot Leicester

Directed by Jane Howell and John Dove
Designed by Hayden Griffin
Lighting by Nick Chelton

PART ONE
One: Garden
Two: Garden
Three: Hill

PART TWO
Four: Inn
Five: Fields
Six: Room

There is an interval after Part One.

Warwickshire 1615 and 1616

Part One

ONE

Garden. A hedge runs across the top of the stage. Left, a passage-way opening through it. Far right, an opening with a low gate leading to the road. A bench. The house is unseen, off left.

Emptiness and silence. SHAKESPEARE *comes in. He carries a sheet of paper. He sits on the bench. He silently reads part of the paper. An* OLD MAN *comes through the gap in the hedge. He cuts the hedge with shears as he comes through and goes on cutting this side of the hedge. Silence.* JUDITH *comes out of the house left. The men don't react. The* OLD MAN *goes on cutting.*

JUDITH (*to* SHAKESPEARE). Isn't it cold for you? (*Slight pause.*) Mr Combe's here.

> SHAKESPEARE *nods.* JUDITH *looks round and then goes back into the house.* SHAKESPEARE *lets his hand hang down with the paper still in it. Silence.*

OLD MAN (*contentedly*). Last toime this year.

> *Silence. The* OLD MAN *goes on cutting. A* YOUNG WOMAN *comes along the road and stops at the gate. She smiles archly at the* OLD MAN.

YOUNG WOMAN. How yo' now?

> *The* OLD MAN *nods at* SHAKESPEARE. *The* YOUNG WOMAN *sees him.*

YOUNG WOMAN (*politely*). Nicet mornin', sir, thank the lord. (SHAKESPEARE *nods. The* YOUNG WOMAN *holds out her hand. A moment's silence.*) Just a little summat. Yo' yont notice.

OLD MAN. Where yo' from, gal?

YOUNG WOMAN. On my way through.

OLD MAN. Where to?

YOUNG WOMAN. My Bristol aunt. My people died lately. My aunt wed a farmer – they'll hev work for us. (*She turns to go.*) I yont be no trouble.

SHAKESPEARE. Stay, stay. (*She stops.*) You'd rather have money not food?

YOUNG WOMAN. Ah, that I would.

SHAKESPEARE *stands and goes out left to the house.*

YOUNG WOMAN. Hev he gone for authority?

The OLD MAN *smiles at her. He goes to the gate and opens it.*

YOUNG WOMAN. Is that all roight? (*Uncertainly.*) I yont know . . .

The OLD MAN *carefully pulls her through. He shuts the gate behind her with his foot. He glances round and then touches her breast.*

YOUNG WOMAN (*looks round, afraid*). Not here.

OLD MAN. Yo'm a beauty, gal. Let us feel.

YOUNG WOMAN. Got money, hev yo'?

OLD MAN. Wait back a the garden in that bit a orchard.

YOUNG WOMAN (*looks towards the house*). He . . . ?

OLD MAN. No one yont see down there. I got money. You go sharpish an' keep low. I'll be down by-n'by.

The YOUNG WOMAN *goes through the gap in the hedge. The* OLD MAN *picks up his shears and cuts the hedge.* SHAKESPEARE *comes from the house. He carries a purse.*

OLD MAN (*amused*). Her run.

SHAKESPEARE. Call her. She'll be out on the road.

The OLD MAN *goes slowly through the gate, still carrying the shears. He looks right and left, then calls.*

OLD MAN. Gal. (*He comes back through the gate.*) Her run.

SHAKESPEARE *puts the purse in his pocket. The* OLD MAN *starts cutting the hedge again.* SHAKESPEARE *sits on the bench. Silence. The* OLD MAN *laughs a little to himself, just loud enough to be heard.* SHAKESPEARE *doesn't react.*

OLD MAN (*steps back and looks at the hedge*). She yont need lookin' at till next spring.

SHAKESPEARE *doesn't react. The* OLD MAN *goes out through the gap.* SHAKESPEARE *is alone. He sits on the bench. The paper is beside him. A chapel bell begins to peal. It is very close.* SHAKESPEARE *doesn't react. An* OLD WOMAN *comes from the house. She wears an apron.*

OLD WOMAN. Where's Hubby? (SHAKESPEARE *shrugs. The* OLD WOMAN *calls.*) Father. (*To* SHAKESPEARE.) His drink's on table if – (*The bell stops.*) – yo' see him. (*She calls.*) Father. (*To* SHAKESPEARE.) Mr Combe's in the house a-talkin t' Judith. Yo' yont ought-a set out here. That's cold afore you feel it this toime a year.

SHAKESPEARE. It's the last of the sun.

OLD WOMAN. So it may be. (*Slight pause.*) Mr Combe's come arter the land. Mornin', business. If t'was yonythin' else he'd a come on an' evenin'. (SHAKESPEARE *doesn't react.*) There's plenty a talk! Some say summat, some say summat else. (*Slight pause.*) P'raps he'll tell yo' what he's up to. (*Slight pause.*) People kip arksin' me hev I 'eard yonythin'. Yo'll be brought in – you stand t'lose.

SHAKESPEARE. And your son.

OLD WOMAN. An' a lot a others. What'll yo' tell him?

SHAKESPEARE. Your son told you to question me.

OLD WOMAN. They've hed a meetin'. They thought I ought-a arkst.

SHAKESPEARE. I don't know anything.

OLD WOMAN. What'll yo' do?

SHAKESPEARE. There's plenty of time.

OLD WOMAN. Start buildin' bridges when your feet git wet. If he shut they fields up he'll ruin whole families. They yont got a penny put by. My son say he like a speak t'yo' bout it. I told him t'look in this mornin'.

SHAKESPEARE. Did you.

OLD WOMAN. I thought yo'd want t' hear him out.

WILLIAM COMBE *comes through the house.*

SHAKESPEARE. Mornin', Will.

COMBE. Mornin'.

OLD WOMAN. Mornin', Mr Combe.

SHAKESPEARE *nods and the* OLD WOMAN *goes out right through the gate.*

COMBE. Nice garden. Your hobby, is it?

SHAKESPEARE. No. I weed a bit. I get tired. I planted the maples.

OLD WOMAN (*off, on the road*). Father.

COMBE. Quiet for you after London. You should take an interest in local affairs. We could get you on the town council.

SHAKESPEARE. No.

COMBE. Well, no use if you're not dedicated. You have to find time for it. Pity, though.

OLD WOMAN (*off*). Father.

COMBE. How's your wife?

SHAKESPEARE. Much the same.

COMBE. Well . . . sensible to sit here – if you know how to sit. Wears me out, of course. Been listening to gossip?

SHAKESPEARE. I've heard something.

COMBE. The gossip's true for once. There are over four hundred acres of common field out at Welcombe. They're owned by a group of farmers and a crowd of tenants. It's divided up into so many bits and pieces no one knows where they are. We can't farm the way we want – we all have to do what the bad farmers do.

SHAKESPEARE. We?

COMBE. Me – and two other big land owners. We're going to enclose – stake out new fields the size of all our old pieces put together and shut them up behind hedges and ditches. Then we can farm in our own way. Tenants with long leases will be reallocated new land. Squatters and small tenants on short leases will have to go: we shan't renew. That leaves you, and some others, who own rents on the land.

SHAKESPEARE. The rents. I bought my share years ago out of money I made by writing.

COMBE. All the farmers on the common fields pay you a rent based on their earnings – so any change affects you. Quite a large part of your regular income must come from that rent. A sound investment.

SHAKESPEARE. I wanted security. Is it true that when you enclose you're going over from corn to sheep?

COMBE. Mostly. Sheep prices are lower than corn prices but they still give the best return. Low on labour costs! No ploughing, sowing, harvesting, threshing, carting – just a few old shepherds who can turn their hand to butchery. Sheep are pure profit.

SHAKESPEARE. But you know I could lose? I've got no labour costs, I just draw my rents.

The OLD WOMAN *comes through the gate. She crosses the garden and goes out left.*

COMBE (*factually*). Everyone listens to money. (*He looks off left a moment and then turns back to* SHAKESPEARE.) There's another problem: the town council also own some of the rents. They use their share to feed the town poor – seven hundred – not counting gypsies and riff-raff passing through. You see there's a lot of money involved!

SHAKESPEARE. The town will oppose you. A lot of the small holders don't have written leases. They just followed their fathers onto the land – and their fathers had followed *their* fathers. If you get rid of them and the short-lease tenants – there'll be more than seven hundred poor to feed. And if you grow less wheat the price of bread will go up –

COMBE. Then it'll be profitable to grow more wheat and the price will come down. Always take the long view, Will. I selfishly cut down my labour costs and put up prices and the town suffers – but not in the long run. This is the only way men have so far discovered of running the world. Men are donkeys, they need carrots and sticks. All the other ways: they come down to bigger sticks. But there's a difference between us and the beast. We understand the nature of carrots and sticks. That's why we can get rid of the bad farmers who *grow* starvation in their fields like a crop, and create seven hundred poor in a town of less than two thousand. But – in the meantime the town council will oppose me. They don't want to feed the new poor while they wait for history to catch up with the facts. They're writing to you for help.

SHAKESPEARE. Who told you –

COMBE. My friends on the council. You're one of the biggest rent holders. You're respectable. They probably think you've got friends in London. You could make out a strong case against me.

SHAKESPEARE. We've come to the river.

COMBE. We needn't build a bridge if there's a ford downstream. Will you reach an agreement with me?

SHAKESPEARE. You'll get increased profits – you can afford to guarantee me against loss. And the town councillors.

COMBE. I make all the effort, I expect to keep my carrot.

SHAKESPEARE. I invested a lot of money.

COMBE. I'll tell you why I'm here: I'll guarantee *you* against loss, in return for an understanding.

SHAKESPEARE. Yes?

COMBE. Don't support the town or the tenants. When the council write, ignore them. Be noncommittal or say you think nothing will come of it. Stay in your garden. I'll pay for that.

SHAKESPEARE. You read too much into it. I'm protecting my own interests. Not supporting you, or fighting the town.

COMBE. That's all I want. It needn't be written into our agreement, it wouldn't read well: but it will be implied. After all, if we sign an agreement it wouldn't pay you to attack me: you get your present rents guaranteed at no extra cost. Free insurance. It pays to sit in a garden.

SHAKESPEARE. You guarantee me the difference between what my rents are now and what they'll be after enclosure, if they fall. How do we agree the figures?

COMBE. O, you can accept my –

SHAKESPEARE (gives COMBE his sheet of paper). I want security. I can't provide for the future again. My father went bankrupt when he was old. Too easy going.

COMBE (holding the paper). Yes, a nice man, but as you say, too . . . Very well. We'll appoint independent assessors. How many?

SHAKESPEARE. Another thing. I've got over a hundred acres of my own land out there. Are you after that?

COMBE. No, no. We won't touch your private land. This only affects your rents from the common fields.

> The OLD MAN hurries in through the gap in the hedge. He is frightened but defiant, excited and amused. He looks round, backs a few steps towards the hedge and stands there. SHAKE-SPEARE and COMBE don't notice him. COMBE reads SHAKE-SPEARE's piece of paper. A moment's silence. The SON comes angrily through the gap in the hedge. He is excited and tight-jawed. The SON stares at the OLD MAN before bursting out.

SON. Beast.

OLD MAN (laughs briefly). Look at him.

SON. Animal. In daylight. Back on a public high road. Any child could put its yead cross the wall.

> COMBE stands up.

OLD MAN (*pointing at the* SON). Look at him!

SON. Grey hair. Waggin' your boney ol' arse. Slobberin' like a boy with mud pies.

COMBE. He's got a woman in there.

SON. Hev yo' no shame? God an' man see you in the daylight. Yo'm drag creation down t' the beast. Animal. They ugly ol' legs. Runnin' loike a thief. Ugly.

JUDITH *and the* OLD WOMAN *come out of the house.*

Look at him! Where your wife an' child can see yo'.

JUDITH. What is it?

OLD WOMAN. Father, your drink's inside on the table.

OLD MAN. Yont sendin' me indoor. Look how red he go!

COMBE (*goes to the hedge and calls through*). Girl! Come here.

SON. Git her out. Thass her. Runnin' round them trees. Tried a climb the wall. I shut the gate on 'em when I saw what t'was. (*He goes to the gap and calls through.*) Come out. (*He turns to the* OLD MAN.) Loike an animal. Ugly. (*To the others.*) He yont hed the shame t'cover her yead with her skart.

COMBE (*calls*). You won't get out there. It's locked.

Silence. The YOUNG WOMAN *comes through the gap in the hedge.*

You're not a local girl.

YOUNG WOMAN. On my way t'Bristol, sir.

COMBE. Got work there?

YOUNG WOMAN (*nods*). Can I go, sir?

COMBE. No doubt your family's dead and your husband's left you?

YOUNG WOMAN. Not wed, sir. My family's dead though. Can I go?

COMBE. Who've you got in Bristol – your sister, uncle?

OLD MAN (*laughs*). Her auntie. Mr Combe almost got 'an roight.

COMBE. Dear me, we're in a bad way. Half the country's suddenly bereaved and they're marching round England to stay with relatives who live as far away as possible. The law says you can't leave your parish without a pass. Where's your pass?

YOUNG WOMAN. I yont no beggar woman, sir.

SON. Mr Combe's on the bench. Yo' hed it now. Yo'll be punished.

SHAKESPEARE (*to the* SON). Why were you in my orchard?

They all turn to look at SHAKESPEARE.

SON. I come t'see yo'. Mother say I . . .

The YOUNG WOMAN *starts to cry. They all turn back to her.*

YOUNG WOMAN. My aunt's waitin' in Bristol. My family's dead.

JUDITH. Where?

YOUNG WOMAN. Coventry.

JUDITH. Could you point out their graves?

YOUNG WOMAN. They'm buried in poor ground. Nothin' t'show.

COMBE. We have her sort in front of us every week, Judith. Do anything for money – though they'd rather do nothing. Lie when they learn to speak. First time they say father it's a lie. (*He laughs shortly.*) The law says you're to be whipped here in the shopping place till the blood runs and then sent back to your parish in Coventry, was it?

YOUNG WOMAN. Yont whip us, sir? I were whip afore an' that hurt my yead sorely. I couldn't go with people arter. I walked okkard an' fell down in the road. I were a gal then an' that's only better now.

COMBE. If there's something wrong with your head it'll do it good. Doctors whip mad people. I'd like to follow my own inclinations and let you off but I have to protect the public. You're a healthy girl, sleeping rough hardens your skin. You'll be all right. If you lead your sort of life you must learn to pay for it. (*To the* SON.) Take her to the lock-up.

The SON *starts to take the* YOUNG WOMAN *out.*

YOUNG WOMAN (*earnestly, not crying*). Yo' yont whip us, sir. That destroy my yead. The Constable's wife long a 'cester say that's a shame t'whip me. (*The* SON *takes her out through the gate. She is heard off on the road.*) I fall over the road, sir. Yont whip us.

COMBE. Tch, locusts or the blight. (*To* SHAKESPEARE.) I'll show this paper to my lawyers and be in touch. Goodbye.

COMBE *goes out left.* JUDITH *goes with him.*

OLD MAN. He git cross!

OLD WOMAN. Father, go in an hev your drink.

The OLD MAN *goes into the house.*

I'm sorry my boy shouted. Young people yont got no patience – worse'n us. I hope he yont upsit his father.

SHAKESPEARE. They're going to enclose.

OLD WOMAN. What'll you do?

SHAKESPEARE. Wait and see.

OLD WOMAN. Yo' give him a sheet a piper.

SHAKESPEARE. Nothing's decided. Has this shouting woken my wife? See if she's all right.

The OLD WOMAN *goes out left.* SHAKESPEARE *sits on the bench. He stares in front of him for a moment.*

TWO

Garden. Six months later.

The OLD WOMAN *and* JUDITH *are sitting alone on the bench.*

JUDITH. Has your marriage been happy?

OLD WOMAN. 'Twas. We had seven good year first off. Then the press men come t' church one Sunday mornin' an' hid back a the tomb stones. When the men come from the lord's supper out they jump an' tak em over sea t'fight. I still think a them times on an off. Time 'fore the flood.

JUDITH. Seven years out of a life. Most people don't have that.

OLD WOMAN. He were gone three year. Then two men bot him hwome. He'd bin hit top the yead with an axe. Some man were killin' a man lay on the ground front on him an' when he swung his axe back he hit father top the yead. Not the sharp end, though. That'd a kill 'un. Now he hev the mind of a twelve year ol' an' the needs on a man. I'm mother an' wife to him.

JUDITH. He should be happy. No responsibilities. No duties.

OLD WOMAN. He's a boy that remember what's like t'be a man. He still hev a proper feelin' for his pride, that yont gone. Hard, that is – like bein' tied up to a clown. Some nights he come hwome an' cry all hours. I git on with my work now. You hear him all over the house. Every room. An' the garden.

JUDITH. It was harder for your son. He had a child for a father.

SHAKESPEARE *comes out of the house.*

OLD WOMAN. No coat?

SHAKESPEARE. Is it cold? It looked warm from the house.

The OLD WOMAN *stands and goes off left into the house.*

JUDITH. Have you been up to mother?

SHAKESPEARE. What?

JUDITH. Shall we carry her down? The spring weather will help her.

SHAKESPEARE. She's happy in her room.

JUDITH. When are you going back to London?

SHAKESPEARE. I don't know.

JUDITH. I thought you were buying some property at Blackfriars.

SHAKESPEARE. That's done.

The OLD WOMAN *comes from the house with a wrap. She drapes* SHAKESPEARE.

SHAKESPEARE (*irritated*). Don't fuss!

> SHAKESPEARE *pulls the coat off and pushes it back to the* OLD WOMAN.

OLD WOMAN. I'll leave it there.

> The OLD WOMAN *puts the wrap on the bench and goes off into the house.*

JUDITH. Aren't you going away at all this year?

SHAKESPEARE (*still irritated*). I don't know.

JUDITH. Have you told mother?

SHAKESPEARE. She's not interested.

JUDITH. You'll get old sitting there all day.

SHAKESPEARE. I *am* old.

JUDITH. You used to be so busy. Striding about. Laughing. It's all gone. You look so tired these days.

SHAKESPEARE. I didn't sleep last night. So many people on the streets. All that shouting. And the sky – like day.

JUDITH. Someone's starting the fires. Everyone says so.

SHAKESPEARE. I'll put buckets on the stairs and by the doors. You must keep them filled. Thank god we're not thatched.

JUDITH. Why don't you tip the watch and tell them to keep an eye on us?

SHAKESPEARE. I have.

> *Silence.* JUDITH *looks at* SHAKESPEARE. *Then she gets up and goes silently into the house.* SHAKESPEARE *is alone. He leans back and slightly to one side with his head up and his hands in his lap. He closes his eyes. Silence. The* OLD MAN *comes silently through the gap in the hedge. A pair of shears hangs from his hand. He pays no attention to* SHAKESPEARE. *He stops and feels along the side of the hedge with the flat of his hand, as if he was blind. Then he begins to cut. Suddenly* SHAKESPEARE *notices him. He is shocked – but he doesn't make a sound or move violently.*

SHAKESPEARE. How long have you been there?

OLD MAN. Juss cuttin' back the young growth. That need air t' thicken out. Hev I woke you up then? Your daughter bin rowin', that it? Yont want a take no woman-row. Yo' got a fist. Thass only two piece a man's anatomy a woman understan', an' a fist's one. She yont hold with yo' set there all day.

The YOUNG WOMAN *comes to the gate. The* OLD MAN *looks at her, goes to the gate, opens it. She comes in quickly and stands close to the hedge.*

SHAKESPEARE (*looks at the* YOUNG WOMAN. *There's a slight pause before he knows her.*) They sent you home.

OLD MAN. Her yont got no hwome. Her go back there her'll get whip again. So her run for it.

SHAKESPEARE. You mustn't walk in the streets. You'll be recognized.

YOUNG WOMAN. I mostly come out a night. I were frightid by meself t'day. I were clever, mind. When someone got by I stoop down an' do as though I brushin' my skart.

SHAKESPEARE. Where d'you live?

YOUNG WOMAN. Barns. They ol' burned 'ouses.

SHAKESPEARE. You're shaking.

YOUNG WOMAN. Ah, I do shake an' all! I bin took so since they whip us. I warned 'em straight. (*She shrugs.*) I yont feel cold but my arms an' legs do shake an' my teeth go a-clatter. (*She holds out her fore-arm.*) Yo' look, see 'ow the skin go in that arm, like a bud peckin'.

SHAKESPEARE. How did you get through the winter?

OLD MAN. I fed her.

YOUNG WOMAN. Sometime. I yont allus count on that. Sometime the boys come a-lookin' for us in they empty houses. Not s'much now. They say I have a sickness. I tell 'em I'm whole, thass only the whippin'. But they only come when they'm drunk. You yont heard a no cure for shakin'?

SHAKESPEARE. No.

YOUNG WOMAN. I cover meself proper but I still shakes. I try holdin' me yand tight. I set in the heat of a fire. But I still shakes. An' when that's cold the same. Well, there. I yont thrid needles for a livin'. I can larn t'live with it. Least it yont touch my yead.

SHAKESPEARE. You give her bread and lie with her.

OLD MAN. She's a poor creature. But us still hev some fun.

YOUNG WOMAN. O ah, us's allus laughin'.

SHAKESPEARE. At what?

OLD MAN. O – people?

YOUNG WOMAN. What they put on t' wear.

OLD MAN. They hats!

YOUNG WOMAN. An' what they say.

OLD MAN. Try t' tell yo' yo' yont know your own name.

YOUNG WOMAN. Gallopin' arter this an' that – but they mustn't pant! 'Howdedo.'

OLD MAN. 'Howdedo.'

The OLD MAN *and the* YOUNG WOMAN *laugh.*

YOUNG WOMAN. Us laugh so us hev t' cover us yeads –

OLD MAN. So us yont git caught.

The OLD MAN *and* YOUNG WOMAN *laugh.*

YOUNG WOMAN. Well. (*She holds out her hand.*)

SHAKESPEARE (*calls*). House!

The YOUNG WOMAN *runs towards the gate.*

OLD MAN. Don't frit. He'll give yo' proper fettles sit out on a table like a christian.

JUDITH *comes out of the house.*

SHAKESPEARE. Let her eat. Give her a shawl or a dress. Both. Give her your mother's things. They're only gathering dust.

JUDITH (*unsure*). I know her. (*She recognizes her.*) She – . (*To* SHAKESPEARE.) No. If we feed her once we'll never get rid of her.

YOUNG WOMAN. That's roight enough. Give us some money an'
I'll away t' go. I yont need feedin'.

SHAKESPEARE. She must be looked after.

JUDITH. She'd steal if we had her here, the poor thing.

YOUNG WOMAN. Missis is roight. It yont do t'trust me. Give us a
bit a money. Yont notice that.

The bell starts to peal.

JUDITH (*to the* OLD MAN). D'you often have her in the garden?

OLD MAN. No.

JUDITH. How often?

SHAKESPEARE *sits on the bench.*

SHAKESPEARE (*to the* YOUNG WOMAN). Wait in the orchard till
it's dark. Then go away. (*To* JUDITH.) Give her some money.
No, bring my purse.

YOUNG WOMAN (*looks at the gap in the hedge and hesitates*). I
yont go down there agin–

SHAKESPEARE. The back gate's locked now.

The YOUNG WOMAN *goes through the gap in the hedge.*

JUDITH. Why is she so frightened?

SHAKESPEARE. She shakes because she was whipped.

JUDITH *goes left into the house.*

OLD MAN. Now she's cross with the two on us. My boy's cross
too. He rage up an' down all hours. Say yo' agin poor people.
Ol' Combe tak the best land, an' do he give yo' any that yont
be good enough t' grow stones in. (*He shrugs.*) I tell 'im yo'
live a rare ol' life but there's no harm in yo'. He's allus talkin'
t'god – so stands t' reason he never listen to a word I say.

SHAKESPEARE. Why is your son afraid of the devil? God judges,
not the devil.

OLD MAN. When my boy's took in a hoolerin'-bout he say the
devil look arter his own.

SHAKESPEARE. By putting them in the fire? You never sell everything. That's what he punishes. Hell is full of burning scruples.

The OLD WOMAN *comes out of the house.*

OLD WOMAN. Mr Combe.

SHAKESPEARE *nods.*

OLD WOMAN. (*to the* OLD MAN). Let the gen'men talk, father.

The OLD WOMAN *goes into the house. The* OLD MAN *takes
another cut at the hedge and then follows her.* SHAKESPEARE
sits alone for a moment. He raises his head as COMBE *comes
out of the house.* COMBE *carries a bottle of ink, a pen and a
document.*

COMBE. In your garden? The day for it. I haven't seen you
since winter. Busy. (*He puts the pen and ink on the bench and
hands the document to* SHAKESPEARE.) From my lawyer.
(SHAKESPEARE *starts to read the document.*) Pity you didn't go
into business before. You can bargain. That guarantees you
against any loss arising from my action.

SHAKESPEARE. You'll enclose?

COMBE. My men start digging – (*The bell stops.*) – round my
land on Monday. I've signed it.

SHAKESPEARE (*reading the document.*) Bells love silence.

SHAKESPEARE *signs the document.* COMBE *picks it up and
looks at it.*

COMBE. I'll have it witnessed. Must keep you on good behaviour,
living by the chapel.

JUDITH *comes out of the house.*

JUDITH. Mr Combe – I thought it was! How is Mrs Combe?
(*She shakes* COMBE's *hand.*) . . . No. I won't have it. (*Icily cold.*)
Father, where is he? It's shameful.

SHAKESPEARE. No.

JUDITH (*icy*). Don't shield them. You're morally as guilty as they are.

COMBE. What is it?

JUDITH. Our garden man. In that hedge.

COMBE (*amused*). With a woman? (*He goes to the hedge and looks through the gap. Then he looks back at* SHAKESPEARE.) I know why you like your garden!

> COMBE *goes out through the gap in the hedge.*

JUDITH. I'm sorry, father, I will not allow that woman – (*She points left to the house.*) – to be abused. How can you behave so badly? It's irresponsible! Why d'you make it necessary for a child to speak to its parents in this way?

> *The* YOUNG WOMAN *runs through the gap in the hedge, over the garden and out through the gate.*

How sordid. Ugly. (*She stares angrily after the* YOUNG WOMAN *but doesn't try to stop her. She is still like ice.*) On one's own property.

> JUDITH *goes to the gate and shuts it.* COMBE *walks through the gap in the hedge. He is still amused.*

COMBE. Gone?

JUDITH. Yes. Thank you.

COMBE. She was hiding behind the trees. Bolted like a rabbit when I said boo. I had a clear sight of her. (*He turns to* JUDITH.) There was no one with her.

SHAKESPEARE. She wants work. I told her she could work in the scullery.

COMBE. No, she can't. She was sent away from here to her proper parish, and she's come back. Tch. The lord chancellor's told the benches they aren't firm enough. Well, I am. I'll have the barns and burned houses searched. I know where they lie up. (*He goes towards the gate.*) The law says it's an offence to give alms to anyone without a licence. So don't be tempted.

Goodbye. I'll get my men on to her. She won't make herself a nuisance anymore.

COMBE *goes out through the gate.*

JUDITH. Last time they . . . So of course I thought . . .

SHAKESPEARE. I came out here to rest. People coming and going. (*He sighs.*) Haven't you any work in the house?

JUDITH. How could I let him enjoy himself while his wife . . .? She's had a hard life, father. You don't notice these things. You must learn that people have feelings. They suffer. Life almost breaks them. (*She picks up the pen and ink.*) I'll take these in. You don't need them? You sit there and brood all day. People in this town aren't so easily impressed, you know. We can all sit and think. (SHAKESPEARE *is silent.*) I feel guilty if I dare to talk about anything that matters. I should shut up now – or ask if it's good gardening weather. D'you know why mother's ill? D'you care?

SHAKESPEARE. Judith.

JUDITH. At last, a word. I'll tell you why she stays in bed. She hides from you. She doesn't know who she is, or what she's supposed to do, or who she married. She's bewildered – like so many of us!

SHAKESPEARE (*flatly*). Stop it, Judith. You speak so badly. Such banalities. So stale and ugly.

JUDITH. I can only use the words I know.

The OLD WOMAN *and the* OLD MAN *come out of the house left. She wears her outdoor coat. He carries the basket.*

OLD WOMAN. We'm away now. There's nothin we'm forgot?

SHAKESPEARE (*to the* OLD MAN). Combe found her.

OLD WOMAN. Oh dear.

JUDITH (*to the* OLD WOMAN). That girl was –

OLD WOMAN. Hubby told me. Us were goin' t'put her up for a few days, now I know on it. Then p'raps summat could be worked out. Surely there's summat?

SHAKESPEARE. Combe's men are looking for her.

> *The* OLD MAN *sits on the bench. He rests his elbows on his knees and his hands hang down between his legs. He rocks like a little boy. The basket is on the ground beside him.*

JUDITH. They'll flog her! O, why wasn't I more careful? You all think I should be in her place. (*To* SHAKESPEARE.) You could have warned me! You ignore me – you always do! You talk to the servants more than to your family.

OLD MAN. That's worse'n that. She lit they fires. I yont know why. She wait up in they empty houses till that's dark then out she go an' back she come an' set down in the corner. She yont tell but I knew what t'was. Her face blacked up an' she smelt of smoke. Smell it for days.

OLD WOMAN. No one else know.

OLD MAN. They'll find out. When they lock her up. Her'll tell.

OLD WOMAN. You're not t' fault. Us won't let em touch you.

OLD MAN. They'll hang her. (*He starts to cry.*) O dear, I do hate a hanging. People runnin' through the streets laughin an' sportin'. Buyin' an' sellin'. I allus enjoyed the hangings when I were a boy. Now I can't abide 'em. They conjurors with red noses takin' animals out the air an' coloured things out their pockets. The soldier lads scare us. The parson an' 'is antics.

OLD WOMAN. Mr Shakespeare yont like yo' cryin in his garden. (*She helps the* OLD MAN *to his feet.*) I'll manage the basket. (*To* JUDITH.) Goodbye then. He'll be round for work in the mornin'. (*To the* OLD MAN.) We'll soon be hwome. (*To others.*) I'll git him t'bed early.

OLD MAN (*crying as he goes*). People pushin' t'see in they empty coffins. Allus so quiet fore the rope go so's yo' hear babbies an dogs cry – an' when it thump the people holla.

> *The* OLD MAN *and the* OLD WOMAN *go through the gate.*

OLD WOMAN (*out on the road*). Hush now. I hev a noice surprise indoor for yo', my lad.

OLD MAN (*out on the road*). That better be good.

OLD WOMAN. That's good. I hid un so yo'll hev t' find it first.

The OLD MAN *and the* OLD WOMAN *go away down the road.*

JUDITH. I can't leave you out here. It's against common humanity. You'ld better come inside and learn to put up with us.

SHAKESPEARE. Go in.

JUDITH. You'll catch cold and expect to be nursed. I've enough
to do with mother on my hands. Why are you so stubborn?
Your family's tearing itself to bits and you sit in the garden
and –

SHAKESPEARE. Yes, yes.

JUDITH. Yes, yes – it's easy to make us sound stupid. You ignore
the people you share a house with and when they try to talk, you
sneer.

SHAKESPEARE *goes out through the gate.* JUDITH *follows him
onto the road. She can be heard calling after him.*

If we bore you why don't you go away, father? Go back to your
interesting friends. Or are they tired of you now?

THREE

Hill. A pleasant warm day. Slight fresh wind. The YOUNG WOMAN
*has been gibbeted. An upright post with two short beams forming a
narrow cleft. The* YOUNG WOMAN's *head is in this and her body is
suspended against the post. A sack is wrapped round her from hips to
ankles. A rope is wound round the sack and the top half of her body
to steady her against the post. (Rembrandt, New York Metropolitan
Museum of Art, inv. 76487. 'Rembrandt's Drawings' Schedig, W.
Ill. 121.) She has been dead one day. The face is grey, the eyes
closed and the hair has become whispy.*

A bench downstage left. SHAKESPEARE *sits on it facing away from the body, out into the audience. He is alone.*

Two labourers come in. Both middle aged. They watch the body for a moment.

JOAN (*reflectively*). By roights they ought- a put her on a bonfire, for lightin' fires. Or starve her in a cage for beggary.

JEROME. Set yo'self down, gal'. I'm tired.

They sit on the ground, unpack their lunch and eat.

JOAN (*quietly as she points to* SHAKESPEARE). Is the gen'man all roight?

JEROME (*nods and eats*). Gen'man from big 'ouse: New Place gen'man.

They eat in silence for a moment.

Good.

JOAN. Like it?

JEROME (*nods and eats*). Good stuff.

JOAN. Take some a mine.

JEROME. No, gal.

JOAN. Go on, I offered, yo' yont arkst.

JEROME. Yont yo' 'ungry?

JOAN. I got extra. I know hot weather allus give yo' an appetite.

JEROME. Yo' pick your grub like a bud with a wart end on its beak. (*He puts his arm round her waist.*)

JOAN. Hold your noise, boy. An' give over throwin' crumbs down the front a my dress. (*She takes his arm from her waist, uncorks a bottle and gives it to him.*) Grab hold a that. Yo' need two hand a feed yo'self.

JEROME (*drinking*). Yo'm a hard woman.

JOAN (*eating*). So'd yo' be if yo' kip gettin' crumbs down the front a your dress. (*She takes crumbs from her bodice and feeds the birds.*) Cheep-cheep, chuck-chuck, my beauties.

The SON *comes on with* WALLY. WALLY *is tall and quite thin.*

SON. Mornin', brother, sister.

WALLY. Morn'. (*He stares at* JOAN *and* JEROME.)

JOAN. We'm on us way t' work. Stonin' our strip a field out at Welcombe. We'm just cooched-ed up for us bit a fitter.

JEROME (*eating*). Which we'm carnt. Sorry yont none left t' hand round. (*He drinks.*)

JOAN. Hev yo' see her drop? (WALLY *shakes his head.*) Proper state her were in. Yont heard a word parson say, poor chap. But she went good as gold.

JEROME (*eating*). He say up yo' git, my gal, an' up she git.

JOAN. Tryin' a help 'em hang her. (*She finds more crumbs in her bodice.*) Cheep-cheep. How the wicked disguise themselves. Her could a bunt the town t'death. When her toime come she couldn't hold a candle straight t' see where she were goin'. She die summat slow. No family or friends t' swing on her legs. I sin mothers an' fathers help their young a go easy afore. She yont afford a pay the hangman t' do it.

SON. A festival a dark. Singin', dancin', layin' money how long she'll live. The sexes going back a hedges. Is that reverence? Lord god is wherever there's justice. When a soul go satanways lord god come t'watch an' weep. Reverence, friends. That ought-a be a festival a light an' prayer.

JOAN (*quietly. Feeding birds*). Chuck, chuck, chuck.

WALLY. P'raps they'm makin' a great show for the presence a lord god, brother. Soundin' the psalter an the joyful harp.

SON. You'm too good natured, brother. Let us talk with lord god.

The SON *and* WALLY *shut their eyes and clasp their hands. They don't kneel.* JOAN *bows her head, stops eating and takes the last crumbs from her bodice.* JEROME *bows his head and goes on chewing and putting food in his mouth.*

Lord god, lord god. The covetous man laugh in 'is secret yeart but thou art not mocked. Thou sent the whore t' the rich man's yate an' the poor man fell in her way but thou art not mocked.

WALLY. Amen.

JEROME. He yont finished yet, brother.

SON. Lord god, thou set thy cross for a sign-post afore the two ways. Lord god, shear the sheep in winter that he feel the blast. Amen.

WALLY *and* JOAN. Amen.

> SHAKESPEARE *has stood up and walked slowly away. His movements and face express nothing.*

JEROME (*wiping his mouth with the back of his hand*). That'll do grace. (*He stands.*) We'm off t' labour in the lord's vineyards.

SON. Yont do need t' laugh at good people, brother. You hev pains an' reasons for 'em I yont know, an' I hev mine. Only the sinner's branded front t' yead – an' that's sometime hid.

JEROME. Nothin' under my yat bar my yead.

> JEROME *and* JOAN *go out. The* SON *stands in front of the gibbet.* WALLY *watches him.*

WALLY. What is it, brother?

SON. I'm larnin' t' face a sin so I know it in the street.

WALLY. Her's terrible changed.

SON. Death bring out her true life, brother. Look, her eyes be shut agin the truth. There's blood trickle down the corner a her mouth. Her teeth snap at her flesh while her die. Be solemn, brother, think a lord god. That's the face us turn to him even when us prays. Day an' day an' day he set the sun t'rise an' shine a way for his saints on earth an' us throw us shadow cross it. God weep.

WALLY. Halleluja! O rapture in the lord!

SON. ⎤ Us sin an' go on all four in the grass. Us face is turned
    ⎟ to dirt away from lord god.

WALLY. ⎦ (*jumping*). Israel. Israel. Israel. Israel. Irsael. Israel. Israel.

WALLY. Praise an' glory. O tis terrible t' die so.

JUDITH (*off*). Father. Father.

SON } Worse, worse to live in sin. Lord god send death t' free his sinner. Damnation's bliss when yo' know he chose it for you.

WALLY } (*jumping*). Israel. Israel. Israel.

JUDITH *comes on right.*

JUDITH. My father.

SON. He were here. I sid a prayer but he turn away from the word.

WALLY. Spurned lord god like the roman in the judgement hall.

SON. Amen.

JUDITH (*calls*). Father.

JUDITH *stops in front of the* YOUNG WOMAN.

WALLY. She'll hev her full a fire now.

SON (*quietly. Watching* JUDITH). Harden your yeart for lord god, sister. Dost matter t' him her beg when all eat out his yand? No. Dost matter her burn the proud man's hall when he break t' earth from toime t' toime? Dost matter her love a man when he love all men –

JUDITH (*calls*). Father.

SON. Even the sinner's innocent. O harden your yeart with a glad-some mind, good people. Tent for us t' question lord god's way. Sin were 'er cross an her bore it afore us for a sign. Lord god send the wolf an' the shepherd to the sheep.

WALLY. Amen.

SON. Amen.

The SON *and* WALLY *go out right.*

JUDITH (*calls*). Father.

SHAKESPEARE *comes on left.*

Are you blaming me? Is that what I've done now?

SHAKESPEARE. No. She'd have been caught. Burning . . .

JUDITH. Come home.

SHAKESPEARE. Later. (*He sits.*)

JUDITH. You're hungry.

SHAKESPEARE. Why do . . .? I thought I knew the questions. Have I forgotten them?

JUDITH. People will stroll out here to look after work. They'll talk if you sit there. We know what she was. (SHAKESPEARE *doesn't react.*) You were out all yesterday. Did you see her hang?

SHAKESPEARE. The baited bear. Tied to the stake. Its dirty coat needs brushing. Dried mud and spume. Pale dust. Big clumsy fists. Men bringing dogs through the gate. Leather collars with spikes. Loose them and fight. The bear wanders round the stake. It knows it can't get away. The chain. Dogs on three sides. Fur in the mouth. Deeper. (*The* OLD WOMAN *comes on upstage right.*) Flesh and blood. Strips of skin. Teeth scrapping bone. The bear will crush one of the skulls. Big feet slithering in dog's brain. Round the stake. On and on. The key in the warder's pocket. Howls. Roars. Men baiting their beast. On and on and on. And later the bear raises its great arm. The paw with a broken razor. And it looks as if it's making a gesture – it wasn't: only weariness or pain or the sun or brushing away the sweat – but it looks as if it's making a gesture to the crowd. Asking for one sign of grace, one no. And the crowd roars, for more blood, more pain, more beasts huddled together, tearing flesh and treading in living blood.

JUDITH. You don't like sport. Some bears dance.

SHAKESPEARE. In London they blinded a bear. Called Harry Hunks. The sport was to bait it with whips. Slash, slash. It couldn't see but it could hear. It grabbed the whips. Caught some of them. Broke them. Slashed back at the men. Slash, slash. The men stood round in a circle slashing at it. It was blind but they still chained it to the ground. Slash, slash. Then they sent an ape round on a horse. A thin hairy man or a child. You could see the pale skin under its arm when it jumped. Its teeth. The dogs tore it to pieces. The crowd howled. London. The queen cheered them on in shrill latin. The virgin often watched blood. Her father baited bears on the Thames. From boat to boat, slash, slash. They fell in and fought men in the water. He was the man in a mad house who says I'm king but he had a country to say it in.

JUDITH. I must go down. Someone must watch the house, count the glasses, knives, spoons. I shan't ask you to listen any more. You're only interested in your ideas. You treat us as enemies.

JUDITH *walks upstage to the* OLD WOMAN. *The* OLD WOMAN *puts her arm round her and silently tries to comfort her.*

SHAKESPEARE. What does it cost to stay alive? I'm stupefied at the suffering I've seen. The shapes huddled in misery that twitch away when you step over them. Women with shopping bags stepping over puddles of blood. What it costs to starve people. The chatter of those who hand over prisoners. The smile of men who see no further than the end of a knife. Stupefied. How can I go back to that? What can I do there? I talk to myself now. I know no one will ever listen.

The OLD WOMAN *comes down to* SHAKESPEARE.

OLD WOMAN. A gen'man's come from London. At the Golden Cross. (*She hands a note to* SHAKESPEARE.) He sent this up by me.

SHAKESPEARE. There's no higher wisdom of silence. No face brooding over the water. (*The* OLD WOMAN *glances helplessly up at* JUDITH.) No hand leading the waves to the shore as if it's saving a dog from the sea. When I go to my theatre I walk under sixteen severed heads on a gate. You hear bears in the pit while my characters talk.

OLD WOMAN. Now, sir. That's bin a longish winter. That's brought yo' down.

SHAKESPEARE. No other hand . . . no face . . . just these . . .

OLD WOMAN (*to* JUDITH). I'll bring him hwome.

JUDITH *goes out.*

SHAKESPEARE. Stupid woman! They stand under a gallows and ask if it rains. Terrible. Terrible. What is the right question? I said be still. I quietened the storms inside me. But the storm breaks outside. To have usurped the place of god, and lied . . .

OLD WOMAN. Why torment yo'self? You'm never harmed no –

SHAKESPEARE. And my daughter?

OLD WOMAN. No, no. Yo' yont named for cruelty. They say yo'm a generous man. Yo' looked arter me an' father. Give us one a your houses t' live in.

SHAKESPEARE (*points*). There's a coin. I saw it when I came up. Glittering in the grass.

OLD WOMAN (*goes immediately to where* SHAKESPEARE *pointed*). Here?

SHAKESPEARE. Perhaps the hangman dropped it.

OLD WOMAN (*picks up the coin*). We'm put a little by for later. Times change. Read your note.

SHAKESPEARE *is silent*. He doesn't move.

If yo' yont allow yo'self t' be helped, what shall us do? I'm afraid I'm like your daughter. I yont had no one t' talk to, no one t' share my loife. Juss father's prattle – an' he stay by me out a fear. Nothin' else. O a child love but he yont even a proper child. He yont more'n a wounded bud in a road. Tread on or go under a cart. I fed him. Kep him clane. Tak the washin' back when he steal it. Scare him so he yont hide t'much. I took a stick to him afore now, or he yont got no tay. But one day when he steal summat they'll be roight cross: shops're doin' bad or that's the weather. Then they'll hang him! His 'ole loife's a risk. I hope he die afore me. (*She shrugs.*) What'm I supposed a make a that? I yont afford arkst questions I yont know y'answers to. Well, you'm summat at peace now.

SHAKESPEARE. I went to the river yesterday. So quiet. They were all here. No fishing, no boats. One boy to mind the cattle – he was being punished. I watched the fish jump for flies. Then a swan flew by me up the river. On a straight line just over the water. A woman in a white dress running along an empty street. Its neck was rocking like a wave. I heard its breath when it flew by. Sighing. The white swan and the dark water. Straight down the middle of the river and round a curve out of sight. I could still hear its wings. God knows where it was going. So quiet and then silence. (*He gestures round.*) And here it was hot – (*He stands.*) – noise – dust . . . she saw none of this – (*He gestures to the horizon.*) the view . . . Where shall I go? London? Stay here? (*He goes to the gibbet. The* OLD WOMAN *watches him.*) Still perfect. Still beautiful.

In the far distance a bell peals briefly.

OLD WOMAN. No. Her's ugly. Her face is all a-twist. They put her legs in a sack count a she's dirty.

SHAKESPEARE. The marks on her face are men's hands. Won't they be washed away?

OLD WOMAN. She smell. She smell.

SHAKESPEARE *goes out. The* OLD WOMAN *goes to the place where she found the coin. She searches for a moment. She doesn't find anything. The bell stops. The* OLD WOMAN *looks across at the* YOUNG WOMAN. *Then she goes out.*

Part Two

FOUR

The Golden Cross. A large, irregular shaped room. Stone floor. Left, a few tables and benches, Right, a table and three chairs. A large open fire between them. Burning wood. Night. Lamps.

SHAKESPEARE and JONSON are at the table right. Bottles and two glasses on the table. No one else in the room.

SHAKESPEARE. How long did the theatre burn?

JONSON. Two hours.

SHAKESPEARE (*tapping the table*). When I was buying my house the owner was poisoned. By his son. A half-wit. They hanged him. Legal complications with the contract. My father was robbed by my mother's side of the family. That was property too.

JONSON. Coincidences.

SHAKESPEARE. But that such coincidences are possible . . . Jokes about my play setting the house on fire?

JONSON. What are you writing?

SHAKESPEARE. Nothing.

They drink.

JONSON. Not writing?

SHAKESPEARE. No.

JONSON. Why not?

SHAKESPEARE. Nothing to say.

JONSON. Doesn't stop others. Written out?

SHAKESPEARE. Yes.

They drink.

JONSON. Now, what are you writing?

SHAKESPEARE. Nothing.

JONSON. Down here for the peace and quiet? Find inspiration - look for it, anyway. Work up something spiritual. Refined. Can't get by with scrabbling it off in noisy corners any more. New young men. Competition. Your recent stuff's been pretty peculiar. What was The Winter's Tale about? I ask to be polite.

SHAKESPEARE. What are you writing?

JONSON. They say you've come down to study grammar. Or history. Have you read my English Grammar? Let me sell you a copy. I've got a few up in my room.

Silence. SHAKESPEARE *pours drinks.*

What am *I* writing? You've never shown any interest before.

SHAKESPEARE. Untrue.

JONSON. O, how many characters, enough big parts for the leads, a bit of comedy to bring them in - usual theatre-owner's questions. Trying to pick my brains now? Run out of ideas?

They drink.

Nice to see you again. I'm off to Scotland soon. Walking. Alone. Well, no one would come with me. Might be a book in it. Eat out on London gossip. The Scots are very credulous - common sense people are always superstitious, aren't they. Can't imagine you walking to Scotland. That sort of research is too real!

SHAKESPEARE (*smiles. Starts to stand*). Well.

JONSON. Don't go. Sit down. Would you like to read my new play? It's up in my room. Won't take a minute.

SHAKESPEARE. No.

JONSON. Nice to see you again. Honest William.

SHAKESPEARE. I wouldn't read it. It would lie there.

JONSON. What is it? Tired? Not well? (SHAKESPEARE *starts to stand.*) Sit down. (*He pours drinks.*) Wife better?

SHAKESPEARE. No.

JONSON. Wrong subject. D'you like the quiet?

SHAKESPEARE. What quiet?

They drink.

JONSON. What are you writing? (*Slight pause.*) The theatre told me to ask.

SHAKESPEARE (*shakes his head*). Sorry.

JONSON. What d'you do?

SHAKESPEARE. There's the house. People I'm responsible for. The garden's too big. Time goes. I'm surprised how old I've got.

JONSON. You always kept yourself to yourself. Well, you certainly didn't like me. Or what I wrote. Sit down. I hate writing. Fat white fingers excreting dirty black ink. Smudges. Shadows. Shit. Silence.

SHAKESPEARE. You're a very good writer.

JONSON. Patronizing bastard.

Slight pause. They drink.

You don't want to quarrel with me. I killed one once. Fellow writer. Only way to end a literary quarrel. Put my sword in him. Like a new pen. The blood flowed as if inspired. Then the Old Bailey. I was going to hang. That's carrying research too far. I could read so they let me off. Proper respect for learning. Branded my thumb. A child's alphabet: T for Tyburn. I've been in prison four times. Dark smelly places. No gardens. Sorry yours is too big. They kept coming in and taking people out to cut bits off them. Their hands. Take off their noses. Cut their stomachs open. Rummage round inside with a dirty fist and drag everything out. The law. Little men going out through the door. White. Shaking. Even staggering. I ask, is it necessary? What's your life been like? Any real blood, any prison? Four times? Don't go, don't go. I want to touch you for a loan. I know I'm not human. My father died before I was born. That desperate to avoid me. My eyes are too close together. Look. A well known fact. I used to have so much good

will when I was young. That's what's necessary, isn't it? Good
will. In the end. O god.

Silence. They drink.

Yes.

Silence.

What are you writing?

SHAKESPEARE. I think you're a very good writer. I made them
put on your first play.

JONSON. God, am I that bad? In prison they threatened to cut
off my nose. And ears. They didn't offer to work on my eyes.
Life doesn't seem to touch you, I mean soil you. You walk by
on the clean pavement. I climb tall towers to show I'm clever.
Others do tricks in the gutter. You are serene. Serene. I'm
going to make you drunk and watch you spew. You aren't well.
I can see that! Something's happening to your will. You're
being sapped. I think you're dying. What a laugh! Are you
getting hollow? Why don't you get up? Walk out? Why are you
listening to my hysterical crap? Don't worry about me. I'll
survive. I've lived through two religious conversions. I thrive
on tearing myself to bits. I even bought enough poison. Once.
In a moment of strength. (*He takes a small bottle from his collar.
It hangs round his neck on a chain.*) I was too weak to take it.
Hung the cross here in my catholic period. (*He takes the top off
the bottle.*) Look: coated in sugar. Like to lick my poison? I
licked one once to try. (SHAKESPEARE *doesn't react.*) Well, it's
not the best. All I could afford. Little corner shop in London.

SHAKESPEARE. Give it to me.

JONSON. Sentimental whiner. You wouldn't uncross your legs if I
ate the lot. You're upset I might give it to someone else. (*He
puts the bottle back in his collar.*) I should live in the country.
No – I'd hear myself talk. When I went sight seeing in the mad
house there was a young man who spent all his time stamping on
his shadow. Punched it. Went for it with a knife. Tried to cut

the head off. Anything to be free. The knife on the stone. The noise. Sparks.

They drink.

I helped to uncover the gunpowder plot. Keep in with the top.

They drink.

Your health. I'm always saying nice things about you, Serenity. Of course, I touch on your lack of education, or as I put it genuine ignorance. But you can't ignore an elephant when it waves at you with its trunk, can you. You taking this down? Base something on me. A minor character who comes on for five minutes while the lead's off changing his clothes or making a last effort to learn his lines? Shall I tell you something about me? I hate. Yes – isn't that interesting! I keep it well hidden but it's true: I hate. A short hard word. Begins with a hiss and ends with a spit: hate. To say it you open your mouth as if you're bringing up: hate. I hate you, for example. For preference actually. Hate's far more jealous than love. You can't satisfy it by the gut or the groin. A terrible appetite. Interrupt me. Speak. Sob. Nothing? I'm not afraid to let myself be insulted.

The SON, WALLY, JEROME *and* JOAN *come in right.*

SON (*pointing left*). Over there.

The SON *goes out right again. The others sit.*

WALLY. They'm followed us.

JEROME. No matter. They'll know who t'was.

WALLY. They'm followed us. I were neigh on slaughtered. One a Combe's men heaved a rock at us when I were scramblin' out the ditch. I'm certain-sure they'm followed us. Where's us shovels?

JEROME. I hid they in the hedge out back.

JOAN (*looking across at* SHAKESPEARE *and* JONSON). Careful, there's gen'men here.

JEROME. Too drunk t' hear if yo' shouted.

WALLY. Git the mud off yo'. That show what us bin up to. Us don't ought-a done it. That'll only start more row.

JEROME. That's us land. Shall us sit down an' let 'em rob it? How I live then? How I feed my wife an' little-uns?

JOAN. Hush.

JEROME. I'll break Combe's neck.

JONSON. Where was I? Yes: hate. I hate you because you smile. Right up to *under* your eyes. Which are set the right distance apart. O I've wiped the smile off now. I hate your health. I'm sure you'll die in a healthy way. Well at least you're dying. That's incense to scatter on these burning coals. I hate your long country limbs. I've seen you walking along the city streets like a man going over his own fields. So simple. A simple stride. So beautiful and simple. You see why I hate you. How have they made you so simple? Tell me, Will? Please. How have they made you so good? You even know when it's time to die. Come down here to die quietly in your garden or an upstairs room. My death will be terrible. I'll linger on in people's way, poor, thick, dirty, empty, a mess. I go on and on, why can't I stop? I even talk shit now. To know the seasons of life and death and walk quietly on the path between them. No tears, no tears. Hate is like a clown armed with a knife. He must draw blood to cap the joke, you know? Well, have you got a new play, it has to be a comedy, rebuilding is expensive, they'd like you to invest. Think about it. You may come up with an idea, or manage to steal one. But it must be in time for next season.

Silence.

My life's been one long self-insult. It came on with puberty.

Silence. JONSON *drinks.*

Teach me something.

SHAKESPEARE *falls across the table and spills his glass.*

God.

> JONSON *tries to dry* SHAKESPEARE *with a napkin. He sets him up in his chair.* SHAKESPEARE *slumps forward again. The* SON *comes on with a bottle and glasses.* JOAN *pours.*

SON. They yont give up.

JOAN. No more'll us. (*She hands him a drink. He waves it aside.*)

SON (*rocking slightly*). Rich thieves plunderin' the earth. Think on the poor trees an' grass an' beasts, all neglect an' stood in the absence a god. One year no harvest'll come, no seed'll grow in the plants, no green, no cattle yont leave their stall, stand hud-dled-to in the hovel, no hand'll turn water in their trough, the earth'll die an' be covered with scars: the mark a dust where a beast rot in the sand. Where there's no lord god there's a wilderness.

WALLY. Don't go forth in it now, brother. (*To the others.*) He's allus close t' tears. (*To the* SON.) Don't git took up.

JOAN (*offers the* SON *the drink again*). Yo' hev this. That's cold out there t'night. (*The* SON *doesn't take it.*)

WALLY. The waters a Babylon run by his door.

SON (*rocking slightly*). The absence a god, the wilderness . . . neglect . . .

> COMBE *comes in. He goes to the* SON.

COMBE. You've been here all evening.

SON (*nods*). Even', Mr Combe.

COMBE (*to* JONSON). How long have they been here?

JONSON. When I drink my eyes swim closer together. One, two, nine, ten peasants . . .

> SHAKESPEARE *is still slumped forward on the table.*

COMBE (*to the* SON). I thought the brothers didn't swill.

SON. We may quench thirst in an orderly 'ouse.

COMBE. After labour.

JONSON gets up and goes out right. As he goes he talks. The others ignore him. He is drunk but controlled.

COMBE. Every time you fill my ditches I'll dig them out. Every time you pull down my fence I'll put it back. There'll be more broken fences.

JONSON. To spend my life wandering through quiet fields. Charm fish from the water with a song. Gather simple eggs. Muse with my reflection in quiet water having the accents of philosophy. And lie at last in some cool mossy grave where maidens come to make vows over my corpse. (*He goes.*)

SON (*to* WALLY). Note that.

COMBE. Be very careful on Sunday. Wear the right cap and go to the parish church – not some holy hovel out in the fields. Keep to the law. Don't come up in front of me on the bench.

SON. Whose interest's that protectin'? Public or yourn?

COMBE. You trespass on my land. Fight my men. Trample my crop. Now you turn me into the devil. The town will benefit from what I'm doing. So will the poor.

JEROME (*quietly*). S'long's they'm still alive.

COMBE. What? (JEROME *doesn't answer.* COMBE *turns to the* SON.) There's a division in this country. We're not just fighting for land. Listen. I've seen suffering, I've caused some of it – and I try to stop it. But I know this: there'll always be real suffering, real stupidity and greed and violence. And there can be no civilization till you've learned to live with it. I live in the real world and try to make it work. There's nothing more moral than that. But you live in a world of dreams! Well, what happens when you have to wake up? You find that real people can't live in your dreams. They don't fit, they're not good or sane or noble enough. So you turn to common violence and begin to destroy them. (*He stops.*) Why should I talk to you? You can't listen. (*To* JEROME.) You hold your farm on a lease. When you die your son has to pay a fee before he inherits it. That fee isn't fixed – it's decided by the landlord, my brother-in-law. We work with anyone who shows good will. But there can only be one master.

JONSON *comes back. He carries a bottle.*

SON. A sexton's diggin' your ditches, Combe.

WALLY. Amen.

SON. An' yo'll be buried in 'em.

JOAN. So dig 'em deep. Israel.

WALLY. Israel. Israel. Israel.

JONSON. Where can you buy a good spade? I'm sure there's a book in it. Should find a sale. Sound practical manual in a good, simple, craftsman's style.

COMBE. Grown men acting like children.

COMBE *goes out.*

SON. God take us on a long journey. That man's prophetical. We see the same truth from odd sides but us both know tis the truth.

WALLY (*softly*). Glory. Glory.

SON. I looked cross a great plain into his eyes. A sword were put into my yand. The lord god a peace arm us. We must go back an' fill up they ditches agin t'night.

JEROME. T'night?

SON. Whenever he turn his back. Every toime.

JEROME. Us'll come.

JOAN. No.

JEROME. Ah! There's only one master. When yo' put your yand in your pocket now yo' find another yand there.

The SON *and* WALLY *go towards the door.*

JONSON. Shepherds –

The SON *and* WALLY *ignore him and go out.*

JONSON (*to* JOAN *and* JEROME). – fill your bowls.

JOAN (*to* JEROME). That's a full bottle. Wasted on them in that state.

JEROME. While us wait.

> JOAN *and* JEROME *go to* JONSON's *table.* SHAKESPEARE *is still slumped forward.* JEROME *recognizes him.*

JONSON (*shaking* SHAKESPEARE). The pilgrims have come.

JEROME. We yont better sit with the gen'man.

SHAKESPEARE. Sit down.

> JONSON *starts to fill their glasses.*

JONSON. Was that man your enemy? Call him back and let me kill him for you.

SHAKESPEARE. You've been filling the ditches.

JEROME. No.

SHAKESPEARE. Lie to me. Lie. Lie. You have to lie to me now.

> WALLY *runs in. He has a shovel.*

WALLY. Snow! Snow!

JOAN. Snow!

WALLY. Late snow! A portent! A sign!

JEROME (*seeing the shovel*). Git that shovel out!

JOAN. Snow! Shall us still go?

JEROME (*pushing* WALLY). Git that out! Yo' fool!

WALLY. What? Snow! Snow!

SHAKESPEARE. Lie to me. Lie to me.

> WALLY *and* JEROME *go out.* JOAN *follows them.*

JONSON. They went? Was it my talk? I talk too much. (*He sits. They drink.*) I hope you're paying. I certainly can't afford to drink like this. You said something about a loan. (SHAKESPEARE *puts money on the table.*) I thought it was just the drink talking. (*He counts the money.*) In paradise there'll be a cash tree, and the sages will sit under it. You can't manage anything better?

You wouldn't notice it. I had to borrow to bury my little
boy. I still owe on the grave. (*He puts the money in his pocket.*)
I suppose you buried your boy in best oak. Sit down, sit
down.

FIVE

*Open space. Flat, white, crisp, empty. The fields, paths, roads,
bushes and trees are covered with smooth clean snow. It has stopped
snowing. Shakespeare comes on drunk.* JONSON's *poison bottle hangs
from a chain in his hand.*

SHAKESPEARE. My house. There at the bottom of the fields. No, I
won't go in. How dark it is. No lamps. The door is a hole.
The windows are ditches with water in. (*He pauses. Looks
round.*) How clean and empty the snow is. A sea without life.
An empty glass. Still smooth. No footprints. No ruts. No marks
of weapons or hoes dragged through the ground. Only my footprints behind me – and they're white . . . white . . . (*He looks
towards the house again.*) How long did I live there? So dark.
No footprints up to the door. No one's gone down the path
brushing against the hedge. The snow's still on top. In the
morning there'll be dead birds under the hedge. Their winter
colours will be bright in the snow. Their wings folded in for
warmth, not stretched out to fly between the snow and the
moon . . . The water and the earth are frozen together . . . One
piece of ice . . .

A snowball hits him. The OLD MAN *comes on. He is excited,
running in the cold has made his voice high.*

OLD MAN. A hit. A hit.

SHAKESPEARE. Where have you been?

OLD MAN. A hit. I bin aimin' snowballs at a snowman. (*He throws a snowball at* SHAKESPEARE.) A hit. A hit. (*He dances.*) Look at that snow, boy. I heard yo' talkin' things t' yo'self.

SHAKESPEARE. Are you cold?

OLD MAN. No. I play. I flap my arms an' run up an' down. Come t' see my snowman.

SHAKESPEARE. Too far.

OLD MAN (*Throws a snowball at* SHAKESPEARE). A hit. Ten, nothin'. Try t' hit us, boy. (*He puts a snowball in* SHAKESPEARE's *hand.*) Try. Try. Please.

   SHAKESPEARE *throws the snowball at him.*

SHAKESPEARE. It hit.

OLD MAN (*laughing derisively*). The legs, the legs, the legs yont count. Still fourteen, nothin'. Throw for the neck.

SHAKESPEARE. Were you on the hill?

OLD MAN. Ah. For a last see. A last toime. Then I saw summat come cross t' fields. A great white thing. That were a cloud I thought! Low. Then that turn t' snow. O pretty! That did fall fast. I saw the fields turn white. (*He laughs.*) She had a little heap set top on her yead. Like a cap. I made a slide down side t' hill. Whee! I hed such a toime. I like snow. Yont yo'? Then they rabbits all come t' see. You charm a rabbit by your play. They set theyselfs round in a circle. Heads on one side. I grabs one an' broke his neck for'n. (*He holds out a dead rabbit.*) Bad. Some'un elsen. Mustn't take. (*He grins.*) But my wife yont row me out when I come hwome. She'll hide it in the pot smart. (*He pats his pockets.*) I got onions here. Carrot here. Egg. Us'll hev a feast. Early greens.

   Four of five dark FIGURES *pass quickly over the top of the stage. They are huddled and quiet. One stops and points at* SHAKESPEARE *and the* OLD MAN.

FIGURE I (*low*). 'Oo's that?

FIGURE II (*stops, low*). Drunks.

All the FIGURES *go out right.*

SHAKESPEARE. A light's on in my house. They're trying to get in my room.

OLD MAN. They'll be out arter yo' now. I flare up do my wife come after me. She know the shape a my fist. Now her wait up till I'm in an' lock up arter us. I yont see no sight a my snowman in this snow.

The OLD MAN *wanders out.*

SHAKESPEARE. The door's opened. I drank too much. I must be calm. Don't fall about in front of them. Why did I drink all that? Fool! Fool! At my age . . . Why not? I am a fool. Why did I come back here. I wanted to meet some god by the river. Ask him questions. See his mouth open and the lips move. Hear simple things that move mountains and stop the blood before it hits the earth. Stop it so there's time to think. I was wrong to come – mistakes, mistakes. But I can't go back. That hate, anger –

JUDITH *comes in. She wears a green cloak.*

JUDITH. Walk all night in the fields if you like. I don't mind. But not when it's snowed. Mother's crying.

SHAKESPEARE. Who woke her?

JUDITH. It's late and I'm tired.

SHAKESPEARE. Who?

JUDITH. Another scene.

SHAKESPEARE. Why did you do it? What can she do? Cry!

JUDITH. When you behave like a child you'll be treated like one.

SHAKESPEARE. Listen. You'll get my property between you when I'm dead. When I ran away from your mother and went to London – I was so bored, she's such a silly woman, obstinate, and you take after her. Forgive me, I know that's cruel, sordid,

but it's such an effort to be polite any more. That other age
when I ran away, I couldn't cut you out, you were my flesh, but
I thought I could make you forgive me: I started to collect for
you. I loved you with money. The only thing I can afford to
give you now is money. But money always turns to hate. If I
tried to be nice to you now it would be sentimental. You'd have
to understand why I hate you, respect me for it, even love me
for it. How can you? I treated you so badly. I made you vulgar
and ugly and cheap. I corrupted you.

JUDITH. Go on. I'm not listening. I'm young and this coat's
warm. I'll wait till you drop and then have you dragged in.

SHAKESPEARE. Don't be angry because I hate you, Judith. My
hatred isn't angry. It's cold and formal. I wouldn't harm you.
I'll help you, give my life for you – all in hatred. There's no
limit to my hate. It can't be satisfied by cruelty. It's destroyed
too much to be satisfied so easily. Only truth can satisfy it now.
I don't think all this matters to you, I can't hate you more than
when I say that.

    JUDITH *goes out.*

The last snow this year. Perhaps the last snow I shall see. The
last fall. (*He kneels on the ground and picks up some snow.*) How
cold. (*He half smiles.*) How perfect, but it only lasts one night.
When I was young I'd have written on it with a stick. A song.
The moon over the snow, a woman stares at her dead . . . What?
In the morning the sun would melt it into mortality. Writing in
the snow – a child's hand fumbling in an old man's beard, and
in the morning the old man dies, goes, taking the curls from the
child's fingers into the grave, and the child laughs and plays
under the dead man's window. New games. Now *I'm* old.
Where is the child to touch me and lead me to the grave?
Serene. Serene. Is that how they see me? (*He laughs a little.*) I
didn't know.

The dark FIGURES *run back across the top of the stage. Their heavy breathing is heard. They go off left.*

Snow. It doesn't melt. My hand's cold. (*He breathes on the snow in his hand.*) It doesn't melt. I must be very cold. Serene. How? When you're running from hangers and breakers and killers. The mad clown still nurses the child.

Far upstage a shot and a spurt of flame.

Every writer writes in other men's blood. The trivial, and the real. There's nothing else to write in. But only a god or a devil can write in other men's blood and not ask why they spilt it and what it cost. Not this hand, that's always melted snow . . .

SHAKESPEARE *lies forward on the ground. A dark* FIGURE *appears upstage. It cries and whimpers weakly and then vanishes.*

I didn't want to die. I could lie in this snow a whole life. I can think now, the thoughts come so easily over the snow and under my shroud. New worlds. Keys turning new locks – pushing the iron open like lion's teeth. Wolves will drag me through the snow. I'll sit in their lair and smile and be rich. In the morning or when I die the sun will rise and melt it all away. The dream. The wolves. The iron teeth. The snow. The wind. My voice. A dream that leads to sleep. (*He sits up.*) I'm dead now. Soon I shall fall down. If I wasn't dead I could kill myself. What is the ice inside me? The plague is hot – this is so cold. The truth means nothing when you hate. Was anything done? Was anything done? I sit in a wound as large as a valley. The sides are smooth and cold and grey. I sit at the bottom and cry at my own death.

The OLD WOMAN *comes in.*

OLD WOMAN. Your daughter come a-knock-knock at my door. Darlint, I say, yont no call t' fret, I'm set up waitin'. Fetch him

in, she say. That's twice t'day, I say. Last toime yo' was an
okkard fuss. Father's out too.

The OLD WOMAN *helps* SHAKESPEARE *to his feet.*

'Ow yo' people carry on. (*She feels him.*) Good lor, you're froze.
SHAKESPEARE. Silly. Staying out here. What have I done?
OLD WOMAN. Yo' had your reasons.
SHAKESPEARE. Drunk.
OLD WOMAN. Hev yo' yeard summat a while back? I yeard a
  noise, blowed if I yont. I yeard thunder in snow one toime.
  Toime I were a gal. They say I were a dazzler. That seem afore
  your father step into the world! – but I remember on it. I
  thought I saw summat run long the lane a while back. These
  eyes . . . I wish father yont stop out when that's jippy. Yont
  make no wish yo' can't grant yo'sel.
SHAKESPEARE. Take me in, take me in.
OLD WOMAN. Yes, sir, I'm sorry.
SHAKESPEARE. Light a fire in my room. I'm cold.
OLD WOMAN. O'course. Yes, yes.

The OLD WOMAN *helps* SHAKESPEARE *out.*

SIX

*Bedroom. Left, a bed with a needlework cover. Close to it a bedstand.
A wooden chair. Right, a door.* SHAKESPEARE *lies in bed. The* OLD
WOMAN *stands in the room.*

OLD WOMAN. I ought-a go down. (SHAKESPEARE *doesn't answer.*)
  I'll stay a while longer. My son'll say when that's toime.

(*Silence. She sits on the chair.*) Shall us set down? I'm that tired. (*She spreads her fingers and looks at her hands.*) I wanted him t' die first. Seem wrong now. He were lyin' in that snow an' I walk by him. Hed he say where he'd bin? (*No answer.*) Nicet if he sid summat a show he know he'd bin looked arter . . . Could yo' eat summat? Shall us let yo' sleep?

SHAKESPEARE. Was anything done?

OLD WOMAN. Yo' ought-a sleep. Why yont yo' try? . . . That all come out a closin they fields. I told yo' long ago in the garden: that'll cause trouble. Yo' yont listen. Sign a piece of piper an' that's all yo' thought on. Call that 'elp? Our house's quiet now he's gone. No one come or go, do they knock first an' ask if I'm in. A stranger's house. All they years.

SHAKESPEARE. Was anything done?

OLD WOMAN. Your daft questions. I yont harm no one's far's I could stop it. I look arter the two on us well's I might. (*Slight pause.*) He'd bin t' see that dead woman, that's 'ow it ended. (*She shrugs.*) He warnt greedy for money loike some men. I yont know . . .

SHAKESPEARE. It's so cold.

OLD WOMAN. That yont his woman neither. That warnt n'more'n his game. 'I want t' go out t' play. I'm tired a playin' indoor.' He wanted summat a child want. I yont know what. (*She shrugs.*) Well, yo' break a cup yo' put it t'gither. Yont kip arksin' 'oo brok it. That's all as is.

JUDITH (*off*). Father.

SHAKESPEARE *motions the* OLD WOMAN *to be quiet.*

JUDITH (*off*). Mother's here to see you.

SHAKESPEARE (*quietly to the* OLD WOMAN). I'm asleep.

JUDITH (*off*). Father..

Silence.

SHAKESPEARE (*quietly to the* OLD WOMAN). Has she gone?

OLD WOMAN (*goes to the door and calls softly*). Judy, dear?

No answer SHAKESPEARE *gets out of bed, goes to the door and listens.*

SHAKESPEARE (*quietly to the* OLD WOMAN). She's there.

The OLD WOMAN *goes to the chair and sits down again.*

OLD WOMAN. They'll level with me for this.

SHAKESPEARE *walks away from the door. Silence. There is a knock on it.*

JUDITH (*off*). Father, mother's here. (*Knock.*) Father. (*Knock.*) Open this door.

Outside an OLD WOMAN *begins to cry. More knocking on the door. The door handle is rattled. The knocking gets louder.*

JUDITH (*off*). Father, unlock this door. Mother's crying. Father, I know you can hear.

Outside the two women bang on the door. The crying is louder and wilder. Suddenly it becomes hysterical. The OLD WOMAN *gets up and slowly and methodically makes the bed.*

JUDITH (*off*). Father. Let us in. How dare you. You treat us like animals. Father. Why don't you come and hit her. You're cruel enough. You've done it before. Open the door and kick her. Father. We hate you. You're cruel. Wicked. Ugly. You beast.

The door is violently banged, kicked and shaken. Someone scratches it. Outside the OLD WOMAN *gasps and shrieks hysterically.*

JUDITH (*off*). Mother, get up. She's fallen down. Don't cover your ears – I'll make you hear. Make you. Make you. Make you. She's on the ground tearing her clothes. Look, her hands are bleeding.

SHAKESPEARE (*almost to himself*). It's so cold now.

JUDITH (*off*). Mother dear! Stop it! No. Don't. Help. Father.

SHAKESPEARE (*as before*). Cold. Cold.

OLD WOMAN (*quietly*). I'll open the door.

SHAKESPEARE. No. It's put on. Thirty-five years. All like this. (*He points to the bedside stand.*) My will. There. Fetch it.

JUDITH (*off*). You'll be punished. There's a god in heaven. She's tearing her hair. Terrible. Terrible. All my life. This. Time after time. I'll kill myself.

> *The* OLD WOMAN *rummages through papers on the bedside stand. She finds three sheets lying together.*

SHAKESPEARE. Those. Yes, yes, those.

> *The* OLD WOMAN *brings the sheets to* SHAKESPEARE. *They both stand by the door.*

JUDITH (*off*). She's clutching her heart. What is it?

> *Outside the* OLD WOMAN *gasps stertorously.*

SHAKESPEARE (*quietly, with amused contempt*). Clutching! (*He pushes the sheets under the door.*) It's all there. Your legal share. And the bed.

> *The sheets are snatched through from the other side. The crying becomes lower but goes on.*

JUDITH (*off*). Stand up. I'll help you. Try. (*The voices start to move away from the door.*) He won't let us in. I told you not to come down. I won't let you any more. We'll never speak to him again. He'll learn when it's too late. There.

> *The crying dies away. It is quiet.*

OLD WOMAN. Is that what her come for?

SHAKESPEARE. No. She'll be quieter now.

OLD WOMAN. Bed's made.

SHAKESPEARE. The chair. (*He sits in the chair. He closes his eyes. He is weak and tired.*) Cold. There's a draft. That door. Did they break it? (*The* OLD WOMAN *glances at the door.*) I must be quiet. White worms excreting black ink. Scratch. Scratch.

OLD WOMAN. What?

SHAKESPEARE. Was anything done? Was anything done?

A knock on the door.

OLD WOMAN. Yes?

SON (*off*). Mother.

The OLD WOMAN *opens the door. The* SON *comes in.*

'Oo's bin a-scratchin' your door? Half the paint's took off.

OLD WOMAN. Are they ready?

SON. Ah.

OLD WOMAN. I'll git into my coat. (*She pauses.*) I'll arkst summat first. Hev yo' took a gun with yo'?

SON. Us yont shot him. Us warn't armed.

OLD WOMAN. Then I'll walk t' church with yo'. (*To* SHAKE-SPEARE.) Goodbye.

SON. I'll follow directly.

The OLD WOMAN *goes out. The* SON *locks the door behind her.*

What hev yo' see?

SHAKESPEARE. Nothing.

SON. Yo' must hev. That were snow an' moon. Like day.

SHAKESPEARE. I wouldn't choose to lie while I'm dying. (*The* SON *watches* SHAKESPEARE *for a moment.* SHAKESPEARE *closes his eyes again.*) You can tell. Can't you. My face.

SON. Yo're very poorly.

SHAKESPEARE. I spent so much of my youth, my best energy . . . for this: New Place. Somewhere to be sane in. It was all a mistake. There's a taste of bitterness in my mouth. My stomach pumps it up when I think of myself . . . I could have done so much. (*The* SON *goes to the door and listens for a sound outside.*) Absurd! Absurd! I howled when they suffered, but they were whipped and hanged so that I could be free. That is the right question: not why did I sign one piece of paper? – no, no, even when I sat at my table, when I put on my clothes, I was a hangman's assistant, a gaoler's errand boy. If children go in rags we make the wind. If the table's empty we blight the harvest. If the roof leaks we send the storm. God made the elements but we inflict them on each other. Everything can be stolen, property and qualities of the mind. But stolen things have no value. Pride and arrogance are the same when they're stolen. Even serenity.

The SON *has come to* SHAKESPEARE.

SON. Everyone looked the same in the moonlight. I shot him.

SHAKESPEARE. So you met. The son and the father.

SON (*quietly*). I yont give meself up. Us'll foight for us land. Outside a me they'd give in. I'll go off later. When mother's settled. T'ent easy t'be with her now. T'ent decent.

SHAKESPEARE. A murderer telling a dead man the truth. Are we the only people who can afford the truth?

A knock at the door.

SON (*calls*). What?

COMBE (*off*). Combe here.

SHAKESPEARE. Unlock it.

The SON *unlocks the door.* COMBE *comes in. The* SON *locks the door behind him.* COMBE *stares at the* SON *and then turns to* SHAKESPEARE.

COMBE. Not disturbing you, I hope? Everything all right?

SHAKESPEARE. Some tablets. There. On the table. Please.

COMBE *goes to the bedside stand and picks up* JONSON's *poison bottle.*

COMBE. These?

SHAKESPEARE. Thank you.

COMBE (*gives the bottle to* SHAKESPEARE. *To the* SON). I'm
   sorry about your father. Decent man. This won't stop the
   enclosure.

SON. Your side shot him.

COMBE. I told my men no guns, only sticks. One of them may
   have disobeyed me – out of fear of you. Perhaps it was your own
   people. (*To* SHAKESPEARE.) I came to ask if you saw or heard
   anything. I'm told you were there.

SHAKESPEARE. Nothing.

COMBE. Pity. It's the magistrate's duty to ask.

   THE SON *laughs.*

If it's one of my men he'll be punished.

   SHAKESPEARE *starts to take the tablets.*

SON. What difference is that to us? Yo' take us land an' if us foight
   for'n – we'm criminals.

COMBE. You've a right to justice on your father's behalf. It's my
   duty to give it to you. Even though you're morally responsible
   for his death.

SON. Morally responsible! (*He laughs.*) He yont see! He yont see!
   He talk 'bout his law loike that had summat a do with justice!
   How can yo' give us justice, boy? Yo'm a thief. When yo' hang
   the man that kill my father, what yo' doin'? Is that justice? No –
   yo'm protectin' your thievin'.

COMBE (*to* SHAKESPEARE). I hope you're on your feet soon.

   The SON *unlocks the door for* COMBE. COMBE *goes out.*
   The SON *locks the door again.* SHAKESPEARE *takes more*
   tablets.

SON. I'll go away – where there's still space. I want t'be free. I cry
   for that. Sometoime when I'm out in the fields I climb a tall
   tree an' set stride the top an' cry. Let me be free. Liberty. Where
   no one stand 'tween me an' my god, no one listen when I raise

the song a praise, an' I walk by god's side with curtesy an' fear
nothin', as candid loike a child. (SHAKESPEARE *takes more
tablets.*) So us'll go away. Us plans is laid. Us'll take nowt bar
bible an' plough. (*Pause. His voice changes.*) I yont had no
proper toime t'reflect orderly on my father's dyin' – what with
the land an' arrangements an' that. I kill him. That'll have t' be
go over proper in my yead. Lord god'll say. Likely he done it a
purpose. Why else'd he afflict one a his chosen with a harsh
cross? The yand a god's in it someplace. (*He goes to the door and
unlocks it.*) The key?

SHAKESPEARE. Go and bury your father.

The SON *opens the door. He stops in the doorway.* SHAKE-
SPEARE *takes more tablets.*

SON (*quietly*). . . . When yo' think on't, t'ent so sure I shot him
neither. I fire a gun – I yont hide no truth. That yont mean I
shot him. Someone else'n moight a fired. Death on an un-
armed man – that's more loike the sort a think Combe'd get up
to. That want sortin' out in my yead. I may have done meself a
wrong.

The SON *goes out. He leaves the door open.*

SHAKESPEARE. How long have I been dead? When will I fall
down? Looking for rings on beggars' fingers. Mistakes . . .
mistakes . . . Was anything done? (*He takes another tablet.*)
Years waiting . . . fed . . . washing the dead . . . Was anything
done? . . . Was anything done? (*He looks at a tablet in his
hand.*) Dead sugar. (*He swallows it.*) Was anything done?

He falls from the chair onto the floor. JUDITH *comes into the
room. She sees* SHAKESPEARE. *She controls her panic. The
funeral bell begins to toll. It is close, but not so loud as in the
garden.* JUDITH *goes to* SHAKESPEARE *and quickly makes him
comfortable on the floor. He twitches and jerks.*

JUDITH. Nothing. A little attack.

> *She hurries to the bedside stand. She searches through it agita-*
> *tatedly. She throws papers aside. She tears some.* SHAKESPEARE
> *whimpers and shivers.*

JUDITH (*to herself as she searches*). Nothing. Nothing.

> JUDITH *runs to the door and shouts up.*

Nothing. If he made a new will his lawyer's got it.

> JUDITH *runs back to the bed. She is crying. She searches under*
> *the pillows.* SHAKESPEARE *has killed himself.*

JUDITH (*crying*). Nothing.

> JUDITH *searches under the sheets. She kneels down and searches*
> *under the bed. She cries. She stands and searches under the*
> *mattress.*

The Fool

Scenes of Bread and Love

INTRODUCTION

CAPITALISM

Not all communities have a culture. Some have only an organization. The members of an organization are often only monkey-people, who can organize and run advanced technologies and elaborate institutions and governments – but these things don't make a culture. An organization is concerned only with efficiency (though it is finally inefficient). Its technology tries to tell men how they can live. A culture does this too, but it also tells them how they ought to live and ensures that whatever is possible is done to make that ought practical; and the grounds for my optimism are that finally that is the only way men are content to live. Obviously we don't live in a culture. There is a discrepancy between what we have to do to keep our society running and what we're told we ought to do to be human. Our economy depends on exploitation and aggression. We expect business to be *ruthlessly* aggressive. At the same time we expect people to be generous and socially considerate. And we expect trade unionists to be dutiful workers and moderate in their demands – when they're at work. When they're consumers we expect them to be aggressive, to be competitive, greedy egotists – our way of life demands it. Advertising goads workers into needing more – *needing*, because its images are attached to human dignity, and so we need after-shave lotion for the reasons that we once needed salvation. Advertising tells the worker as consumer to be a master without responsibility to anyone but himself, a placid worker but a rampaging, selfish consumer demanding all the latest adult-toys and life-styles – which are his only rewards for reducing himself to a tool for two-thirds of his awake life. We're confronted with deep and destructive ironies: advertising is an incitement to strike and so capitalism destroys its organizational basis. We need anti-social behaviour to keep society running but this behaviour destroys society. The worker must 'know his place' in the factory but be an insatiable egotist outside it. The good citizen must be schizophrenic. And capitalism is incompatible with law and order. Ideally, capitalism would like to take a commodity out of one can – a tin – and put it into another can – a person. And although capitalism feeds on technocracy it is itself devoured by it, because technocracy destroys the acquiescing basis of society throughout the entire world – and while it grows rich on the poor it teaches them that the customer is always right.

Capitalism is competitive and its members use whatever power is at hand to extend and protect it. It's liberal, so far as it needs to protect itself from revolt, and when possible it substitutes affluence and moral and psychological pressure for force, because these are more easily justified and apparently (but only apparently) provoke less opposition. If it could supply enough goods, would it create complete satisfaction? No, it depends on dissatisfaction and by its nature it imposes the only means of meeting this dissatisfaction: consumer goods. Capitalism cannot satisfy the acquisitiveness it creates to maintain itself.

It tries to solve its dilemmas in many ways. Fascism is one way. It is the rational form of capitalism and tries to save it by consistency. This would work *if* we were prepared and able to behave permanently worse than animals. I say worse because animals are constrained by instincts and rigid physical limitations and men are not. But fascism can't have a culture because it's forced to equate that with driving people back to what it mistakenly regards as their instinctive nature.

Affluence is another attempt at salvaging capitalism. But this really only accelerates its decay. Affluence isn't well-being but a form of aggression. It makes consumption a form of competition. It makes the greedy hungry and the warm cold. Nothing is valued for itself but only for its consumption or possession. This is perpetually dissatisfying and the greater the dissatisfaction, the greater the business of stuffing things in the 'maw'. This can't create a culture because, firstly, it destroys its physical basis by squandering natural resources and in this way creates an ecological crisis in which we waste these resources to increase our dissatisfactions. And, secondly, because the more wealth that's put into the business of feverishly creating and stoking-up private dissatisfactions, the less there is to spend on the public fundamentals of culture or of any human society. The richer our organization becomes, the more impoverished are our schools, hospitals and welfare and social services. We abandon the old, we can't afford to socialize our children, our cities decay and our streets become the playground of violence, because we have neglected the necessities and decencies of life for the trivializing and ultimately despairing consumption of ersatz satisfactions. That is another irony: affluence impoverishes and produces the social conditions of scarcity.

TECHNOLOGY

We fail to solve our problems because we're dazzled by our technology and think there's a scientific solution to everything. Neither technology nor science can by themselves or together create a culture. They can both be misused. Auschwitz and a hospital are both scientific-technological institutions. Our technology doesn't make us highly civilized. We live in a scientific barbarism, the most irrational society that's ever existed. A society's rationality isn't measured by what it knows or has, but by the use it makes of these things. Knowledge, technical skills – the more of these there are, the more crucial the question of use becomes. It's quite possible that in a rapidly developing technocracy the gap between society and reason may widen. How rational a community is it in which technology can imitate the Black Death and there are no reliable political or social safeguards to stop it? Or in which an audience can sit in a theatre while a few miles along the road men are sitting before the gadgets that fire nuclear weapons? Collectively we have never been so insecure. This doesn't mean that we can do without science – even to try would be barbarous. Science and technology are essential to our future. But left to the wrong people they can become a source of social irrationality. We need a culture that can use them wisely.

It's said that technocracy will usher in the age of freedom and real community because it will create such abundance that people won't need to compete and so their destructive human-animal nature will remain dormant. But technology by itself won't give us security through abundance. Apart from anything else society changes more slowly than technology, and so the gap between the initial successes of technology and its utopian apotheosis may be so great that it allows the irrationality of society to get out of hand and become so powerful that our species is destroyed. Technology can't produce utopia out of a hat. Culture must be fought for on its own ground as well. And cultural struggle, although of course it doesn't exist in a vacuum, can't be reduced to anything else. Without technology and science there could be no abundance, no welfare, no hope, no destruction of false myths. But without cultural struggle technocracy will be irrational and destructive. Morality can exist only in a culture or be forged in the quest for one. Outside that there are only superstitions, as in primitive societies, and hypocrisy, as in Western democracies.

Left to itself technology develops in relation to its own needs. 'Let's do X because it's possible to do it'. Of course X will be related to human needs, otherwise technology would exist in a vacuum, but human needs may increasingly be determined according to technological convenience. 'If there's a problem let's solve it in the way technology already knows. If there are many problems let's give them priorities based on present technological possibilities'. In this way technology may be progressing when human beings are only being processed. This has of course often happened in the past. But it becomes dangerous in an advanced technocracy. People must always be fitted into technological structures – rickets and other slum diseases have been among the negative signs of this – but now technology could go further, the tool could modify the user not in a real historical development but simply in an inhibition. The fantasy behind this is of Robots taking over. But you don't need Robots, you need only give the wrong priority to technology in general. We have to make choices about technology. These can only be properly made when they're guided by culture.

Human beings live by biological systems, most of which were developed and tested in lower animals. Evolution has been a self-disciplining system for millions of years. This has produced species that function well and relate well to their environment. We're living through fast technological and political changes and these must be constantly tested. Again, this can only be done properly in a culture.

HUMAN NATURE

We don't have a fixed nature in the way other animals do. We have a 'gap' left by our freedom from the captive nature of other animals, from the tight control of instincts. The gap is filled by culture. Human nature is in fact human culture. The degree of culture is measured by its rationality. Rationality is the basis for discriminating between good and bad cultures. As human nature is human culture, human nature is social.

Men who live in an irrational society are driven to a kind of madness because such a society isn't in a static state, it deteriorates and ends by actively cultivating ignorance and combating knowledge. It can't be stabilized by its technology, however brilliant. On the contrary, its technology can be a danger. The neglect of social institutions, which I've already mentioned, affects us in many ways. It doesn't just divide individual against individual, it divides the individual against himself and tears him apart inwardly. An irrational man is frightened of himself as well as others. Irrationality is a state of *possession*. An animal doesn't know it's an animal but when men are irrational they know or sense that they are worse, more lost, than animals. They are not frightened of the strength and extent of their instincts – as it's often said – but of their weakness and limitation. A human being needs a culture to attach himself to real things in the outside world. When this doesn't happen, his unattached passions and emotions become self-parasitical. He either simply goes mad – and enters a state of false inventiveness which is unable to imagine the real (I shall try to explain this) because it finds it meaningless or unbearable – or he attaches his passions and emotions to substitute objects. He heaps possessions round him. He marks things as his possessions, his money, his property. Then the fulfilments of his passions are like crimes at the ends of cul de sacs. He is like a miser, he can never be rich, or like a glutton, he can never be fed, and he is cut off from creativity, which is the discovery of other people.

We need rationality not only to cope with our heightened self-consciousness, but also to answer questions about our existence. Everyone must answer some of these questions. Irrationality is never a harmless eccentricity. It is destructive. We don't have an animal nature which is violent, aggressive, egocentric, and which we must constantly fight in order to maintain a veneer of civilization. These destructive things are only *capacities*. We're born with many capacities and potentialities and these can be developed rationally so that we become socialized members of a culture. Disaster only occurs when we neglect to do this. Imagine a stack of bricks, floorboards, doors, tins of paint and bags of cement on a building site. They could be assembled into a strong, sound house. Instead they're left to rot and crumble. The glass is broken, the bags of cement ripped, it rains, weeds grow over the heap and then the rats move in. We didn't build Auschwitz because our animal natures made us do it, but because we neglected to create our nature.

Capitalism uses force and morality to try to restrain change, but it can't. Not only does it destroy its social basis and the characters of its members, it is itself destroyed by its own myths. An irrational organization needs myths to maintain itself. In this it's unlike culture, which seeks truth. Obvious myths are, from the past, the dogma of original sin, and in our day the dogma of original violence – the idea that violence is a necessity of human nature in the way eating and sleeping are, and not just a capacity such as fear or pain. Both these myths have been used to justify force to preserve social relationships. As the toys of affluence become brighter and faster and noisier, so it becomes necessary for capitalism to take an increasingly pessimistic view of human nature. Original violence is, of course, a far more pessimistic doctrine than original sin because there is no redemption in earth *or* heaven. This increasing pessimism isn't accidental. Capitalism creates a schizophrenic society of tension and aggression, and because 'consumerism' can't calm or restrain this (on the contrary), so more force and control and scrutiny are necessary. Authoritarianism and myth will penetrate deeper into human and social relations, not because capitalism can't imagine other methods and dream of different horizons, but because it's unable to achieve them. When conservatives ask for more privacy they only want it, like the burglar, for business hours.

If human nature is a vacuum waiting to be filled by culture, not a tabula rasa but a set of biological expectations, and if these expectations aren't met, then not only do people become haunted by disembodied passions in the way I've described, but whole societies are condemned to live out the myths they create to maintain their injustice. Our myth is that we are essentially violent but that there are scientific and technological means of controlling our violence – and we live out our myth by creating the weapons of death. In this way the first world war can be seen as the myth of the nineteenth century. The dreams of the old enlightenment have been lost and we see our society becoming more violent, despairing and uncultured. Science in the service of profiteering won't create a new enlightenment. We won't achieve that till we change our political and social basis. And in passing I would add that the idea of a society of hedonists stimulated (or is it pacified?) by a technology of lights, smells, sounds and feels – that is pure science fiction, based on the illusion that to be happy we have only to satisfy our instincts. The bright people would murder one another on the streets, and they wouldn't wait for the cover of darkness.

Animal instincts are concerned with survival, and as men aren't guided through life by instincts, they have no alternative, if they're going to survive, but to understand their lives. If they refrain or are prevented from doing this, then their condition is as absurd as a dog's would be if it could ignore its instincts. Such a man would be very like a dog chained up and starved. The dog dies because its need for food has a direct relation to an appropriate activity, eating, and if this doesn't occur the need is removed: the dog dies. But if a man's need for a rational understanding isn't met, the end is postponed, because the man must invent something to meet the need. The object of any biological structure is to orientate itself and perpetuate its kind. For man this means the need to relate himself to society, his individuality to the community, and to observe the relationship. When a man can't do this, his passions and emotions turn inward, in the way I've described, and relate only to himself. He invents a fantasy reality. He's like a chained dog who takes to devouring himself. Such a man soon pulls reality down on his head, and whole classes do the same.

CULTURE

Culture is the rational creation of human nature, the implementation of rationality in all human activity, economic, political, social, public and private. A culture must unite technology, science, and political and economic organization, and relate them to our environment in such a way that we can continue our lives and broaden them socially and humanely. It must show us how we can live and how we ought to live so that there is a future for us. When it uses myth it does so not for Plato's reasons, but as working hypotheses in matters not yet fully understood. Our species must order its nature rationally because irrationality is a state of accelerating decay leading to destruction. Even if this were not so, a man left to his instincts could still only use a small number of his potential abilities. He might grub for roots for a while but he could never build a farm. Instincts can't produce culture. Culture is built into the gap in human nature – the open brain, the awareness that develops itself exponentially, the capacity for thought that needs to learn in both a disciplined and a playful way.

How does the artist help to create culture? Technology says what's workable, and politics what's possible, at a particular time. And as most scientists aren't mad, and most politicians aren't power maniacs, the artist can understand political necessity and sympathize with political compromise, just as much as he enjoys the benefits of technology. But culture isn't made from these things alone. Everyone has a creative imagination, the faculty that's used, among other things, to create and understand art. I think that creative imagination is related to rationality and through this to human values. I don't know of any fascist 'art' – book, film, picture or anything else – that isn't tawdry and ludicrous. I shall say more about art later. Here I want to stress that it can only be rational and have a social meaning and purpose.

Just as culture is the way a society meets its fundamental needs, and not something it adds later, so it isn't a veneer a well-fed, secure person adds to his life as a luxury. Culture is what he is and what will become of him. It is the cause and consequence of his daily life. Art helps to monitor the creation of culture and reflects the past and future in the present. Without some form of creative imagination we probably can't be human beings at all, not because we wouldn't be nice and civilized but because we couldn't function biologically in such a way as to remain sane and create a future for our species. Creative imagination is a necessary element in culture, and without it we are denatured animals without even the security of belonging to nature: not a species being shaped by natural selection, but the victims of a vicious chaos *we* have created.

Art is usually taken to be a very private experience. This goes back to the nineteenth century, the first age that tried to take art away from the masses of people. The nineteenth century pursued a lop-sided development, not the mutual cooperation of technology, politics and art, which is essential to culture. Of course most art falls short of its aim. But the honesty of its aim can be recognized in its intellectual rigour, and because nothing false is added to heighten or sensationalize it. There is a specialism in art just as there is in technology and politics. It only becomes embarrassing when the artist suggests he's a specialist in another, finer world. He's a specialist in describing this world, and all art is realism. We're the product of material circumstances and there's no place in art for mysticism or obscurantism. Art is the illustration, illumination, expression of rationality – not something primitive, dark, the primal urge or anything like that. Science can work irrationally but art never can, because it must always show what it is doing. Its truth is written on its face. That *is* art. But we must learn how to look, and teaching about art is as important as creating it. The S S Commandant didn't read Goethe, he admired himself reading Goethe.

Art can't be judged by the literal images it creates – that's the danger of propaganda whether of the Royal Academy or the Left. Surely most artists know of circumstances in which they'd want to produce propaganda of the directest, simplest sort? Propaganda can be good art. Looked at properly a Rembrandt portrait is a propaganda poster. But propaganda ceases to be art when it becomes the mechanical duplication of images. Then it trivializes the information it conveys and can produce bewilderment.

Sincerity is a necessary element in art, and the contemporary religious artist in a revolutionary state may be sincere. But kitsch is also sincere. Art is finally judged not on its sincerity but on its rationality. Well, if art is rational, it clearly can't be judged solely by what it criticizes. It must show the standards by which it criticizes, and these must be illustrated in the work of art. To say 'X is wrong', in the perpetual crisis of political necessity, isn't enough. The right course or emphasis must be illustrated. Art is responsible for the relation between the present and its vision, and this has to be shown in the work of art or its utopia becomes kitsch. We must be able to recognize ourselves somewhere in the people in the artist's utopia, and to relate its freedom to our necessity. Politics can be escapist, technology can, but art never can. The artist can't create a utopia and oppose that abstractly to the present. He must explain on the surface of his art the relationship between his utopia and the present. If he is a religious artist he must explain what god is up to now – and this means that in our age religious art is in fact anti-religious or kitsch.

Art isn't just the articulation of utopia, or even a foretaste of it. It also helps to monitor the consequence of change. Outside utopia art can be critical. The aim of this criticism is to ensure that the necessities of the present don't reproduce the future in their own image. To put it in contemporary jargon, part of culture is feed-back. A society that excluded the critical part of creative imagination would *pharaohize* itself. I'm not asking for the voice of the individual against the collective, but in what way can each individual learn how to speak for the collective? We can't function efficiently as ant-like units in an organization, because each of us carries the whole community in himself. We must represent it, not just belong to it. Human nature is culture, and culture is social because it develops through social experience and practice. So human nature is social nature or (as I've said) worse than animal. Our species has a future only as a self-conscious collective, and this will extend the individual self-consciousness which has developed in the past. Culture will be each individual's understanding of his community and his commitment to it.

WHAT IS ART?

I've given some indication of what I think the artist's role should be, and of what society should ask from him. I would like to be able to answer the old question 'What is art?' more fully, but I can only offer the inadequate suggestions that occurred to me when I wrote *The Fool* – and even these are really questions rather than answers. Nowadays art is often dismissed as irrelevant to the solution of social problems. It will be clear that I don't believe this. If creative imagination exists in all people, it must have a use. It's too potent, and in the past has been too effective, to be an accident of nature.

Our whole biological being is a means of orientating and perpetuating ourselves. So our passions and emotions are part of the means of doing this, and of obtaining knowledge of the world (especially in the sense of 'canny' knowledge or insight), just as much as our five senses are. And the same is true of our creative imaginations. (Whether creative imagination is a separate faculty, or the effect of the working of other faculties, doesn't matter.)

The 'gap' in our natures is filled by our understanding and experience of the world. This understanding and experience make us what we are, and what we are can be either chaotic or rationally ordered. If it's rationally ordered, it is a culture (or is involved in creating a culture). A culture isn't just an assemblage of knowledge, because in the context of culture what we know becomes the ground for action. It's a way of recognizing the world which involves both our emotions and our rational minds. A simple metaphor (not in any-way literal) is that of the 'gap' as a stomach, the stomach walls as emotions and reason as the digestive juice. This metaphorical stomach works on what is put into it and creates a sane culture – an emotionally evaluated, rational understanding of the world. It is the individual's summing up or balancing of himself as a relationship between the world, his society, and his instinctive capacities. It is a human being's intellectual and canny knowledge of reality – but he has built reality through his creative imagination, not merely observed it or borne its brunt. It is a process of self-creation. The result can be intellectual or simple, but not stupid. Art is the images, sounds, dynamics of this rational process of creation – and that's why I say that art is the imagination of the real and not the invention of fantasy. If, on the other hand, the process is passive, because the individual is paralysed by neglect, fear, or anything else, then a culture is not created.

Creative imagination need not always be expressed in art – there are other expressions of it – but it must be expressed in art some-times. The artist's job is to make the process public, to create public images, literal or figurative, in sight, sound and movement, of the human condition – public images in which our species recognizes itself and confirms its identity. There are obvious parallels with species-identification in other animals, but art, by being associated with rationality and value, goes further than these.

Art is a direct record of the creation of human nature. It places the individual in the world, and interprets the world in accordance with possibilities and human needs. It expresses the real within the limits of knowledge at a particular time and in this way it has always been rational, even when this meant dancing for the rain.

The artist should look as closely and comprehensively as he can at the developing creation of human nature, and do this without excuse or fear and without being gratuitously shocking. The complexity is usually in the skill, the vision should be simple; it gets some of its strength from the absence of illusion. Art helps to create meaning and purpose in what is in many ways an apparently irrational world. In a culture, or the struggle for a culture, a cry, a tear, a death become rational. Art is beautiful only in the broadest sense because it can include death and ugliness. But it can never commit itself to despair or the irrational. Art is the human being claiming a rational relationship with the world, perhaps even especially when what it portrays might have otherwise seemed absurd or tragic. No one can look questioningly at a work of art and not be made freer, even when faced with promethean necessity and when making those judgments that turn into calculations.

The last scene of *The Fool* is set in an asylum. In this scene I've tried to show that rational processes were still being worked out even in the apparently insane world of nineteenth-century Europe. The English slums of that time were like slow-motion concentration camps – death takes longer in slums than in concentration camps. Art has always looked at the atrocities of the age in which it was created. What Adorno and Auden said about poetry and Auschwitz misses the point. They would have hit it only if Auschwitz had been the summing up of history – and of course it wasn't.

1976

for Irene

The Fool was first performed at the Royal Court Theatre on 18 November 1975 with the following cast:

JOHN CLARE Tom Courtenay
MILES David Troughton
DARKIE Nigel Terry
LAWRENCE Mick Ford
PATTY Bridget Turner
MARY Caroline Hutchison
LORD MILTON Nicholas Selby
THE PARSON John Normington
LORD MILTON'S GUESTS
  Peter Myers
  John Boswall
  Malcolm Ingram
  Robert Lloyd
  Shiela Kelley
  Avril Marsh
WADLOW, LORD MILTON'S
  GAMEKEEPER Roger Hume
HILARY, THE ASSISTANT KEEPER
  David Ellison
BOB Roderick Smith
PETER Malcolm Ingram
BETTY Shiela Kelley
HAMO Brian Hall
GENTLEMEN Peter Myers,
  Robert Lloyd, John Boswall

HICKS, A WARDER Tony Rohr
GOVERNOR Peter Myers
PORTER Ken Gajadhar
JACKSON Brian Hall
PORTER'S BACKERS
  Malcolm Ingram, Mick Ford
JACKSON'S BACKERS
  David Troughton
  Roger Hume
REFEREE David Ellison
A BOY Roderick Smith
MRS EMMERSON Isabel Dean
CHARLES LAMB Robert Lloyd
MARY LAMB Gillian Martell
ADMIRAL LORD RADSTOCK
  Bill Fraser
DR SKRIMSHIRE John Boswall
TOMMY Tony Rohr
MICHAEL Roger Hume
ARNY Brian Hall
NAPOLEON John Normington
A MAN IN A STRAITJACKET
  Mick Ford
AN ATTENDANT David Troughton

Directed by Peter Gill
Designed by William Dudley

One: The porch of Lord Milton's house; *Two:* A wood near Helpstone; *Three:* A lane at Littleport; *Four:* A cell at Ely; *Five:* Hyde Park; *Six:* Clare's garden; *Seven:* Open ground; *Eight:* A drawing room
There is an interval after Scene Four
Note: In Scene Five the fight is played simultaneously with the rest of the action. The placing of the rounds is the one used at the first production. In the same production the mummers' parts in Scene One were played in this way:

Enterer-in – MILES
St George – LAWRENCE
Bullslasher – DARKIE
Doctor – CLARE

SCENE ONE

Porch of LORD MILTON's *house. Winter. Evening.*

A bench.

CLARE, DARKIE, LAWRENCE *and* MILES *come on. They are dressed as mummers. They carry lanterns.* PATTY *follows them.*

CLARE. We'll start then.

> CLARE *knocks on the door.*

MILES. Hear anythin', boy?

CLARE. Howd your row so's I can listen. (*Knocks.*) Summat's comin'.

> *The door opens.* MARY *stands in the doorway. She is dressed as kitchen staff.*

MARY. On't hev t'knock our door down old chap. (*Laughs.*) You do look a spectacle.

> MARY *goes back into the house. She shuts the door.*

DARKIE. Shut door smart so's you on't git a proper see in.

PATTY. On't start.

MILES. Who told you t'come gall?

PATTY. Told meself.

LAWRENCE. Thass lads only t'night.

MILES. Know what she's after.

PATTY. T'on't you.

DARKIE. None on us ought-a come.

MILES. Lordship allus give us silver.

DARKIE (*knocking*). Waitin' all night.

PATTY (*sudden warning*). On't shout down the keyhole boy!

> MARY *opens the door.*

MARY. Told you not t'knock. Housekeeper'll send you packin' lads.

DARKIE. Howd your row woman.

MILES. Thass Christmass. On't hev no rows.

> MARY *laughs at their costumes. She goes back into the house. She shuts the door behind her.*

LAWRENCE (*looking through the keyhole*). Drat great roomy old place. (*Sudden warning.*) Hey up!

> *The* MUMMERS *line up.*

PATTY. Goo hot when he look at me.

> *The* MEN *laugh nervously. The door opens.* LORD MILTON, PARSON *and a few* LADIES *and* GENTLEMEN *come on to the porch.* LORD MILTON *is a giant. The* MUMMERS *raise their lanterns and bow.*

MUMMERS (*chorus*). Please you t'want the mummers this season a good will my lord.

MILTON. Welcome at Christmas tide good friends.

> MILTON, *his family and guests hiss, boo, laugh and whistle in response to the mumming. They hold glasses and empty them, but they are not refilled.*

The Play

ENTERER IN.
> We hope your favour we shall win
> For acting time is come and we appear
> Let merriment begin
> This joyful time a year
> We are not of the ragged sort
> But some of the royal trim,
> An if you on't heed what *I* say
> Let Saint George enter in.
> > *Enter* SAINT GEORGE.

ST GEORGE.
> I am Saint George the parfick knight
> An this is my golden sword.
> I met the dragon in terrible fight

An killed him as you've heard.
England's Champion am I
An anyman here I do defy.

Enter COLONEL BULLSLASHER.

BULLSLASHER.
I am Colonel Bullslasher
Otherwise known as Boney.
This is my crusher an basher an hasher
I'll kill Saint George an take his money.

They roar and fight. SAINT GEORGE *is wounded.*

MILTON. Carrie stand out of the wind.

A GENTLEMAN *puts a shawl round a lady's shoulders.*

ST GEORGE.
O pardon Saint George the parfick knight
For he is wounded sore.
BULLSLASHER.
I will not pardon you Saint George
I'll kill you ten times more.

COLONEL BULLSLASHER *kills* SAINT GEORGE.

ENTERER IN.
Alas Saint George you hev died this day.
By Colonel Bullslasher slain.
In the cold earth you will lay.
Your friends are left in ruin.

Enter the DOCTOR.

DOCTOR. I am the Doctor.
ENTERER IN. Doctor can you cure this man?
DOCTOR. Ten pound if he's rich, twenty pound if he's poor.
ENTERER IN. He's very poor.
DOCTOR.
I've a bottle of pills from my auntie in Spain.
They are good for the wind an' better for rain.

I cured a squire who neighed like a horse.
Now he bray like a donkey an he's very much worse.
The queen had a fit so I gave her a pill.
She never felt better an' she's constantly ill.
Saint George here is my magical potion-lotion-notion
    commotion. Take ten drops on a fork an' stir it with a knife.
Then see what my brew
Can doo for you.

The DOCTOR *pours a bottle down* ST GEORGE's *throat.* ST
GEORGE *stands.*

ST GEORGE.
Hello good people, now give three cheer!
The like was never seen –
When I died I had my seven wits
An now I hev seventeen.

Song and dance:

Hal-an-tow.

Where are the Spaniards
That made so great a boast-o?
For they shall eat the grey goose feather
An we shall eat the roast-o.
    Hal-an-tow jolly rumble-o
    For we were up as soon as any day-o
    An for to sing for summer come
    The summer an the may-o
    For summer will a-come-o
    The winter will a-goo-o.

As for Saint George-o
Saint George he was a knight-o
Of all the knights in christendom
St George he has the right-o
In every land-o
The land where'er we go
    Hal-an-tow etc.

God bless Aunt Mary Moses

With all her power and might-o
An send us peace in Merry England
Both by night an day-o
In every land-o
The land that e'er we go
 Hal-an-tow etc.

PATTY. }
MILES. } Wren. Wren.

  Others, including the people on the porch, shout 'The Wren'.
  'Hunting the Wren'.

THE MUMMERS (*sing*).
    Hunting the Wren
We'll hunt the wren says Robin the bobbin,
We'll hunt the wren says Richie the robin,
We'll hunt the wren says Jack a the land,
We'll hunt the wren says everyone.
Where o where? says Robin the bobbin,
Etc.
In yonder green bush says Robin the bobbin,
Etc.
How git him down says Robin the bobbin,
Etc.
With sticks an' stones says Robin the bobbin.
Etc.
How'll we eat him? says Robin the bobbin,
Etc.
With knives an' forks says Robin the bobbin,
Etc.
Eyes to the blind says Robin the bobbin,
Legs to the lame says Richie the robin,
Scraps to the poor says Jack a the land,
Bones to the dogs says everyone.

The wren the wren is king a the birds,
Saint Stephen's Day he's caught in the furze,
Although he is little his family is great,
We pray yoo good people to give us a treat.

The hat has been passed round. Applause.

MILTON. A fine Saint George and a terrible Bullslasher.

GENTLEMAN. Try my gout on that doctor.

PARSON. In this year of our lord eighteen hundred and fifteen
England is beset by troubles. The tyrant Bonaparte has been
put down. But we are entering a new age. An iron age. New
engines, new factories, cities, ways, laws. The old ways must
go. The noble horse and the hand are slow. Our land must be
better used. Forests cut down. Open spaces put to the plough. All
of us must be patient and understanding. We must work for the
common good. God bless you.

DARKIE. On't heard you give a sermon afore parson.

PARSON. Come to church and you would.

DARKIE. Too tired. Sit on me arse after work not me knees. I'd
fall asleep an' they'd blame your sermon!

PARSON. Well it's Christmas so you're pleased to joke.

DARKIE. On't pleased at nothing. My Christmas's spuds an'
greens.

The LADIES *go into the house.*

MILTON. The war made us all prosperous but prices have fallen
with the peace. Wages must follow. Not because I say so. That
is a law of economic science. Wages follow prices or civil
institutions break down. Civilization costs money like everything else. Put too much in your own pockets and what's left to
pay for our state institutions? Well, now you have something to
think about. They'll give you hot pies and punch in the kitchen.
Thank you for your play. Goodnight.

MILTON *and the* GENTLEMEN *go into the house.*

PARSON. You offended his lordship Turner.

MILES. On't mean no damage sir. Allus talk straight out.
Worried for his old ma. She hev t'give up work on the land.
Lad his age ought-a git married. But thass on'y takin a woman
in t'beggary!

PARSON. I'm surprised at the turn this festivity's taken. Our
rulers guide our affairs in such a way that each of us reaps the

best possible reward for his labours. Without their guidance –
though you might not understand it – there'd be chaos.

DARKIE. We're headed that way now.

PARSON. Turner, Christmas is the gift of god. A time as serene
as this night sky. Can nothing lighten your dark spirit?

LAWRENCE. Hard times all round.

PARSON. My prayers will be very long tonight. All of you have
friends Turner. We shall come through. Let that be the Lord's
will.

DARKIE. Six day a week I goo t'work in the dark an' come home
in the dark – for what? Ten shillin'. Even Judas got thirty – but
he come from a good family an' wouldn't work for less.

PARSON. Goodnight.

> *The* PARSON *goes into the house.* MARY *shuts the door from the
> inside.* DARKIE *sits on the bench.*

PATTY. Let's goo round the kitchen. Warm there.

DARKIE (*puts his head in his hands*). His drink'd choke me.

CLARE. Can't afford t'feel like that boy. Spite yourself. (*To*
MILES.) Goo an' fetch it. I'll kip an eye on him.

> LAWRENCE *and* MILES *go out.* PATTY, CLARE *and* DARKIE
> *are left.* CLARE *sits on the bench beside* DARKIE.

PATTY. Serve you right Darkie. My feet's froze. Upset everyone
else an' end up upset yourself! Well thass Christmas, I on't
goo on. Sit yourself up boy an' look on the bright side. No
crack heads yit.

> DARKIE *doesn't move.*

CLARE. He all right?

PATTY. Pay no notice.

> PATTY *sits between* CLARE *and* DARKIE. DARKIE *stays
> completely motionless. He has his head in his hands.*

PATTY (*to* CLARE). Cold hands, boy! (*Laughs.*)

CLARE (*puts his arms round her*). You look all right – (*Puts his
hand in her dress.*)

PATTY. What yoo lost, boy?

CLARE (*feeling her breasts*). Togged up special t'set me on.

PATTY. On't need settin' on. Git that all the time when we're wed. On't hev t'kip grabbin' –

CLARE. On't mind grabbin'.

PATTY (*giggling as* CLARE *unbuttons her*). Darkie make your mate behave.

    DARKIE *remains motionless.*

CLARE (*nodding towards the house*). Hush.

PATTY. When we're wed –

CLARE. On't rush in t'weddin'. Hev t'afford a wife an' family fore I wed.

    DARKIE *doesn't move.* MILES *and* LAWRENCE *come back. They carry mugs, a jug and pies.*

MILES. Is his lordship hangin' out the winder? Darkie your mate hev his hand up your sister's dress.

LAWRENCE. Knew what she come after.

PATTY (*taking* CLARE'S *hands away and buttoning her clothes. Nods at* DARKIE). Sulks. Told him off. What they give us?

LAWRENCE. Hot punch.

PATTY. Drunk half hev yo'u?

MILES (*pouring*). Left you a drop in the bottom.

    They drink.

  All the best.

CLARE. Health and wealth.

PATTY. O – good drop a stuff.

DARKIE (*drinking*). Thanks all round to his lordship.

    The door opens. MARY *comes out.*

MARY. On't allowed make that row out here.

PATTY. On't heard no row gall.

MARY. That chair on't for sittin' on this time a night neither. We're lock up. You're supposed t'goo round the back.

DARKIE (*to* MARY). On't got no quarrel with you gall. (*Turns to the others.*) She's just an ijit.

MILES. Git off home, mates.

> MILES, LAWRENCE *and* DARKIE *go.* MARY *goes in and shuts the door.* PATTY *watches her.*

CLARE. Run them round the back. I'll howd on an' see you home.

> PATTY *takes mugs and jugs off.* CLARE *is alone. He stands and stares at the door. He puts his hand on his crutch. The door opens slightly.* MARY *comes out. She stays by the door.*

MARY. What you watchin'?

CLARE. Come over here.

MARY. On't try your tricks on me. Saw you with your gall.

CLARE. On't my gall.

MARY. On't look like it.

CLARE. She'll be back soon.

MARY. O ay.

CLARE (*still holding his crutch*). When they let you out?

MARY. All accordin'.

CLARE. Hev t'walk her home. Said I would. When'll I see you?

MARY. Depend.

CLARE. When?

MARY On't promise. (*Beckons with her head.*) Hall's dark though.

> CLARE *follows her into the house. She shuts the door behind them.* PATTY *comes on.*

PATTY. Look at the stars boy. Ah them. Bet people goo t'school ten year an' still can't count so far. (*Looks round.*) Boy? (*Pause.*) Drat!

> PATTY *hurries out after the others.*

SCENE TWO

Wood. Night.

CLARE *alone. He sits. His lips move and his fingers tap a rhythm. He is saying something noiselessly to himself. He has a piece of paper in his hand but he doesn't read it. Suddenly he turns his head.*

PATTY *comes in.*

PATTY. I know what's gooin' on.

CLARE. Bats up there. Hundreds an' hundreds. Listen. Sky full.

PATTY. Creepin' round the wood at night. On't born yesterday.

> PATTY *starts to cry. Slight pause.*

CLARE. There! – they've gone. Great hole gapin' right on top of
us. You cry like a bat gall. Driv 'em off.

PATTY. Know sort a gall meet fellas out here. Cost more'n you've
got. Gloves an' hankies. An' you on't git nothin' worth hevin'.
My head screw on I'd let you git on with it. Learn you a lesson.
(*Pause.*) Us'll git along all right. Make a good wife s'long's you
behave.

CLARE. I know.

PATTY. On't want no one bar you. Never hev since I set eyes on
you. On't ashamed a that, thass just a fact. Wish I had a kid.
We'd hev t'git wed then.

CLARE. On't you goo on gall!

PATTY. On't force you. You on't keen, we'll let the matter drop.

CLARE. On't be daft gall.

PATTY. On't hev that flung in me face every time there's a row:
you had your arm twist. Goo off with some gall if thass what you
want. On'y on't live my end the village. On't want see the two
of you every time I goo t'the winder.

CLARE. You doo goo on gall!

PATTY. Just sayin' so it's understood. (CLARE *kisses her.*) My ma
think good on you John. Say you on't be no trouble outside the
drink. Thass a question of can us afford it? Like a drop myself
as you know. But I *on't* howd with wastin' flesh on drink when
you on't afford t'eat. On't see the –

CLARE. On't *drink*. Likely I had you t'come home to I on't touch
drop gall.

PATTY. Now on't start putting that on me. I on't say give up.
Man's a man. Thass a question a lettin' your glass empty afore
your purse.

> DARKIE *comes in.*

PATTY. Well I'll goo t'buggery. You allus follow us boy.

DARKIE. On't follow you. Come after John.

PATTY. How'd you know where we were?

DARKIE. Bin up his house.

CLARE. What's up boy?

DARKIE. I wondered hev you heard? They're cuttin' the forest down t'make fields.

CLARE. What boy?

DARKIE. Milton want the land for corn.

CLARE. Why's that?

DARKIE. Sell t'the old factory boys. They on't grow corn.

CLARE. But not *so* much!

DARKIE. Ay. More. They'll drain the common fen an' turn off the river.

CLARE. Thass a lot a old scare talk.

PATTY (*nervously*). Thass true boy. They saw chaps gooin' round the fields this mornin with chains an' writin' books. Thass how it all come out. Wrote the river down in the books.

DARKIE. An' the forest.

CLARE. *You* heard a this gall? (*She nods.*) How'd you git rid of a river – (*Laughs.*) turn the river off!

PATTY. Dam her up an' pump her out boy!

CLARE. Can't – thass our's much as his. An' the fens. An' the trees. What's it mean boy? We'll lose our fishin' – our wood – cows on the fen common. How'll we live? Not on the few bob they pay us for workin' their land. We need us own bit a land.

DARKIE. They take all the land they'll hev t'pay us proper wages.

CLARE. Like factory boys? They git proper wages?

DARKIE. Ah ... An' I said my piece too often. On't even offer me work.

PATTY. On't howd that agin you.

DARKIE. No?

PATTY. Talk's no harm. They – (*She stops.*) You bin up t'summat?

DARKIE. No.

PATTY. Fightin'!

DARKIE. Push. Thass all.

PATTY. Who? Who?

DARKIE. Milton's gaffer.

PATTY (*frightened*). O you bloody fool boy!

DARKIE. Ask him what his chaps were up to with chains an'
 books. Took howd a my coat. I say I on't your cattle boy!
 Push, thass all. Goo down so's he could say I hit him. On't
 stun a fly.

PATTY. Doo ma know? (DARKIE *shrugs*.) I'll soon tell her.
 Rowin', fightin' - thass all you know about Darkie. She'll hev
 summat t' say.

DARKIE. Say what her like.

CLARE. Give over rowin'.

DARKIE. Rowin'? Wait till you wed her - then you'll know what
 rowin' is! I'm sick a rowin'. Allus rowin'.

PATTY. Whose fault's that?

DARKIE. O Patty you know ma's like an adder gooin' for a
 stoat.

PATTY. On't ought a say that.

DARKIE. You know it's true. She hev- her reasons. On't easy
 bringin' up hungry kids. That on't make her easier t'live with
 now we're growed up.

 The KEEPER *comes in. He wears a dark suit and cap. He carries
 a gaming gun.*

KEEPER. What you up to in this wood?

CLARE. Walkin'.

KEEPER. Trespassin'.

PATTY. On't come so soft boy. Allus use this wood.

DARKIE. Who're you?

KEEPER. Lord Milton's keeper.

CLARE. On't got no keeper s'far's I heard.

KEEPER. Hev ten now.

CLARE. This on't private land. If that was we still hev rights a
 way.

KEEPER. Move on, there's good lads. New here. On't want start
 trouble. An' you ought a be home makin' your old people easy
 miss. Know the sort a gall goo out with two lads this time a
 night.

DARKIE. Yoo jump out a cess pit! You're fit t'be Lord Milton's
 keeper.

KEEPER What's your name lad?

PATTY (*to* DARKIE). No boy! You come home with me. 'Nough trouble for one day!

DARKIE (*to* KEEPER). You on't last long in this village boy!

KEEPER. On't in village. Live on estate.

PATTY (*to* DARKIE). You come home. (*To* CLARE.) An' you John. Straight home. I'll come round t'morra.

> DARKIE *and* PATTY *go out right.* CLARE *out left.*

KEEPER. Want keepers a people round here.

> *The* KEEPER *follows* DARKIE *and* PATTY *off. Almost immediately* MARY *comes on.*

DARKIE (*off*). On't walk back a me pointin' your gun boy. On't a criminal yet.

> CLARE *comes on. He stands some way away from her.*

MARY. Saw me in the trees on't you.

CLARE. Bin here night after night.

MARY. Housekeeper saw you playin' with yourself. Crep' up on the landin and watch. Jealous old bitch. Say I on't fit for servants' hall. Threw me out. After prayers next mornin'.

CLARE. Waited every night. All hours. For weeks.

MARY. On't hev no proper job now. Old cow warned all the big houses. Got in with some travellers.

CLARE. Gypsies?

MARY. T'on't your fault. On't last *there*. Done a violence with the silver cutlery fore long. Git a lot more laughs now. On'y I on't sure bout the winter yit. Saw your gall.

CLARE. Her brother took her home.

MARY. Thought he was her fella way he was gooin'. Keep an eye on you doo he?

CLARE. No life campin' in ditches.

MARY (*sits*). I live with one a the gypsy bosses. Keeper on his rounds.

CLARE. Soon tell him t'bugger off. (*Squats beside her but doesn't touch her.*) On't bin out my head. That night. Never forget you.

MARY. Hungry?
CLARE. Allus hungry.

> MARY *takes out bread and gives him some. They eat.*

MARY. Stole it.
CLARE (*touches her breast while he eats*). Well built gall. Never
    seen a gall like you. Like t'live in this forest. The two on us.
    Tread the reeds an' creep in.
MARY. Damp. Gypsies know better'n that.

> CLARE *pushes her onto the ground.*

All right.

> *Off*, KEEPER *whistles. One short blast.*

MARY. Shall us wait?
CLARE. Come on.

> *A young* ASSISTANT KEEPER *comes on left.*

KEEPER (*off*). Hilary?
ASSISTANT KEEPER. Hear that Mr Waddlow? (*Points.*) There.

> KEEPER *comes on right.*

KEEPER. Galls. On't git caught up Hilary. Hev you down here
    while their husbands robbin' the hatches.
MARY (*quietly to* CLARE). Goo on.
ASSISTANT KEEPER (*points*). There Mr Wadlow.
KEEPER. Let him draw her boy. Never drive that out the wood.
    Animal in rut. Under your feet, step over 'em, worms rolled
    up, birds gallivantin', fishes on top a each other. Gills goo as if
    they're drownin'.
ASSISTANT KEEPER (*hears something*). Again Mr Wadlow.
KEEPER. Sights I've seen. (*Laughs.*) Chop rabbits down while
    they do it in the graveyard. Seen two stoats at it in a broken
    gravestone.
CLARE (*quietly*). Bugger's mad.
ASSISTANT KEEPER (*points*). There.

> MARY *and* CLARE *groan.*

KEEPER (*calls*). On't waste a shell! (*To* ASSISTANT KEEPER.) Think a the cost. Hev a skin t'show each time you shoot. (*He reaches the* ASSISTANT KEEPER'*s side.*) Git the vermin gibbets up t'morra. Keep a good line a carcas hung up. Old crows, rats, owl. Boss creep round on the sly an' count the corpses. Check up you're keepin' busy. Show you how t'fix em so they on't drop off when they rot.

> *The* KEEPERS *go out.*

CLARE. Bugger's gone.

MARY (*quietly amused. Looks down at her crotch*). You made little drops on my hair. Silver in this moonlight.

CLARE. On't goo.

> MARY *stands. She and* CLARE *fasten their clothes.*

MARY. My boss is waitin'.

CLARE. Don't.

MARY. Come back your place then?

CLARE. Well. (MARY *laughs*). Yes. Us'll manage. There's on'y my old people.

MARY. Rather be stoned out the village than look down on respectable. Your gall on't put out the flags neither. 'Night boy.

CLARE. Us'll work out summat.

MARY. What?

CLARE. Marry me.

MARY. On't talk so far back.

CLARE. What you called gall?

MARY. Mary if you must know.

CLARE. Where's your camp?

MARY. On't hev you there.

CLARE. You be here t'morra night or I'll come round.

MARY. Git a crack head.

CLARE. I'll walk you back.

MARY. Bugger off if you want t'see me t'morra.

CLARE. They move camp where'll you goo?

MARY. On't tell me. Move sharp sometime. Folk come out an' stone us off.

CLARE. I'll be here t'morra.

    MARY *goes out right.*

What should I have said?

    Silence. CLARE *puts on his hat. He goes out left.*

SCENE THREE

Littleport.
Road.
Night.

BOB *and* MILES *carry* LAWRENCE *in.* LAWRENCE *is crying.*

BOB. The bushes.
PETER (*off*). Miles. Miles.
MILES (*shouting back*). Lawrence is hurt.
BOB (*to* LAWRENCE). Git crep in they bushes boy.
MILES. His row! They'll hear!

    PETER *and* CLARE *come on.*

PETER. Who?
MILES. Lawrence. Cut 'bout the head. (*To* LAWRENCE.) Howd
    your row boy. You on't die.
PETER. We'll doo all the big houses. (*Blows his horn.*)
MILES. Ijit! (*To* CLARE.) See that gall from Milton's house?
CLARE. Mary?
MILES. That what they call her? Gall up there last winter.
CLARE. You see her?
MILES (*indicating*). Runnin' across them fields.
PETER. Mr Wicken – screw a pound out a him.

    CLARE *hurries out.*

BOB. Then Mrs Hadchit's.
MILES. No, her first. She on't no bother. Wicken! – that can-
    tankerous bastard'll need workin' over.

BOB (*to* LAWRENCE). Howd on boy. We'll be back.
CLARE (*off*). Mary!

    PETER, BOB *and* MILES *start to go.*

BOB. Then parson!
PETER. ⎫
MILES. ⎬   Ay parson!
PETER. Thass the laddo. (*Blows horn.*)

    DARKIE *and* HAMO *come in.*

DARKIE. Whole village up t'night!

    BETTY *comes in from the opposite direction. She is laughing.*
    She carries a sheet.

BETTY. Silver. Look. (*She shows them three candlesticks.*)
MILES. Mrs Hadchit's next.

    PETER, BOB *and* MILES *go out.*

HAMO. Git hung takin' property.
DARKIE. Don't talk so far back boy! (*To* BETTY.) Keep 'em out a
    sight. Give 'em t'the carter when thass all over. He'll sell 'em
    up London.
BETTY. Proper silver. (*Looks at her reflection.*) See yourself in the
    side, twist up. On't need candles in 'em. Light the room up by
    themselves.
HAMO. Put them away, gall. Scare me.
BETTY. Mrs Hadchit's. Git inside her cupboards!
HAMO (*going.*). There on't be nothin' left.

    BETTY *is hiding the candlesticks in the bushes. She screams.*

HAMO. ⎫   What?
DARKIE. ⎭   Soldiers?
BETTY. Dead man.
DARKIE. The bushes!
LAWRENCE. Betty I'm alive.
BETTY. Oh god it's young Lawrence Star. Whatever's happen,
    Lawrence?
LAWRENCE. My head's cut about.

DARKIE. Tie him up, gall.

BETTY. Should us git a doctor?

DARKIE. They'd hand him over.

BETTY. My linen off Farmer Fab's. Gooin' a dye that an' run up a
skirt. On't tell where it's come from then. Smart clean stuff.
(*Binds* LAWRENCE'*s head in the sheet*.) Shame! . . . Never had
nothin' like that afore an' I on't had that ten minutes. Well
that'll keep the blood in. Hurt on't harm. You keep an eye on
my candlesticks. Anyone come sit up an' goo like a ghost. They'll
soon run. I got 'em first: they're mine.

    MILES *comes on.*

MILES. Darkie! Darkie! Darkie!

DARKIE. What's that, boy?

MILES. On't you come t'parsons?

    MARY *comes on.*

MARY. All the big houses. The Mill. Old Mrs Shaft's the harlot.
Straight up the front gate an' pick the roses –

BETTY. An' cabbage.

MARY. On't allowed in afore 'cept t'work. Tap front door. Say
the poor's collectin'. Git off they say! Break the winders.
Howd out your apron. Where's the silver under your floor?
No silver here! Tap their heads with a stick. See the silver
then. Jump out their pockets! Gold teeth out their heads!
Tap tap. We'll be rich t'night. (*Stops.*) I smell silver!

BETTY. Silver on't smell.

MARY. Red pumice powder. Clean silver every day in Lord
Milton's house. Know that smell. Money lender's guts!

    MARY *goes into the bushes.*

BETTY. Leave that gall!

MARY (*finds candlesticks*). Silver. Knew t'was. On't touch your
stuff gall. But you tie 'em on the end a rope an' drop 'em in the
river out a my reach.

    DARKIE, MILES *and* HAMO *laugh.*

Come on. Parson's.

MARY *goes out.*

MILES. I'll knock the landlord up the Globe. Thirsty work!

BETTY. Nose on her like an animal. On't hide 'em in the river for her t'goo fishin'. Bury 'em.

MILES *goes out right. The others go out left.* LAWRENCE *is alone.*

JAMO (*off*). Split both ways lads case he bolt. You goo the lanes. We'll cut across the fields.

Off, the distant sound of the horn. The GENTLEMEN *come in.*

FIRST GENTLEMAN. Listen. Children.

THIRD GENTLEMAN. We'll cut them off before they reach the parsonage.

FIRST GENTLEMAN. No – don't meddle. Wait for Milton.

THIRD GENTLEMAN. What? If we let them get the bit between their teeth –

FIRST GENTLEMAN. What can they do? Enough damage to bring them to Assizes. This has been coming on long enough. Strangers creeping over fields, burning ricks, breaking machines, laming cattle – and vanishing. No one's seen them. No one knows anything. Well after tonight we'll have names.

SECOND GENTLEMAN. Yes. We'll watch from a safe distance.

THIRD GENTLEMAN. If they come on my land I shoot.

The GENTLEMEN *go out.* LAWRENCE *sits up. His head is wrapped in the sheet. It seems an enormous bundle. He starts to cry.*

LAWRENCE (*crawling*). Hev t'goo ... (*Tries to stand. Falls. Lies and cries.*) O god ...

MILES *comes on with some bottles. He looks round for* LAWRENCE.

MILES. Lawrence? (*Sees him.*) Where you gooin' boy?

LAWRENCE. Gen'men. We'll git hang Miles.

MILES. How many?

LAWRENCE. Gen'men. Tell from their voices.

MILES. How many?

CLARE *comes on.*

CLARE. I can't find her Miles!
MILES. On't time goo chasin' galls. Gen'men here. Lawrence?
LAWRENCE. My head. That on't stop bleedin'.
CLARE. Which way she goo?
MILES (*to* LAWRENCE). Drink some a this boy.
CLARE (*calls*). Mary! – Hev she say anythin'? Were she lookin' fo
me?

LAWRENCE *drinks from the bottle.*

MILES. Hev they talk a soldiers boy? Think!
LAWRENCE. Blood run down my ears.
CLARE (*going*). Mary! Mary! Mary!

CLARE *goes out.*

MILES. Git back under that hedge. (*Helps* LAWRENCE *into th*
hedge.) I'll git the others. Pick you up on the way back. (*Of*
the horn sounds in the far distance.) Damn ijit row!

MILES *goes out.* LAWRENCE *starts to crawl again.*

LAWRENCE (*crying*). Miles . . . They'll hang us . . . Hev t'goo . . .

PARSON *comes in. He is out of breath.*

PARSON. O dear dear. (*Stands still. Looks round.*) The moon wi
come out. O dear dear dear.

LAWRENCE *starts to cry. He tries to stop it.*

Who's that? Who's laughing at me? (*Whimpering.*) Cowards
Hunting an old man! O god how many?
PARSON *tries to hide in the hedge and quieten his breathing.*
Who's there? Lord Milton's men? Don't shoot. (*Stands*
What is . . .? A little boy crying? I'm not used to being ou
without a lantern. Stop it? (*He trips over* LAWRENCE.) Ah!
bottles. How foolish and disgusting. Lying there in beer an
your own blood. Will you find peace in a bottle? Stop cryin
boy. God knows who'll hear – your people or mine. Are yo
badly cut? Not if you can still cry.

The PARSON *sits on a tree stump.*

Lord Milton's men will get you to a doctor – *your* people can't help you now. Stop it! (*Slight pause.*) And after this terrible night? – when I ride down a lane and meet a labourer can we look each other in the face? I baptized him and we can't give each other a decent good morning. They'll raise their hats like an insult. O try to stop crying! The whole system will go out of their lives. We'll be reduced to relying on anger or strength or our wits – master *and* servant. And then what are we? – animals trying to live in houses. For one night's violence and a handful of silver to spend on drink!

DARKIE, MILES *and* BOB *come in.*

DARKIE. If I believed your lies I'd say we were meant to meet· Left your place an' was off home – an' there you are stood cross our way.

PARSON. Your friend. See to him. He can't stop crying. Some nervous reaction.

BOB. We're collecting.

MILES. From rich farmers, shopkeepers –

BETTY *comes in.*

BOB. He farm.

DARKIE. Spend more time writin' pigs in his book than readin' the Bible.

PARSON. I have nothing on me.

DARKIE. Shall us escort you back t'parson's?

PARSON. I shall not give way to violence –

DARKIE. Turn your pockets out.

PARSON. – and go against every principle I've lived by. How could I call you my flock if I betrayed the good shepherd's laws – from cowardice?

BOB. Git up.

PARSON (*not moving*). An old man powerless before you. I do not want to think I've blessed savages from my altar –

MARY *and* PETER *come in. They all stand some way from the* PARSON.

MILES. Show us your pockets!

DARKIE (*goes to the* PARSON, *jerks him to his feet and searches his pockets. The others begin to move in closer to the* PARSON). Silver in this pocket. Notebook in a silver case. Corn prices in that. Silver pencil. Gold ring. (*Pulls it from the* PARSON's *finger.*) Cross on chain. Gold. (*Yanks chain free.*) Silver knob end his stick. (*Snaps the walking stick over his leg and throws the knob to the others.*)

BETTY. They buttons! Pearly buttons!

MARY. Fasten them on the back with a gold stud. Show you how thass done.

> MARY *and* BETTY *start to take off the* PARSON's *buttons.* LAWRENCE *crawls slowly out of the hedge. He tries to drag himself away. He is weaker. He cries. The sheet is soaked in blood.*

PARSON. Aren't you ashamed?

BETTY. No. No. No. No. I on't ashamed. I'm ashamed I can't feed my kid.

MARY (*working at buttons. Laughs*). Let me. Thass it.

PETER. I'm ashamed I work in parson's field an' crawl home like an animal.

MILES. I'm ashamed the sweat roll off me while you git fat!

MARY (*laughing*). Thass five.

HAMO. I'm ashamed t'goo t'sleep with the dirt out your fields on me hands every night.

MARY (*searching the ground*). Drop one.

PARSON. I'm an old man –

> PETER *blows his horn.*

MILES. Git his collar!

MARY (*searching on the ground*). Irish linen!

BOB. Git his shoes!

HAMO. You on't wear leather like that.

PARSON. People of my parish. Stripping an old man –

BETTY (*touching the shoes*). Softer'n gloves.

MARY (*searching on the ground*). Mind that stud. (*Picks it up.*)

DARKIE. Git his coat. Git it off.

PARSON. O god look down and judge –

MILES. Under that he's same as us.

DARKIE. You cold now?

PETER. Take his shirt.

BETTY. Git it off.

BOB. Off.

HAMO. Off.

BETTY. Pull it off.

MARY. Mind that tear!

BETTY. I'll hev it.

MILES. Pull it off.

DARKIE. Your flesh cold now boy? 'Fraid I put my fist in your face? Hev a fist in my face all day. On't like my fist wave in your eye? Hev a fist stuck in my eye every day.

BOB. More clothes under that.

BETTY. Walkin' shop!

> PETER *blows his horn.*

MILES. Vest off.

HAMO. Git that off.

BOB. Let's see his flesh.

BETTY. Off. Off.

PETER. Off.

> The PARSON *stands stripped. His long grey hair falls over his face. He shivers. They stare at him for a moment.* LAWRENCE *still crawls slowly over the stage.*

BOB (*child-like innocence*) . . . How they wash an' care for that!

MARY. Let's goo. Thass all he's got. Gen'men about.

> MARY *picks up shoes, clothes and bottles. She runs out while they talk.*

BETTY. My baby. My baby on't got proper baby skin like that. Look how soft that is. Like silk lace. My baby's born hard – hev animal skin like summat live in the road. (*Pinches the* PARSON'*s flesh.*) Look at that. Come away in handfuls.

MILES. Look! Handful a flesh!

HAMO. Handfuls!

PARSON (*yells as they grab his skin*). Ah! Ah!

DARKIE. Our flesh. That belong t'us. Where you took that flesh
boy? You took that flesh off her baby. My ma. They on't got
proper flesh on em now.

> *They pull at his skin.*

BETTY. My flesh.

BOB. Her baby's flesh.

PETER. Our flesh.

DARKIE. Where you stole that flesh boy? Your flesh is stolen
goods. You're covered in stolen goods when you strip! How
you climb your altar steps like that? What god say when you
raise Chriss flesh in service? – more flesh they stolen doo he
say? You call us thief when we took silver. You took us flesh!

> BETTY *cries.* LAWRENCE *stops crawling. The sheet has un-*
> *wound from his head and dragged over the ground. He lies and*
> *cries.*

BETTY. My baby. My baby.

> *The others cry. The* PARSON *weeps and mumbles prayers.*

DARKIE (*in tears*). When you laugh you use our voice. When you
goo straight you took us backs. Thass why we're bent.

MILES (*in tears*). O god o god how shall us ever git our things
back. All the things they stolen.

BOB (*in tears*). What shall us ever do?

PARSON. God of the merciful . . . father of heaven . . . (*He stops.*)

DARKIE. Nothin' t'say? He hev the truth now. More truth than
all the bishops an' lords'll tell him. An' he say nothin'. Ay well:
we said the truth t'night an' he can't answer.

BETTY (*crying quietly*). Baby. Baby.

MILES. The truth.

HAMO. Ay.

BETTY (*throws* LAWRENCE'S *blood-stained linen at the* PARSON).
Cover yourself. (PARSON *doesn't move. Angrily.*) Cover it!
On't you throw charity back in my face!

> *The* PARSON *covers himself with the linen.*

You stood there two minute boy. I'm made a mock of all my

life. (*Quietly again, she holds a button up between her thumb and index finger.*) Yes, yes. Look at the buttons t'cover his thievin.' An' my little un on't never git a morsel she on't cried for. He'll bury her, will he feed her?

LAWRENCE *crawls back into the bushes.*

DARKIE. You lay charge against us or give evidence?

PARSON. The cross is always humiliated. What have I suffered? A little humiliation and cold. I shall stand to the truth. I cannot betray the life I've lived till now. How could I go on living? From now on my thoughts shall only be of death.

BETTY (*to* PARSON). Hush your row boy. You on't a child. Don't talk so scandalous – an' you hush Lawrence.

MILTON *comes on with the three* GENTLEMEN.

MILTON. Give Mr Twice your coat.

THIRD GENTLEMAN (*covering* PARSON *with his coat*). A mob destroying in a minute the work of centuries –

MILTON (*calmly*). Quiet.

THIRD GENTLEMAN. – broken windows, old folk in tears, looting –

MILTON (*calmly but decisively*). Be quiet. Mr Twice stay the night at my house. I sent your family and servants on ahead. Mr Harvington will take you to the house.

PARSON (*looking at his bare feet*). My lord, my feet . . .

MILTON. Mr Harvington will carry you.

THIRD GENTLEMAN *picks the* PARSON *up*

PARSON. Thank you.

THIRD GENTLEMAN *carries the* PARSON *out.*

MILTON. These gentlemen are special constables. I swore them in tonight. I was called away from dinner – and I find you misbehaving like children. Go home. Let us avoid any more violence.

DARKIE. You steal from us. Parson steal from us. What we doo t'parson? Make a mock. Took – what? Trinkets! When I steal

from parson what you doo t'me? Law hang us. Thass the on'y
difference 'tween you an' me: you on't think twice 'fore you use
violence.

MILTON. Take your cap off.

MILES. Don't. He want you recognized.

> *A shot.* LAWRENCE *yells and dies. The* GENTLEMEN *aim
> their guns.*

MILTON. Stop!

BETTY. Lawrence! (*Starts to go to him.*)

MILTON. Stop! (BETTY *stops. To* SECOND GENTLEMAN.) Go
and look.

> SECOND GENTLEMAN *goes to the body.* BETTY *cries.*

MILES. Bastards.

DARKIE. He's dead.

SECOND GENTLEMAN (*looking up*). I'm afraid my bullet went
through his temple.

MILTON (*orders*). Bind his head. That sheet. You and you – carry
him to the horses. All of you march behind. You'll be covered
with the guns. (*To* SECOND GENTLEMAN.) Yes?

SECOND GENTLEMAN. Sir.

> MILES *and* HAMO *carry* LAWRENCE *out. The two of them
> cry quietly.* LAWRENCE'*s head is wrapped in the sheet.*

MILTON. Follow them.

> *The rest go out.*

SCENE FOUR

Ely.
Cell.
Evening.

*Quiet. Dark. Pale light from two small high grated windows. Bench.
Blankets.*

DARKIE, MILES, BOB *and* HAMO *looking towards the door as it opens.* WARDER *comes in. He gives each man a bowl of soup and a lump of bread.*

WARDER (*to* DARKIE, *as he gives the food out*). Your mates outside on a visit.

    WARDER *goes out.*

BOB. On't touch it.

MILES. Eat. Sorry you starved when they let you out.

    BOB *eats. The door opens.* PATTY *and* CLARE *come in in travelling clothes. The door is shut behind them.* PATTY *carries a jacket.*

PATTY (*puts her arms round* DARKIE). O dear my boy.

BOB, MILES. } 'Lo gall.
HAMO.

PATTY. My dears. All.

CLARE. On't let us interrupt your grub.

    They eat while they talk.

DARKIE. All right at home? (PATTY *shakes her head.*) Ma?

PATTY (*nods*). Took t'bed. On't git up. Lie by winder. I on't know. (*Silence.*) Say I hev t'bring your good jacket. On't goo like a tramp an' disgrace the family.

    PATTY *cries for a few seconds. They eat.*

DARKIE. Quiet pal?

    CLARE *smiles and nods.*

BOB. Never thought it'd come t'this. Thing like this . . .

    Silence.

DARKIE. Mum ill then?

PATTY. Git old.

DARKIE. Lot a talk outside?

PATTY. Ely's full a army.

HAMO. Say bishop'll give a sermon. All judges goo in cathedral arm in arm. Proper sight.

MILES. Bishop like t'fix the rope his-self. On'y way he git satisfaction. Great hog. Twenty four. No they on't goo through with it. What people say?

PATTY. On't rightly tell. Stand on street corners like the whole week's market. On't understand n'more.

MILES. On't they say –

PATTY (*irritated*). How'd I know *what* they say? (*Silence. She collects the bowls and stacks them neatly by the door before she speaks.*) O boy *I* don't know what t' say. Thass a fact. (*Trying not to cry.*) Allus a good boy Darkie. Stood up for the right. On't hurt a fly out askin' pardon. All a you. They on't know.

MILES. An' you can't tell em.

DARKIE. On't goo through with it. Ship us off t'Australia. (*To* CLARE.) Lucky you dodged off before the law got us.

PATTY. He's had another drop a luck – so p'raps your's'll change.

DARKIE. What's that?

PATTY. Scribblin' come t'summat. Gen'man bin. Talk 'bout a book.

DARKIE. O.

PATTY. Says he'll travel. If that goo well. London.

DARKIE (*after a pause*). Who's that?

PATTY. You on't know. Gen'man.

MILES. What you git boy? Hev t'pay you summat.

CLARE *shrugs.*

DARKIE. No thass good John. On't be ashamed a that.

MILES. What you write boy? Write 'bout this place. What goo on.

CLARE. Who'd read that?

PATTY (*pride*). Gen'man come though on't he boy? (*Silence.*) Well thass a long way gettin' here but I'm glad I made the effort. Hev t'goo soon Darkie. Git a start fore it's dark. Any errands? Miles?

MILES. No, gall.

Silence. CLARE *starts to laugh. He tries to stop.*

PATTY. John. What's up boy?

CLARE. On't – (*He stops laughing but starts again.*) – nothin' –

DARKIE (*smiles*). Thass right. On't goo through with it.

BOB (*giggling*). Twenty four.

DARKIE (*laughing slightly*). On't allow. Government stop it.

MILES (*to* CLARE, *a bit frightened but grinning*). What you laugh at boy?

PATTY (*giggling with embarrassment*). Behave John an' give over. (*She folds the jacket on her lap and pats it.*) Look good when you're all dress up Darkie. Stickler for being clean.

> PARSON *comes in. They stop laughing.*

PARSON. I was visiting the others and I thought ... May I? (*He comes into the room. He shuts the door.*) I have not come to offer hope. If you don't die at the end of the week you will all die in time. To those outside this prison that would sound like cant. But you inside can understand it now. When you stripped me in the forest I stood with naked feet on the earth that will be my grave. I heard the devils laugh at my sins. I saw myself judged and condemned – as we all are. If not tomorrow then soon. (PATTY *makes an awkward gesture with the coat.*) Do you understand that my dear?

PATTY (*confused*). Just visitin' sir. Brought my brother's new coat. Believe in church though.

PARSON. How small and impotent we are. We clear a few fields, build a few houses, twist a few rods of iron, and think our laws are everlasting. But the world is the Lord's for he rules time. Forget this world, its misery and waste, all luxury and vice, its painted vanities. Think only of the brightness of god. Rejoice! His mercy welcomes. His joy is to forgive. Do you understand at last? (*Slight silence. He begins to plead.*) Die to this dark world. Live in eternal day. (BOB *cries a little. The* PARSON *turns to him eagerly. He takes the crying as a sign.*) Yes, yes. (*Quietly.*) God is here. God enters through these bars. Reach out. Touch his garments.

> WARDER *comes in.*

WARDER. Step outside sir.

PARSON. This is not –
WARDER. Governor says outside.

PARSON and WARDER go out. WARDER shuts the door behind them.

MILES. On't a scratch on him.

Outside a woman's laugh spirals up inside the prison. Another woman joins in. A group of people laugh.

MILES (*looks at* CLARE). You got 'em all gooin' boy.

The laughter fades out. Then a man laughs closer and the group laugh again. Everyone in the cell stands.

DARKIE. Lettin' us off.
BOB. Listen.
HAMO. Why on't they come here?
BOB. Hev they goo pass?
HAMO. On't they let us off?
DARKIE. Quiet! Other rooms first.

MILES *listens at the door. Everyone in the cell is silent. The laughter goes on.*

MILES (*calling*). Shut up! (*To others.*) Laugh too loud. On't hear.
DARKIE (*to* CLARE). Goo out boy. They'll let you out.
BOB (*banging on the door*). Here! Here! Here! Here!
DARKIE (*to* BOB). Shut up, boy!

HAMO, BOB *and* PATTY *beat on the door and shout.*

HAMO.
BOB.   } Here! Here! Here! Here!
PATTY. Let's out! Let's out! On't a prisoner!

Outside the laughter goes on and on. Screams, shouts, peals, groans – of laughter. No one laughs in the room. Their hysteria is dry. They stop banging. They move away from the door. They go to the other side of the room. They stare at the door. They huddle together. The door opens. GOVERNOR, WARDER and PARSON come in. WARDER gives BOB a thumbs up sign.

GOVERNOR. I have received a document from London. Listen carefully. Noise Hicks.

> WARDER *goes out through the door. He leaves it open.*

After studying the proceedings of the special assize that last week –

WARDER (*off*). Howd your row!

GOVERNOR – sentenced you to hang –

> The WARDER *comes in. The laughter goes on.*

– the authorities have provided me with a list –

WARDER. I told 'em.

GOVERNOR. – of condemned whose sentences have been commuted to such alternative punishments –

PATTY. I knew they had t'let yoo off! On't git coffins in this town. Local shops on't provide. Know what'd happen t'their winders. Had t'send all the way t'Cambridge. On't even git the loan of a cart t' –

GOVERNOR (*talking her down*) – as London deems appropriate. I have still to be informed of these. (*Reads list.*) Miles Cooper.

MILES. Sir.

GOVERNOR. Hamish Cecil Towsey.

HAMO. Sir.

GOVERNOR. Peter Star –

WARDER. Last room sir.

GOVERNOR. Robert Hall.

BOB. O bless 'em. Bless 'em –

GOVERNOR. That is the list for this room.

HAMO. Thanks be t'god.

MILES. Bless 'em. Bless 'em.

PARSON. You men vow now! O vow! Remember this moment. God took you to the graveside –

GOVERNOR. Last room.

PARSON. – and you saw its shadow. O take –

BOB. Bless 'em.

PARSON. – that shadow and let it be the mirror for your minds.

> GOVERNOR *and* WARDER *have gone out.* PARSON *turns to* DARKIE.

They will die of typhus in the galleys. Drown. Spend their
lives in prison. And they laugh!

Laughter goes round the prison. Everyone in the room except
DARKIE *and* PARSON *laugh with nervous hysteria.*

They'll never see the place where they were born. Wives and
children will vanish from their lives. Listen to them laugh!

A closer burst of laughter from the next room.

Their world will be so strange they won't know their face in the
glass or the world outside the window. They'll dig rocks to
plant seed. When they die they'll be buried in shallow graves –
men will have long since forgotten the customs for the dead.
Listen! (*Laughter.*) Abandon this bitter hope. Hope! – it is a
tide that goes in and out and grinds men together till they wear
each other down. Take your scaffold from god's hand. He
crushes a life's despair into a few seconds. I will walk with you
to the scaffold. I'll have a word with the prison ordinary about
it.

The PARSON *hurries out.*

DARKIE (*to* CLARE). Take my coat. Here boy. On't just show,
was it Patty. Good strong stuff. Work hard t'wear that out.
MILES (*involuntary happiness*). O god.
BOB. Saved! On't he said?
HAMO. Must be true. They're laughin'.
DARKIE. Goo on, take it. On't waste it on show. Kep' us in rags,
on't dress up for 'em when I die. On't their circus.

CLARE *takes the coat.*

On't – feel straight in my head. I'll be a bit quiet.

The door opens. BETTY *runs in.*

BETTY. O boys hev you all bin saved! (*Laughs and embraces the
prisoners.*) Boy. Boy. Bob my lad.
BOB. Bless 'em. Bless 'em.

WARDER *comes in.*

WARDER. Git out gall! What you think this is? Cooper, Towsey, Hall: things t'gither an' git next door.

MILES. I'll stay with him.

WARDER. Next door.

MILES. On't right. (*To* DARKIE.) Let us off t'be harder on you.

DARKIE. Bob on't more'n a lad. You got your wife and kids. Best me if it had t'be someone.

WARDER. Move sharp.

MILES, HAMO *and* BOB *collect their things*. BETTY *helps*.

CLARE. Look at the fly gooin' in an' out the bars. You could climb up an kill it but you on't. Patty stay in town t'night. Likely they'll let you lie out in the corridor. I'll come again t'morra.

GOVERNOR (*off*). I ordered quiet!

PATTY (*unsure*). Darkie.

DARKIE. No need t' stay in this place. On'y git upset.

The prison goes quiet.

PATTY. Stay if you ask.

DARKIE. On't want it.

MILES, HAMO, BOB *and* BETTY *go out*.

BETTY (*outside the door*). On't Darkie saved then?

WARDER (*in the doorway*). Five left t'hang.

The WARDER *goes out and shuts the door.* CLARE *sits on the bench with his head in his hands.* DARKIE *and* PATTY *stand.* CLARE *begins to laugh. It is easy, not hysterical, but not calm. It wells up in him and overflows.*

PATTY. Stop it. Shameful.

CLARE (*laughing into his hands*). Can't.

PATTY. Stop it. Doo I goo back on me own.

CLARE lies on the bench. He covers himself with the blanket to muffle the sound.

Allus find some carry on! Wicked!

CLARE *falls on the floor. He rolls about under the blanket. Off, there is a short burst of laughter. It becomes hysterical – like sobbing. It lasts for a few seconds.* CLARE *laughs happily through it.*

CLARE. Hurts. Hurts.

WARDER *comes in. He watches from the doorway.*

WARDER (*nods at* DARKIE). Thought you'd gone off your head. Happens sometime.

PATTY (*giggling politely*). Is he hurt? On't right. Ought a think a Darkie. Not allus self. (*Hands over ears.*) Stop it Mr Clare.

WARDER *comes into the room.*

My head goo. (*Screams*). Stop it!

PARSON *appears in the doorway.*

PARSON. Keep that man quiet. This house has seen enough levity.

PARSON *goes.*

WARDER. Howd your racket.

DARKIE. Let him be. Bad seth t'him, why should I stop him?

WARDER (*to* DARKIE). Stay civil! (*Gestures after* PARSON.) Parson'll rattle t'Governor an' I'll git it in the neck. On't make trouble for me boy, doo I'll make trouble for you! (*Pulls the blanket off* CLARE.) Drunk. Pair a you git off.

WARDER *goes to the door and waits.* CLARE *stops laughing.*

DARKIE. Best mate I had John. Keep your luck. On't fit in at home. Sorry mother's upset but thass a bit late. Well I on't the son she'd hev chose. Look arter my sister. (*To* PATTY.) On't come. Rather you on't. (*No answer.*) Expect you'll doo what you think best.

PATTY. On't ought a said you on't fit in. No cause t'burden us with that. You on't know.

DARKIE. Can't say the right things in this place.

PATTY *goes out.*

CLARE. Had a gall with you that night. Gall worked at Milton's.
DARKIE. What?
CLARE. You on't know her name. Saw her last Christmas.

Off, a short burst of laughter.

DARKIE. What you up to boy?
CLARE. Hev she told you where she were gooin'?
DARKIE (*shrugs*). All that row. Some got away.
CLARE. But on't she said –
DARKIE. Chriss sake boy! (*Slight pause.*) Patty's stood outside.
CLARE (*after a pause*). On't quarrel Darkie.
DARKIE. No.

WARDER *stands aside.* CLARE *goes out.*

SCENE FIVE

Hyde Park.
Day.

CLARE *downstage with* MRS EMMERSON. *He wears* DARKIE'S
green jacket. She is about forty.

Upstage a prize fight. PORTER, *a negro, and* JACKSON, *an Irishman, are stripped to the waist, wear tights, and fight with bare
knuckles. A tubby referee. Backers.* PORTER'S *backers are:* FIRST
a marquis, and SECOND *the marquis's fellow Harrow school friend.*
JACKSON'S *backers are:* THIRD *the young son of a shopkeeper, and*
FOURTH *a greasy old cockney. The* BACKERS' *jackets on the ground
mark the ring.*

MRS EMMERSON. The admiral said we should meet him here on
his afternoon walk. You are nervous, Mr Clare.
CLARE. Ay.
MRS EMMERSON. No need. He subscribed for twelve copies of
your book. Such a subscriber attracts interest.
CLARE. Ay.

The Fight

The FIGHTERS *are fresh. They move lightly on their toes.*

FIRST BACKER. Watch the fella Porter.
SECOND BACKER. Ware the fella's left.
FIRST BACKER. You're not here to bow to each other.
THIRD BACKER. After him Jackson. Get stuck into him.
FOURTH BACKER. Nicely Jackie boy.
REFEREE. Corners Gents.

End of Round One

MRS EMMERSON. See, Mr Clare, we have grass and trees in this
   park. Do they not inspire you? O to be touched by the wings!
   The rushing of the spirit! We earthly ones can but crane our
   necks to watch you soar! Mr Clare, shall I slip into yonder
   hedge and leave you to the muse?
CLARE. Tell-'e-true mam I'd like t'be alone with my thoughts –
   so long as you on't goo too far.
REFEREE. Right lads.

Start of Round Two

MRS EMMERSON. But wait! I promised Patty to stay at your side
   in the great city. I underlined it in my letter.
CLARE. You could kip an eye on me from the bushes mam.
MRS EMMERSON. O Mr Clare, I could hardly come upon the
   admiral from the bushes – even in the company of a poet.
   (*Laughs.*) I will tell the truth. (*Showing.*) Notebook and pencil.
   It is my ambition to be at your side when the muse calls. I shall
   take down your words as you cast them on the air. When I'm
   old with my nieces and nephews gathered at my skirts I shall
   take out this book and turn – commanded by their childish
   piping: it will be their habitual pleasure! – to the oft op't pages
   where I wrote the effusions of John Clare. 'Hyde Park Im-
   promptu'. Now comes tom-sparrow on his feathered wing, the
   city bird that cannot sing, but ah I know within thy heart,
   what thoughts are longing to –. The last line is often difficult to
   bring home.
CLARE. It flew. Like the sparrer.

MRS EMMERSON. Mr Clare, my silly chatter! Well, I've done you some good and I shall do more.

The Fight

FIRST BACKER. That nicked the Irishman's smiling eye.
THIRD BACKER. Use the left. Jab. Jab.
FOURTH BACKER. Nicely Jackie boy.
SECOND BACKER. Hack at him Porter. Up the blackman.
FIRST BACKER. Left jab then tap the solar plexus.
REFEREE. Corners gents.

End of Round Two.

MRS EMMERSON. This is a popular refuge for poets. Away from the hot London streets. The air should be filled with music. I call it poets' corner. Though happily the poets are living. Who's that? My eyes in this bright light. I read too much.
CLARE. Lamb.
MRS EMMERSON. Have they told you about Lamb?
CLARE. They all have.
MRS EMMERSON. His sister killed his mother with the bread knife. They put her away – but Lamb promised to stay with her all the time and they let her out. Poor lamb! The insane live so long. No money – he works as a clerk. He can't support his sister *and* marry – so he drinks. They carry her strait-jacket everywhere. In the ornamental bag.

The Fight

REFEREE. Right gents.

Round Three starts. There is a quick knockdown.

REFEREE. Right gents.

End of Round Three.

FIRST BACKER. Watch his left Porter. Beat you twice. Watch his feet. Irish go in for dancing.
SECOND BACKER. Chip him down.
THIRD BACKER (*to* JACKSON *as he breathes*). Deeper.

FOURTH BACKER. In out. In out.

> CHARLES *and* MARY LAMB *come in.* CHARLES *is young, lean, handsome and dressed as a literary romantic.* MARY *is ten years older than* CHARLES*. She wears a respectable hat and carries the ornamental bag.* LAMB *hesitates when he sees* MRS EMMERSON *but comes forward.*

LAMB. John.

CLARE. Respects brother.

LAMB (*to* MRS EMMERSON). Mam. John, my sister, Mary.

CLARE. Mary had a little lamb. Is that knowed up in London? Everywhere that Mary went the Lamb was sure to goo! (*Laughs.*)

MRS EMMERSON. Hyde Park reminds Clare of his native country. We almost had a poem on it, did we not?

LAMB. Now you've seen us will you desert your village?

MRS EMMERSON. No, John will go back to his wife and cottage. We are agreed.

LAMB. Are *you* agreed brother Clare?

CLARE. Ay. On't afford London.

> LAMB *and* MRS EMMERSON *laugh.*

LAMB. None of us can afford London. Well you're a wise poet. Stay at home where the muse has your address.

The Fight

REFEREE. Gents.

> *Round Four starts*

THIRD BACKER. Move the big clumsy bear.

FIRST BACKER. Let him do his jig Porter. And make him wince so he's got music to do it to.

SECOND BACKER. Fella'll soon lose his puff.

FIRST BACKER. Then you can bend him over your knee and break his back a vertebra at a time.

REFEREE. Part lads.

> *End of Round Four.*

MARY LAMB. The shopping Charles.

LAMB. And my office.

SECOND BACKER. The marquis will see you all right Porter. He's a good judge of flesh. The light in his eye means money.

THIRD BACKER. Move him.

LAMB. I wanted to tell you in the crush last night: I like your verse.

MRS EMMERSON. There'll be another book soon – if our plans prosper.

LAMB. Clare tells the truth.

MRS EMMERSON. What is the truth?

LAMB. Pilate asked Christ that but he didn't wait for an answer. If he had he would have crucified it.

MRS EMMERSON (*uncertain*). Tut tut, Mr Lamb. Is that not free thought?

LAMB. Mrs Emmerson you are the only person who's ever really said tut tut.

MRS EMMERSON. O fie!

LAMB. Truth isn't governed by the laws of supply and demand. When it's scarce its price goes down. So it's not a luxury, it's never found in palaces, or paraded by judges. Truth shelters in the gutter. Only the man who stoops finds it.

MRS EMMERSON. I'm proud to say I didn't understand one word. Mr Lamb, you are a poet. You have no call to go round putting ideas in people's heads.

LAMB. Even the hangman tells the truth when he's drunk. Keats went to Rome to find truth – and beauty and life. He died there. Truth is often ugly. The spit on god's face. Yes, the truth is spat into the golden faces of all idols. God's face is covered in spit. Fools think that's his mask and worship it. Dangerous! But it's even more dangerous when the truth is told by a wise man. The goddess of wisdom is a bird of prey, the owl. But the fools have hunted *her* and put her in a cage. If you try to let her out she savages your hand. Only a wise man tries to do that – or another sort of fool.

He comes downstage and turns his back on the others.

That was the lunchtime sermon. Now the blessing. (*He takes out his flask.*) To truth. (*He shakes it.*) In vino veritas,

The Fight

REFEREE Right gents.

Round Five starts.

SECOND BACKER. Go for the cut on the fella's eye.
FIRST BACKER. Stretch the cut.
THIRD BACKER. Use your science.
SECOND BACKER. He thinks science is the English shillalah.
FIRST BACKER. Keep your fist in his face Porter.
MARY LAMB. In this hot weather the vegetables are covered in dust. It's as oily as soot. The water goes black when you wash them. They're going off before you get them home. I complain to the shopkeepers –

LAMB sees they are listening to her, drinks from his flask and crosses himself.

– but they say they have to display their goods. They soon complain if you touch them or smell them. Goods? – I tell them they should call them bads.

She laughs. She takes a cabbage from the ornamental bag.

I bought this cabbage yesterday. It smells of fish.

She smells it and puts it under MRS EMMERSON's *nose.*

Mackerel or sprats?

MRS EMMERSON. I have no sense of smell.
LAMB. I write on the back of bills and promissory notes when the Governor's out of the office.
MRS EMMERSON. John doesn't know what they are.
CLARE (*smiles excitedly*). Ay. Bills are never paid and promises never kept.

The Fight

FIRST BACKER. Play the fella Porter.
FOURTH BACKER. Ouch.

SECOND BACKER *laughs.*

THIRD BACKER. Lout! Use your feet if you can't use your head!
SECOND BACKER. He's yours now! Ouch!

ADMIRAL RADSTOCK *comes in. Large, dignified, grey-haired.
He watches the fight. The others do not see him at first.*

The Fight

REFEREE. Right lads.

End of Round Five.

THIRD BACKER. Dam' it you give him your eye to carve up!
FIRST BACKER. He'll come like a well trained puppy now and
stand to be whipped. Don't thrash him too soon. No better
pastime than watching a big punchy bruiser taking punish-
ment. Don't let the fella duck it by passing out.
SECOND BACKER. Bang him and keep him raw.
PORTER (*laughs*). I play him suh. Have my piece of fun and hurt
him real hard.
SECOND BACKER (*calls to the other corner*). Send him back to his
Irish bog.
FOURTH BACKER. Yer ain' won yet ol' sport.
THIRD BACKER. I invested in you Jackson. He's over confident.
You can stop that black ape. Just behave.
MRS EMMERSON. Lord Radstock, good day.
LAMB. Servant, sir.

MARY LAMB *bows.*

MRS EMMERSON. Allow me to present my friend. John Clare –
your benefactor.
CLARE. Servant sir.
ADMIRAL. Honoured, Mr Clare. Mrs Emmerson been rushing
you off your feet?
CLARE. Mrs Emmerson's bin most kind.
ADMIRAL (*after nodding approval*). Your verse. Great charm
there. True melody. Fine love of English landscape. (*Looks
at* LAMB.) Nothing mawkish – (*Turns back to* CLARE.) a

sailor or christian may read it with profit. I'm both. When I
was away with the fleet I often had such thoughts. Couldn't
put them on paper though. I'm glad now – with time on my
hands – to be of use. How is Mr Emmerson?

MRS EMMERSON. As well as we may hope.

ADMIRAL. Ah.

The Fight

REFEREE. Gentlemen then.

Round Six starts.

THIRD BACKER. Elbows. Head out the way.

SECOND BACKER. Punish him. Let him smart.

FOURTH BACKER. Ouch!

THIRD BACKER. Hit him! Hit him!

ADMIRAL. I have one reservation. Not serious. The fault of a
narrow horizon. Those remarks in – poem named after your
village –

MRS EMMERSON. Helpstone.

ADMIRAL. (You see we've discussed it) – which criticizes the
landowning classes – smack of radicalism.

MRS EMMERSON (*reciting*). Accursed Wealth! –

ADMIRAL. That bit.

MRS EMMERSON. O'er bounding human laws
                              Of every evil then remainst the cause.

ADMIRAL. And so on.

MRS EMMERSON. Including lines from 'Winter'.
  (*Reciting.*)   What thousands now half pined and bare
                              Are forced to stand thy –
  (*Explains.*) That is, Winters –
  (*Reciting.*)   – piercing air.

ADMIRAL. Now now, sir.

MRS EMMERSON. All day near numbed to death with cold
                              Some petty gentry –

ADMIRAL (*shaking his head*). At it again.

MRS EMMERSON.   – to uphold.

ADMIRAL. Tut tut!

The Fight

REFEREE. Corners gents.

End of Round Six.

FIRST BACKER. Put the fella down now Porter. Good sport but too much is damned sight worse than too little eh?

SECOND BACKER. Dinner wants orderin' properly.

FIRST BACKER (*slaps* PORTER'S *shoulder*). Greek torso under that muck. If you could scrub it off you could stand on a pedestal.

PORTER. I'll do him this time suh.

THIRD BACKER. Keep out of his reach. You've only got to catch him once. He'll go down like an ox.

JACKSON. Ay ay.

FOURTH BANKER. Pecker up old lad.

REFEREE. Gents.

Round Seven starts.

THIRD BACKER. Remember Jackson. Let him thrash you and you're on the way down. No one else will back you. You make your own future.

FIRST BACKER. Do it stylish. It's worth a new suit.

ADMIRAL (*going to* CLARE). I shan't lecture you. Political science isn't parish pump philosophy. But answer this. Who controls the brute in man? Polite society. Well, your verse undermines its authority. There'd be chaos. The poor would be the first to suffer. I understand some hangings have already been necessary in your part of the world. Makes my point for me.

REFEREE. Corners gents.

End of Round Seven.

MRS EMMERSON. The admiral has a stateman's experience.

ADMIRAL. The people you criticize –

MRS EMMERSON. Unwittingly.

ADMIRAL. – are the only ones who can afford books. The only ones who can read! I ordered twelve. Now I can't give them to my friends. I can't tell you how to write verse. But I can spot a blemish. I'm a fellow author. Have you read my 'Cottager's

Friend, or a word in Season to him who is so Fortunate as to Possess a Bible or New Testament and a Book of Common Prayer'?

MRS EMMERSON. I gave John his copy.

ADMIRAL. In its twentieth edition. He should also look at my 'British Flag Triumphant'.

MRS EMMERSON (*writing*). I'll get it for him.

CLARE. The poems'd fall down.

ADMIRAL. Your publishers won't like you to alienate the already limited reading public and –

CLARE. On't see no nymphs in our fields but I seen a workhouse.

MRS EMMERSON. How does it help to shake your fist at heaven when some homeward-wending swain perishes in the snow?

LAMB (*downstage*). Spitting on god's mask?

CLARE. They had a winter coat they on't perish.

ADMIRAL. And the poem 'To Mary'. You can't put a book that contains such lines into the hands of a young lady. *I* don't think they're suitable even for the privacy of the bedroom – and I've been round the world twice – but if you choose to think of Mrs Clare as –

MARY LAMB. The tomatoes were quite blue. You find dust everywhere.

REFEREE. Right, lads.

Round Eight starts.

MRS EMMERSON. There's a mistake. Clare is married to Patty.

ADMIRAL. Then the poem *must* come out.

The Fight

FIRST BACKER. Blood on his gob! Pump the fella's tummy up in his mouth.

SECOND BACKER. Let the fella taste what he had for dinner.

FOURTH BACKER. O dear.

SECOND BACKER. Stand him straight before you hit him.

PORTER *knocks* JACKSON *down.* JACKSON *forces himself to stand.*

FIRST BACKER. And again.

> JACKSON *is half unconscious.* PORTER *knocks him down. He sways slowly to his feet, like a half-drowned man forcing himself to make useless gestures. He's unable to give up.*

ADMIRAL (*politely*). Well done the black man! Had them on our ships. Go to pieces in a storm – all whites of eyes and flashing teeth – but put a cutlass in their hands and bellow at them – what soldiers! Counter attack the devil! Used them against Boney!

MRS EMMERSON (*waving a handkerchief at* PORTER). Bravo the navy!

SECOND BACKER. Thrash the bleeder!

FIRST BACKER. Insolent celtic puppy. Take his feet off the ground. Make him soar. No better sight than watching them knocked through the air.

> JACKSON *drifts to his feet.*

THIRD BACKER. Up! Up! Up!

FOURTH BACKER (*to* CLARE. *Slyly amused. Nods at* THIRD BACKER). My young friend cuts his losses every round the Paddy lasts.

MARY LAMB (*takes a loaf from the ornamental bag*). This loaf smells of onions. (*Sniffs it.*) Can it be onions? It goes back.

> PORTER *knocks* JACKSON *out.*

FIRST BACKER. O class.

SECOND BACKER. What a fight! What a man! An ox!

MARY LAMB. Our shopping, Charles. (*She clutches the ornamental bag threateningly.*) Charles, I feel quite ill.

MRS EMMERSON. Should he see a doctor?

ADMIRAL. He'll only be out a few seconds. Even after that.

LAMB (*to* CLARE). She was shopping three times yesterday. A houseful of food. Rotting on the floor. Is she afraid of starving? Is it some punishment? I can't eat it. The rats are so fat they stroll over it. The cost!

MRS EMMERSON (*to* ADMIRAL). I must get tickets for Covent Garden tonight. Mr Corri has set one of Clare's poems to music.

The Fight

FIRST BACKER (*empties a bottle over* PORTER). Hail!

PORTER. I feel so good an cool lord-suh. I could eat myself. (*Licks wine from his arms.*) Yuh I doo taste sweet.

FIRST BACKER (*slaps* PORTER'S *shoulder*). You're a genius Porter. (*To* SECOND BACKER.) Collect my winnin's from my young shopkeeper friend.

SECOND BACKER *goes to* THIRD *and* FOURTH BACKERS.

PORTER. Exercise! I ain't had my proper exercise chasin' that boy round the grass. (*Laughs.*) Who want a little box? Yes suh!

THIRD BACKER. I'll give you a promissory note.

SECOND BACKER. Last fella welched on the marquis broke both arms goin' home.

THIRD BACKER *pays* SECOND BACKER. JACKSON *gets to his feet.*

THIRD BACKER (*to* JACKSON). A hundred guineas on you! Borrowed money.

FIRST BACKER. We'll take Porter out to dinner – (*Takes* money from SECOND BACKER.) – on this.

REFEREE, PORTER *and* FIRST *and* SECOND BACKERS *go out.*

CLARE (*to* FOURTH BACKER). Yoo lost too?

FOURTH BACKER (*slyly*). Put your money where it works. (*Gestures towards* THIRD BACKER.) Young spark knows it all. Can't learn – 'cept the hard way. (*Smiles.*) I backed the black man.

LAMB (*to* MARY). One shop. Mrs Emmerson. Sir. Clare.

ADMIRAL. Clare. Those lines: out!

MARY LAMB *bows and goes out with* CHARLES.

THIRD BACKER (*to* FOURTH BACKER). Sammy, I paid for his straw and oats and water. See me through Sammy. Fifty quid?

FOURTH BACKER. More broke than you are old man. I went in for his stablin' too remember. You'll earn a few quid if you ain' particular.

> THIRD BACKER *goes out*. FOURTH BACKER *helps* JACKSON *to dress*.

JACKSON. Me gut. Jazuschriss he must chew granite for breakfast.

CLARE. Wow! Seen knockin' at fairs but I on't see a man git to his feet after *that*! On't knew a man could stand so much!

JACKSON. Can yous spare a bob sir? If yous enjoyed your fight yous ought t'pay.

CLARE. On't in the money.

JACKSON. A new coat on your back.

CLARE. That were give us.

JACKSON. Were that give us now? Wish t'god someone'd give me summat!

MRS EMMERSON. John, the Admiral's tea! And Covent Garden tonight. You shall learn Mr Corri's tune and whistle it to Patty.

> MRS EMMERSON *and the* ADMIRAL *go out*.

CLARE. Did he hurt yoo, boy?

JACKSON. What bloody stupid English question is that? D'you think I have no feelin's?

CLARE. You kep comin' back.

JACKSON. Then aren't I the bigger fool? Stayed down a sight bloody sooner if Sammy the hawk hadn't had his eye on me.

FOURTH BACKER (*smiles*). You cost me a packet Paddy but I don't hold a grudge.

> JACKSON *is dressed. He goes out with* FOURTH BACKER. CLARE *follows* MRS EMMERSON *and the* ADMIRAL.

SCENE SIX

CLARE's *garden at Northborough.*
Morning. Pleasant late summer.
Table, bench, small fence. House off left. CLARE *sits at the table. A scrap of paper in front of him. He doesn't write.*

PATTY (*off*). Mr Fab want help. Grubbin' up his ol' orchard an' burn it.

> PATTY *comes on and goes straight to the bench.*

Why on't you goo down an' git took on? Worth a few bob. Time you git down someone else'll hev it.

> PATTY *picks up the basin from the bench and goes into the house.*

(*Off.*) Tired a you sit under my feet all day. Scribble bits a paper. No one on't bother read all that. Thought you was supposed a be clever boy. I'm daft but I know *that.*

> PATTY *comes out of the house. She carries the basin with water, potatoes and a knife in it.*

Scrap *them* boy. Sit there you make yourself useful. On't take much a your time. On't enough for that. On't scrap em thick. Make a proper job.

> CLARE *moves his paper to one side. He starts to peel the potatoes.* PATTY *goes into the house.*

(*Off.*) Shall *I* goo down Fab's an' ask? He were a mate a mine fore I wed. Spot a hard work doo you good boy. Sweat the scribble out a you.

> CLARE *pulls the piece of paper towards him and suddenly writes very quickly.* PATTY *comes out of the house and watches in silence.* CLARE *finishes writing before he answers.*

CLARE. Smell a burnin'd lay on my stomach. You know I on't kip nothin down.
PATTY. Nothin t'kip down! (*Looks at paper. Reads slowly.*) That

say Mary? (*Knowingly.*) I'll catch her out one day. (*Slight pause.*) On't a letter? (*No answer.*) Who is she boy?

CLARE. Gall.

PATTY. Had 'nough sense not t'wed yoo. On't that bake house gall at Maxey? (*No answer.*) One a your London madams.

CLARE. She on't round no more.

PATTY. On't see the point a writin t'someone when they on't round no more even if that is poetry.

BABY *starts to cry in the house.*

She goo in your new book? Allus in your books. What do next-door think? Bin your doormat too long. (*Calls to* BABY.) Chuck chuck darlint. Your ol' mum on't far.

CLARE. There on't a new book.

PATTY. Bin scribblin day-in-day-out for years. House full a it! On't that nough for a new book yit?

CLARE. No new book. Last book on't sold.

PATTY. What?

CLARE *starts to peel the potatoes.*

Told me they like how you write up London.

CLARE. No more books.

PATTY. Well – thank chriss for that! So thass all over then? Now we know where you stand. On't scrap them too thick.

PATTY *goes into the house.* CLARE *goes on peeling potatoes and dipping them in the water.*

(*Off, she tries to control her happiness.*) Can't say I on't said. No surprise t'me. Well now you know who stick by you. Put all that ol' scribble in a big box. I'll scrounge one off the shop. No call t'throw 'em out. Never know. Someday someone might want a buy one. (*To* BABY.) There now shall mummy make him comfy? (*To* CLARE.) God hang the man that invented ink. Wicked shame. Let 'em lead you a proper dance boy. Times I told you what it'd be. You?: no, wouldn't hev it. Well, thass done with. Best thing all round. Now our luck's beginnin' t'change.

PATTY *comes out of the house. She carries the* BABY.

On't say *I* on't grateful. (*Picks up the piece of paper.*) Put her with the rest?

CLARE (*after a slight pause*) ... Leave it ...

PATTY (*frightened*). Thass over boy.

CLARE. Ont goo back labourin'. On't know what I'm at out in the fields. (*Picks up his pen.*) Goo sit back the hedge an' write on me hat. Who'd give us work?

PATTY. Fab for a start.

CLARE. How long that last? Week?

PATTY. Hev t'kip askin'. Got work last harvest. Lads'll jike you first off. They'll soon git tired. On't never give yourself airs.

CLARE. Can't live like that. Can't help what I am. God know I wish I couldn't write me name! But my mind git full a songs an' I on't feel a man if I on't write 'em down. O god I on't even know if thass truth anymore. (*Throws pen down.*) No grip left in me hand! Pain in me head! Gut burn! Thass terrible gall.

PATTY. On't try git round me. My sympathy run out years agoo. On't fed right. Thass all the matter with you. Bring regular wages in the house an' I'll soon hev you fed up. Forgit Mary an' think a me. On't rowin. One kid on my hands an' another on the way. Tired a all this self. You think a someone else. Feed *us*. Thass your job boy. On't goo out workin' while I'm carryin'. An' they on't let you on the parish while you got your health.

CLARE. Health gall? My limbs're on fire?

PATTY. On't talk so daft! Talk straight so a body can hev a proper conversation. If you're on fire you goo up in smoke. On'y smoke I seen out a you's tobacco – when you scrounge it. (*To* CHILD.) There there, ol' mum on't row *you*. (*To* CLARE.) Limbs! Normal people hev arms an' legs. Chriss sake talk like a man. On't comfortable with you in the house. Talk like some little ol' gall so well brought up she can't git her gloves off without the footman. Aches an' pains? I'll know what smartin' is when I hev your kid.

CLARE (*hands her the basin*). Done.

PATTY (*takes the basin. She now holds the basin and the child*). Sick t'death a the whole bloody thing! Like a new pair a shoes like other women doo. A shirt. Or a bit a ribboned. I'm still a

young woman. Sit down to a decent meal. Just once. Tired a
hoardin' every little scrap t'make it look like a proper meal.
Sick an' tired. I'll tell you why you're ill: you're hangin'
about atwix an atween. No mystery there. You on't know what
you're supposed t'be at. No wonder you're sick. All that scribble
scribble drive anyone sick. An' for what? For Chriss sake what?
They on't even read it! Look at this child John Clare. Thass
sick an' pukin since it come in the world – cause thass famished
like its mother. An its father. An' we're famished for what?
Scribble scribble scribble on bits a paper for rats t'eat! Scribble
scribble scribble scribble.

> CLARE *turns away.* PATTY *puts the basin down.*

On't turn your back on me! Tell you straight boy: had enough.
I goo down Fab's an' git you took on. (*She picks up the basin.*)
You borrow a saw next door an' goo down six t'morra sharp
an' show willin'. Or you on't sleep an' eat by my side. I'll
shame you.

> PATTY *takes the basin into the house.* CLARE *sits and stares in
> front of him. Pause.* MRS EMMERSON *comes through the gate.
> She carries a canvas bag.*

CLARE. Mrs Emmerson . . .
MRS EMMERSON. Good day, John.
CLARE. What're you dooin' here?

> CLARE *gets up and goes to her. He moves like an old man.*

MRS EMMERSON. I didn't warn you. You'd have got into one of
your fusses.

> CLARE *impulsively puts his arms round her and starts to cry.*

CLARE. O mam . . . mam . . . Five years. No one t'talk to. I'm so
alone. (*Takes his arms from her.*) Sorry. Mustn't. Sit down.
(*Cleans the bench.*) Sit here.
MRS EMMERSON. You look ill. So tired, John.
CLARE (*puzzled.*) But I warned you. Put everythin' in my letters.
My stomach an' my hands. My mind goo dead.
MRS EMMERSON. But suddenly seeing you.

PATTY (*off*). Hope someone enjoy your scribble. God know I suffered for it.

CLARE. What's the London news? You on't sit down. Had a letter from my publisher –

MRS EMMERSON. I know.

CLARE. He'll hev t'change his mind mam. On't nothin' t'live on bar my books.

PATTY (*off*.) Sleep on your own after this. You hev the pleasure a getting kids you hev the worry a feedin' 'em.

CLARE. I'll tell Patty. She'll want t'smarten up fore you see her. Sit down.

> CLARE *hurries into the house.* MRS EMMERSON *looks round. She puts her bag by the table. She sits on the bench. She reads the poem.* CLARE *comes out of the house.*

MRS EMMERSON. It's as I imagined. Full of peace and stillness.

CLARE. Where you put up?

MRS EMMERSON. Lord Milton's.

CLARE. Oh.

MRS EMMERSON. He's coming here now. I came ahead. I wanted to have a little time with you. On our own.

CLARE. What he want?

MRS EMMERSON. Did you know how I looked forward to your London visits? (*Smiles.*) You were –. When my husband died, our talks were – well, almost my reason for living. You still write?

CLARE. Hundreds a verse. Chorus in my head all day. Each one sing a different tune. Struggle t'git one straight at a time.

MRS EMMERSON. You write too much.

CLARE. Patty'd say yes t'that. Scare her. Like hevin a drunk in the house. Moaned when I drank a bit over the edge. Now it's the words – an' they're worse. (*Moves bag.*) She's heavy. Lug that all on your own?

MRS EMMERSON (*smiles at the paper*). More Mary?

CLARE. My other wife.

MRS EMMERSON. Have you turned Mohammedan, John?

CLARE. Not my real wife. No she is real. But not Patty. My other real wife.

MRS EMMERSON. It's a bag of your books. They won't sell. The publisher's let you have them cost price. That will help you. Take them round your neighbours.

CLARE. But the village on't read.

MRS EMMERSON. There'll be easier to sell where you're known.

CLARE. They on't read woman! Barrin' the parson and a few others – an' they got copies!

MRS EMMERSON. John, you must co-operate with your friends when they try to help you. Don't – (*She searches for an idiom.*) – fly off the handle. Surely *visitors* would gladly purchase a copy at the –

CLARE. On't git visitors now! An' the few that doo come expect a copy free for the trouble a findin' me out! That letter from my publisher – he sold all they books – first book give him three editions – he say I owe *him* money! Hundred an' forty pound! Work on the land you git ten bob a week. On't live on that let alone pay him! Now he dump this on me an say cost price! Cost? Cost? That cost me the earth!

MRS EMMERSON. Publishing is a business. Printing, advertising, copies for critics –

CLARE. Hev the world gone mad? No wonder they say I'm a clown!

MRS EMMERSON. Preparing the text. You don't even punctuate. Your penchant for native words. The foreign languages your readers know are Latin and Greek – not East Anglian! Your – scribble has to be decoded and made accessible to polite society. That has to be paid for.

CLARE. Lord Radstock.

MRS EMMERSON. He's written to your publishers.

CLARE. Lord Milton.

MRS EMMERSON. I'd help, but my husband left so little. He was an invalid and I was never a good manager. A widow of my social standing can't risk any suggestion of want ... Society is so intolerant.

CLARE. Patty you had long enough!

PATTY *comes out of the house immediately. She has straightened her clothes and washed. She stands stiffly by the door.*

MRS EMMERSON. I shall call you Patty straight away.

PATTY (*bobs awkwardly*). Yes'm.

CLARE. Show her Fred.

PATTY (*defensively*). Sleepin'.

MRS EMMERSON. Later. I'm at Milton House for a few days.

PATTY. Yes'm.

MRS EMMERSON. It's a difficult joy being married to a great writer. You're lucky to be the woman in his house.

PATTY. (*to* CLARE). She askin' for a cup a tea?

CLARE (*opens the book and hides his face in it*). All these pages. On'y the author's read 'em. Opened 'em.

MRS EMMERSON. Don't cry on them, John. No one will buy if they're soiled. Show me your new work.

CLARE. Us'll hev t'git a proper job. Somethin' drastic t'bring in proper money. Set up boxin'. They git paid for bein' knocked about. I git knock about. Why on't I paid for it? I know the back a your faces: think I on't up to it. I'd surprise you.

CLARE *goes into the house.* PATTY *tries to follow.*

MRS EMMERSON. Patty our women's talk.

PATTY *stops.*

Well?

PATTY. Pardon'm?

MRS EMMERSON. How is he?

PATTY. On't know'm.

MRS EMMERSON. He still thinks he's a boxer.

PATTY. Sometime'm.

MRS EMMERSON. You don't let him drink?

PATTY (*laughs with nerves so that she snorts*). What on? No one treat him now.

MRS EMMERSON. Lord Milton's coming.

PATTY. Now?

MRS EMMERSON. Don't be alarmed. They'll do what's best. If he has to go into care they'll take him today.

PATTY. That soon'm?

MRS EMMERSON. Surely? If he needs help he must have it before his mind's irretrievably lost. Untoward delays can be fatal.

PATTY. So soon.

MRS EMMERSON. Let us pray in a year this is all over. John will be home again. Well enough to work and support his family.

PATTY. On't know'm.

MRS EMMERSON. Even now all might yet go well. If only you surround him with assurance and support. Surely he can find peace in this garden? (*She stares at the view.*)

PATTY. Yes'm. (*Slight pause.*) Baby cry. Gentry stay all hours. On't seem t'realise you hev t'git up of a mornin' . . . beggin' your pardon'm. That an' the worry.

MRS EMMERSON (*turns to* PATTY. *Uncertain.*) What, dear?

PATTY. The doctor ought a see his pains by right. God knows I on't want him t'goo. Shut up here on my own. He say a visit t'London'd help. But he hev t'come back an' that make it worse. Seen it afore.

MRS EMMERSON. You have this garden. This beautiful view.

PATTY. I look at that an' think a the rent. On't goo an' see him. Hope none a you expect that.

MRS EMMERSON. Patty.

PATTY. Even if I had the fare. On't manage. On't my world. Gentry come here scare me. Hev n'more on it. Never bin off more'n a few miles. How I goo trapsin' round a city askin' strangers the way t'the *madhouse*? On't doo more'n I can.

MRS EMMERSON. You married him.

PATTY. On't-ought-a-had by rights. How'd I know what it'd turn out t'be? He on't harm a fly. But what use is that to us?

> LORD MILTON *and* PARSON *come in.* LORD MILTON *carries two canvas bags and the* PARSON *one. They put them beside* MRS EMMERSON's *bag.*

MILTON. How've you got on Ellen?

MRS EMMERSON. We had our talk.

MILTON. Doctor's down the lane. I brought my keeper in case of trouble. Didn't want to all descend at once.

PARSON. Clare's wife.

MILTON. Afternoon Mrs. Clare. (PATTY *stands stock still.*) Shan't intrude. I'll keep my visit short.

MRS EMMERSON. It's good of you to find the time. We know this touches you as much as us.

> CLARE *comes out of the house.*

PARSON. Good afternoon. Clare. Lord Milton's here to see you. Be on your best behaviour. A credit to the village.

CLARE. On'y got the one behaviour so he'll hev t'make doo. Others hev. On't lookin' for a scrap with the church. (*Makes a boxing gesture.*) You bin in some scraps. Gen'man climb in the ring from time t'time t'defend his title. (*Laughs*). Her dead brother Darkie know. Hev his lordship come for a book? Can hev one cheap. Lower than London rates. Take two or more an' you git a discount. Or if he's hard up like us – thass bad times – tell him I'll let him hev a soil one cheap. Letters smudge but thass still fit t'read. (*Turns to get a book and sees the four bags.*) Four! My word the power of the press! The gospel's spread. The word bore fruit.

> *Turns back to the others. He becomes quiet and laconic.*

Will his lordship take tea? Patty make a good cup a cottage tea. Burnt bread in hot water an pepper t'taste. That on't take t'sugar. (*Slight pause.*) Words, my lord. You hev a poet in your parish parson. You had a poet in your field my lord. Wrote first poem when I were a boy pickin' up stones in your field. Took a stone in me hand an' a poem come in me head.

MRS EMMERSON. Show us your lovely new poem.

CLARE. 'My Mary'?

PARSON. Who *is* she?

CLARE. My wife. My real wife. Not Patty but my other wife. (*To* PATTY.) On't you frit my darlint. Had nowt t'doo with her for years. Look her out all place but she on't be found. Gone. I on't her choosin'. Or likely I doo us both wrong an' she's in the ground. On't Patty's fault she on't the gal I want. Bin a good wife. Good mother. Stood by me. But how'd I live with her? No, I remember *her*: the other one. An' all I want's t'lay my head on her breast. Peace then. Laugh agin. Talk like a sensible man. I'm so alone.

MILTON *nods to the* PARSON. *The* PARSON *goes towards the gate.*

Parson aren't you old! Lie in your churchyard soon stead a lyin' in your church. An ol' man's hair's the colour a bone. Seen 'em stack outside the slaughter house. Goo t'be turned t'glue. Seen a mouse once. Made its home in the heap a' bones an' shoulder blades stood outside the door. There'd bin some bellowin' that day! Slaughter a whole herd. Ox. O he were proud on his little house. Pop in an' out. Took seed in the hole.

The PARSON *goes.*

(*Gestures at* PARSON). He reeks. Glue.

MILTON. Read us a poem.

CLARE. I hev – but you on't know how t'listen. On't write for you. On't be a poet then. No more'n his carpenter's a carpenter. He touch a piece a wood an' it turn t'coffin. His corn's grass. His men are animals – goo round an' round his house on a rope, on a path shape like a sover-in. – I waited an' no one come, or give tuppence without a grudge. An' what I wrote was good. Yes. Worth readin'. Shall I step in line now? No. I on't labour in your fields n'more. Labour in my fields. You cut your fields up small so you could eat 'em better. I've eat my portion of the universe an' I shall die of it. It was bitter fruit. But I had more out the stones in your field than you had out the harvest.

The PARSON *and* DR SKRIMSHIRE *come in.*

PARSON. Clare, this is Dr Skrimshire. Your friends are worried about your pains and stories –

CLARE. Patty!

PATTY. Had me up parson's. Had t'tell what you say. Bein' a boxer an' Lord Byron.

CLARE. Patty thass just men I saw in London! (*Immediately turns to* DOCTOR.) Doctor I doo hev pains in my head! It git covered in boils. Sometimes I start t'goo blind. When I write. Why is that? My head were that hot this mornin'.

MILTON. Painful to see you in this distress. Unlike yourself. Let
   the doctor help you. I shall meet all expense. Mr Twice, as
   representative of the parish.

PARSON (*nods*). My lord.

MILTON. Mrs Emmerson, you're a close friend.

MRS EMMERSON. If the doctor can help.

DOCTOR (*looking at* CLARE). Mr Clare should spend a few months
   with me. At the end of that time I shall begin to know him.
   Then I can start disentangling the truth from the poetry.
   (*Smiles seriously.*) If things went well you'd soon be back. Rest
   and quiet are sometimes difficult to get at home.

   KEEPER *comes to the gate.*

CLARE. Where's your hospital?

DOCTOR. My lord when a mind's poised on the brink of grotesque
   oblivion it must not be offended with lies. (*To* CLARE.) I run a
   house for the mentally ill. Outside London. I don't lock my
   patients up or punish them. That's already been tried before
   they come to me. Your wife needs a rest too. Is she carrying?

MRS EMMERSON. Patty, we'll go into the house.

PATTY. On't budge.

CLARE. Out a my garden! I managed till now –

MRS EMMERSON. John, you haven't managed!

CLARE. Git out!

   MILTON *grabs at* CLARE *and finds himself pinioning him with
   his arms. There is a shocked silence.* MILTON *stops in surprise
   and lets* CLARE *go.*

MILTON. O. (*To* KEEPER *in sudden anger.*) You!

   KEEPER *takes* CLARE. *He winds a short rope round his arms and
   chest.*

CLARE. You can't drag me out my garden! Let us goo!

   KEEPER *takes him to the gate.*

   My kid. My papers, Mrs Emmerson! Patty, fetch next-door!
   (*Calls.*) I'll start work. Call Fab. Patty.

KEEPER. Settle down in the cart.

CLARE (*as he's led off*). Mrs Kemp dear! Git my brothers out the field!

> The KEEPER *takes* CLARE *away.* PATTY *watches in silence.* MRS EMMERSON *cries.*

MILTON. He was so slight. Skin and bone. Like a quail.

PARSON (*looks at his watch*). I'm old. My mind was settled on death long ago. But god sends me home to sleep in my own house.

MILTON. I'll drop you. (*To* PATTY.) Goodbye. I'll have the empty bags collected.

> MILTON *goes out.*

PARSON (*to* PATTY). Come when you need anything. My sister will look in. The world is in shadow because the father stoops so low to nurse his children. (*Shrugs.*) No, no one understands . . . Tragedy is like justice, blind and over pity. Clare didn't ask for help. He scorned us . . . In a way his sufferings condemn him. They protect him with the arrogance of a certain sort of pain.

> PARSON *goes out.*

MRS EMMERSON. Shall I call the neighbours?

PATTY. T'on't necessary. They'll look in. Feed baby or that'll fret. (*Picks up the poem.*) Will you take it? I could let you hev a handful. He'd expect me t'ask.

MRS EMMERSON. No . . . perhaps later.

PATTY. Was he a proper writer?

MRS EMMERSON. One's partiality blinds one. At first – but perhaps they became only ramblings, droolings . . . (*Cries.*) O this terrible day! He was so brave. He did so much – (*Hanky.*) but he couldn't even get a living like any rough you see hanging about the lanes. Why? (*She tears her hanky in anger.*) I'm sorry.

> She takes coins from her purse and gives them to PATTY.
> PATTY goes into the house.

MRS EMMERSON (*dabbing eyes*). Torn hanky.

MRS EMMERSON *puts the hanky away and goes out.* PATTY *comes out of the house. She feeds the baby at her breast.*

PATTY. Dig that. Few rows. Tatties an greens. Mind you grow up quick an' be a help. Us'll cope. Mary? Mary who? What Mary? On't come back n'more. Pair on em. Mary on't drive the sense out your head boy.

She strokes the BABY's *head.*

Safe now. An' your playmate. (*Taps stomach.*) His books learn you how t'starve. On't need books t'learn that. Mary.

SCENE SEVEN

Open space.
Night.
The BOXER *sits on a boundary post, hunched forward in the pose of The Thinker.* CLARE *comes in. He is exhausted and in rags.*

CLARE (*calls routinely*). Mary? (*Sighs.*) Walked so far ... (*Sees* BOXER.) The Paddy! Still fightin' boy – or just dead?

MARY *comes on. She is a tramp. Grotesque, filthy, ugly.*

Mary.
MARY. What?
CLARE. Mary. At last.
MARY. On't make a game a me boy!
CLARE. It's John.
MARY. Who?
CLARE. John Clare.
MARY. I on't ... Yes! – boy got me sacked out the big house! You changed boy. Terrible old.
CLARE. They locked me up.
MARY. Prison?
CLARE. Like a prison. Four years. Then I run for it. Come lookin' for you.
MARY. Why?

SCENE SEVEN

CLARE. I thought a you all the time. On't you think a me?

MARY. Can't say I hev.

CLARE. We was wed.

MARY. On't talk so far back! How'd you look after me? (*Laughs.*) He's hard done by? Lives like a Lord! *I* live like an animal with its hide pull off.

CLARE (*puts his hand on his crutch*). I'm still strong.

MARY (*laughs*). Look at him! Want summat a sight more appetizin' fore I put myself out this time a night. Bin on the road how many days an' what you had t' eat?

CLARE. Some grass. Taste a bread.

MARY. Grass! I look the sort a woman goo with a chap that eat grass? Hell-a-bit! I still git little better class'n escape convict.

CLARE. Marry me.

MARY. Take your hand off yourself. Cut you open doo you bother me.

CLARE. I give it all away for you. Patty, kids, home, my whole life. All away. I had you once. Lived all my life off that. Always hev you in my head. Watchin', talkin', smilin'. All the time. Good an' bad. Never git tired. Never lose hope. Everything goo t'gither in you. An' all those years my life was waste. You on't there. On'y in my head. That drove me mad. I'd a stood the rest with you. Now you're here an' you say ... No, I'm tougher'n you think! Show how I fight. (*Turns to* BOXER.) Hey up, Paddy!

Stands in a boxing pose in front of the BOXER, *dances on his toes.*

Sat there long enough an' on't fall down – stand up two minutes till I knock you down!

Punches the BOXER's *arm.*

Lady want a scrap!

The BOXER *looks up. It is* DARKIE. *He has a burn mark on his neck.*

Darkie ... They hang you boy!

DARKIE. On't see too well. Tell the truth the boxin' give me a squint an' I goo blind. Punch punch or summat – knock all the sight out my head. Sorry if you're an acquaintance. The discourtesy on't intended.

CLARE. Darkie it's John Clare.

DARKIE. John? What you punch my arm for?

CLARE. I'm sorry Darkie I on't –

DARKIE (*groping for him*). On't make a sport a me!

> Tries to hit CLARE *but can't find him.*

Come on!

CLARE. No Darkie. On't know you're blind.

DARKIE. You jabber. I'll git you.

CLARE (*trying to help him*). No Darkie! Sit down ol' chap. Let me . . .

> DARKIE *catches him on the side of the head.* CLARE *half falls.*

DARKIE. That hit summat!

CLARE (*doubles over*). Don't Darkie! Don't!

> DARKIE *throws a violent punch and misses. He throws another and catches* CLARE's *head.* CLARE *passes out.*

DARKIE. An' that! 'Nough boy? (*He gropes round for* CLARE.) Hev he pass out?

MARY (*looking at* CLARE). Knock out by a blind boy? You're all trouble an' no joy! (*To* DARKIE.) I goo off with anyone I'll goo off with you. You're a better piece of flesh than him.

DARKIE (*sitting on the stone marker*). On't git far with me. They torment you for a laugh when you're blind. Need all my strength t'crack their heads. On't eat. No grub for years. Sit here an' try t'forgit. But the cravin goo on.

MARY. I got bread.

DARKIE (*holds out his hands*). Where? Where?

> MARY *takes out bread and gives it to him.*

Hev you got a whole loaf! (*Chews.*) Jaw stiff.

MARY. You dribble like an ol' man.

DARKIE (*chewing*). On't kip in. (*Calmly.*) Chew an' chew but on't

know how t'swallow. My gullet's set. (*In tears.*) I'm hungry an'
I can't swallow.

MARY (*feeds him.*) Here boy. Try.

DARKIE. Summat in my neck. Summat goo crosst or thass a
twist. Can't eat.

MARY (*holding bread in his mouth*). Be a good chap.

DARKIE. My mouth taste a bread –

MARY. Try –

DARKIE – but I can't eat. It hurt. It hurt.

DARKIE *spits out the bread. It sprays on the floor.*

MARY. Risk my life for that!

DARKIE (*holds his neck*). My neck! Hurt!

MARY. Hush boy! Listen! (*Silence.*) Someone there. Quick. Out
the road. Hide till thass safe.

MARY *takes* DARKIE *off upstage.* THREE IRISHMEN *come in:*
FIRST *is older than* SECOND *and* THIRD. *They're muffled in
dark clothes. They carry bundles, parcels and sticks.*

FIRST IRISHMAN. This hollow lads. Sleep here. It's dry. Get
the water on the fire. We'll go on to Bourne t'morra. There's
work there.

FIRST IRISHMAN *starts to light a fire.* THIRD IRISHMAN
fills the kettle.

THIRD IRISHMAN. I'll never git rich: I work too bloody hard.

SECOND IRISHMAN. Give us your mug Tommy. And give us the
kettle here. His tea taste like piss out the udder of a dead cow.

FIRST IRISHMAN. If they bring any more machines on the land
they won't need us. When the harvest's over we'll try the
railroads. Buildin' railroads every bloody where.

THIRD IRISHMAN. You'd think they wanted t' travel away from
theirselves. Iron trains, iron houses, iron cannons. They sleep
in iron beds.

SECOND IRISHMAN. What do they think about when they poke
their little women: nails?

THIRD IRISHMAN. I'm not goin' on no railroad. Work like a
bloody steam-engine yourself.

CLARE *stands up.*

SECOND IRISHMAN. Jazuschriss the lord is risen.

CLARE. Cold night.

SECOND IRISHMAN. Where you goin' laddie? Haven't seen your face round here.

FIRST IRISHMAN. Out of prison?

CLARE. T'wont prison.

THIRD IRISHMAN. He's loony in the head.

FIRST IRISHMAN. On your own, is it?

CLARE. Mate's back there. And a woman.

THIRD IRISHMAN. Jazuschriss have you a woman back there? (CLARE *nods.*) Jazus-be-buggered is chriss wastin' women on you when there's a young fella here with his finger pokin up t'catch the chairman's eye? Is she all roight?

CLARE. Ay.

THIRD IRISHMAN. I mean, is she clean?

SECOND IRISHMAN. Jazus he'd hire himself out as a pitchfork t'git stuck in the muck.

THIRD IRISHMAN. How old would she be?

CLARE. My age.

THIRD IRISHMAN. It's a dark night. I'll make you a proposition now. Let me lay down with your little lady an' I'll give you my bread an' cheese. Is it on? Best cheese, my man.

CLARE. Hang on what she say.

THIRD IRISHMAN. If the lady says yes to you she'll say grace when she sees me.

CLARE *takes the bread and cheese. He eats like a starving man.*

FIRST IRISHMAN. Hang on Arny.

Turns to CLARE *and holds his arm to stop him eating.*

If your lady's any good it's me an' Michael after. Is that agreed sonny?

THIRD IRISHMAN (*after a slight pause*). Great-roarin-dust haven't we all t'share alike? If that's not in the Bible god slipped up.

FIRST IRISHMAN. And there'll be a mouthful for the lady after.

CLARE *starts eating again.* THIRD IRISHMAN *goes off.* CLARE
stands and eats. The other IRISHMEN *watch him.*

SECOND IRISHMAN. Slowly. You won't see Arny a while yit.
(*Slight pause.*) Come up to the fire. (CLARE *steps closer.*) Would
she be blond?

CLARE. Black.

FIRST IRISHMAN. Huha.

SECOND IRISHMAN. Long hair or short?

CLARE. Long.

FIRST IRISHMAN. Huha. An well set up?

CLARE. Huha.

SECOND IRISHMAN. But small inside?

CLARE. Huha.

SECOND IRISHMAN. As Christ's my god I like it small. Where
you make you own room.

The KEEPER *comes in. He is the former* ASSISTANT KEEPER.
He is dressed in dark clothes and carries a gun.

FIRST IRISHMAN. We're resting quietly mister.

KEEPER. Not on Lord Milton's land.

SECOND IRISHMAN. Jazuschriss a man can't put a road in his
pocket! I tell a lie. They put Ireland.

THIRD IRISHMAN *comes back.* KEEPER *steps into shadows.*

THIRD IRISHMAN. You little lyin' English punk! What bloody
woman?

CLARE (*points off stage*). There. (*Wipes his mouth.*)

THIRD IRISHMAN. You gobbled my bloody supper down smart.
Lyin' git. There's no bloody snatch in that wood. I'd find a
snatch if that's twice as dark as black. Lyin' English git! Don't
play games with me, fella-me-lad. I'll break your bloody neck,
you lying' punk. What's up?

FIRST IRISHMAN. Pol-iss.

KEEPER *empties the kettle over the fire.*

Are we supposed t'walk all night?

KEEPER. Village two mile down the road. On't pay for lodgin's –
thass your trouble.

SECOND IRISHMAN. Come to earn not spend. If you had a
starvin' family back home you'd understand.

FIRST IRISHMAN. They won't put us up in the village. We take
their fellas' jobs. That's how your boss keeps his wages down.

KEEPER. You wake my birds up. His lordship hev a shoot an his
London guests on't git a good bag – I'm out. T'on't the easiest
job. I got a wife an' nippers too.

The IRISHMEN *collect their things.*

THIRD IRISHMAN (*pushing* CLARE *out of his way*). Another twisted
thievin' English git.

SECOND IRISHMAN. One night your lord's barn'll go up in flames.

THIRD IRISHMAN. An' his ricks.

FIRST IRISHMAN (*gives* THIRD IRISHMAN *a bundle*). Arny.

SECOND IRISHMAN. An' no one'll put 'em out.

THIRD IRISHMAN *picks up the last bundle. The* THREE
IRISHMEN *go out.*

CLARE (*going upstage*). Mary! Mary!

KEEPER. No woman there. I'd hev heard.

CLARE. I dreamt I saw bread spat on the ground, and her say:
Waste, I risk my life! (*Shakes his head.*) No. Bread on't waste.
Thass on'y seed so you threw it on the ground. Birds hev it.
Or that soak away. Bread goo from mouth t'mouth an' what it
taste of: other mouths. Talkin' an' laughin'. Thinkin' people.
I wandered round an' round. Where to? Here. An' a blind man
git here before me. The blind goo in a straight line. We should
hev come t'gither. She git the bread. He crack the heads when
they come after us. An' I – I'ld hev teach him how to eat. I am a
poet an' I teach men how to eat. Then she on't goo in rags. He
on't blind. An' I – on't goo mad in a madhouse. No. No one
there. Never was. On'y the songs I make up on them ...
Walk four days. What, ninety mile? Head git mix up. Patty
on't welcome me neither.

KEEPER. Village down –

CLARE. I know where the village is. I'll goo home an' wait quiet,

till they come. Nothin' here now. Nice t'set eyes on my boys.
Tell em t'help their mother. P'raps my sons on't hev me in the
house when they grow up.

KEEPER. Down there. (*Treads on the last of the fire.*) Keep on the
path an' git off the land. Night.

They go.

SCENE EIGHT

Home.
Afternoon.
*Simple, comfortable room. Chintz armchairs. Big windows. A glass
door set in them. Sunny and pleasant.*

MARY LAMB *sits at a table opposite* NAPOLEON. *They play chess.*
MARY LAMB *makes a move. Silence.* NAPOLEON *makes a move.*

NAPOLEON. That's the move I made at Austerlitz.
Wellington won because he'd learned to cheat on the playing
fields of Eton.

*They stare at the game in silence. They don't move. The door
opens.* DOCTOR SKRIMSHIRE *shows* LORD MILTON *in.*
LORD MILTON *wears brick-red tweeds and carries a cane.*

DOCTOR (*nervously*). If your lordship waits in here.

MILTON. Pleasant room.

DOCTOR. The south facing drawing room. If I'd known your
lordship was –

MILTON. Spur of the moment.

DOCTOR. Was there any special reason for . . .? (*His voice trails
away in anxiety.*)

MILTON. I was asked to.

DOCTOR starts to go. MILTON *stops him.*

Will he recognise me?

DOCTOR. He may. Er, sometimes they're full of complaints, and
another time everything's fine – so you mustn't take . . . (*He
stops awkwardly.*) Won't you sit down?

DOCTOR SKRIMSHIRE *goes.* MILTON *walks towards the chess.*

MILTON. A demanding game.

> *They ignore him.* MARY LAMB *makes a move.* MILTON *wanders to the windows. He looks out.*

Beautiful grounds. Elms. Shadows on the lawn. Reminds me of home. Will *I* recognise *him?*

MARY LAMB. Don't use the soap. It smells.

MILTON. O I'm only a visitor, not . . . D'you know Mr Clare?

MARY LAMB. He doesn't get visitors. And they don't let him out. Took his key away. Years ago. A girl in the church porch. The mother complained.

> *The door opens. A man in a straight-jacket is pushed into the room. He is old, grey, dressed in grey, and completely unrecognisable. He makes rhythmic sounds. A* KEEPER *follows him. The man writhes from side to side but doesn't resist being propelled. His neck is stretched stiff.*

MAN IN STRAIT-JACKET. Mmm! Mmm! Mmm! Mmm! Mmm! Hup! Mmm! Mmm! Mmm! Mmm!

> *The* KEEPER *propels him over the room and out the other side. A moment later* DOCTOR SKRIMSHIRE *appears in the open doorway.*

DOCTOR. So sorry my lord. Fixing the decorations for the autumn ball. He got into a tizzy.

> DOCTOR SKRIMSHIRE *turns round and pushes* CLARE *into the room. He's in a bathchair. A shrivelled puppet. His head nods like a doll's. His face is white.*

Takes him time to wake up. (*To* CLARE.) Visitor John.

MILTON. Leave us alone.

DOCTOR. Of course. (*Hesitates.*) If your lordship would care to take tea in our rooms? A meat tea. I would be most –

MILTON. How kind.

DOCTOR. I'll alert my wife.

> *The* DOCTOR *hurries out.*

MILTON. Sorry. Didn't mean to wake you. D'you need anything? (*Silence.*) It's a nice garden.

> Silence. NAPOLEON *makes a move.*

Can you remember Mrs Emmerson? She died last week. When they confined her to bed she wrote and asked me to see you. D'you remember us? Seeing you brings it back. The afternoon in your garden. So long ago. Another world. The estate went to church every Sunday. I sat in front in my high pew. The parson read the story of the centurion. The man with authority. I say to this man, Go, and he goeth; and to another come, and he cometh. So be it done unto thee. The Bible. *You* had some books out too. Time to write here? No. It's changed. The village is there. But new houses. Part of the town really. (*Pause.*) What else? I can't sleep. See my wife's grave from the windows. Lie awake. Through the night. The dawn hurts my eyes. I hate my son. A vicious bastard. I was cruel sometimes. Foolish. But did I hate? No. Never a hater. He hates. Flicks his wrist as if he's holding a whip. Don't see much of him – except his back. Busy. In love with his factories. It's changed. D'you know who I am?

CLARE. Ha . . . yer . . .

MARY LAMB (*interpreting*). A new shirt.

MILTON. Yes. Anything else? (*Silence.*) Your wife's downstairs. Wouldn't come up. The journey upset her. Asked me to check first. You ought to see her. She's come a long way. Can I go down here?

> MILTON *opens the door in the windows and goes out. He disappears. The door swings slowly open. It catches the sun. It flashes once into the room. Brilliantly. Silence. An owl calls in the trees.*

NAPOLEON (*calls*). Poet – this is Napoleon. He's fetching your wife. (*Slight pause. To* MARY LAMB.) He's a government spy. He watched my strategy. I fooled him.

CLARE. Wh . . . yer . . . yer . . .

MARY LAMB (*interpreting*). He said What's she like?

NAPOLEON (*looks through window*). Nice little old lady. In black. Bent. Grey hair.

MARY LAMB. Ask him for soap and give it to me. Or I'll tell your wife about the little girl.

> *Pause.* MILTON *and* PATTY *come through the open door in the windows.*

MILTON. Talk. (*He stands by the windows.*)

PATTY. On't want t'come. On't know how you'd feel. Bin twenty-three years. He say I had to. Brought you some a your apple jelly. Apple off your crab tree. (*Pause. Tries to jolly him along.*) Hear you're gettin' a new shirt. There! They all send love.

> *No reply. She goes to* MILTON.

I'll goo home now if you can give me a lift.

MILTON. He's shy. Talk to him.

PATTY (*goes back to* CLARE). Good garden this year. Best sprouts for a long time. Proper journey gettin' here. On't used t'travel. Not like you allus gallivantin' up t'London. (*Terser.*) Well on't you least gooin' say hello, boy? Let's see some a the ol' self.

CLARE. Ha . . . m . . . m . . . b . . .

MARY LAMB (*interpreting*). How are his boys?

PATTY (*goes to* MILTON). Askin' after his boys. Sent a letter when they died. (*Goes back to* CLARE.) You remember your letter? Said they had good funerals an' names on the grave. Anythin' you want?

CLARE. G . . . g . . . g . . .

MARY LAMB. Go home.

PATTY. Here's home now. 'S all changed. New next-door. Nice here. Waited on. Regular food. Kep' clean an dry. I see they on't put you in the poor wing.

CLARE. T . . . t . . . b . . . w . . .

MARY LAMB. Tell the boys to write.

PATTY (*tries to jolly him*). Come by train. There! You on't bin on a train with all your gaddin' about. Line goo by the village. Goo out Sunday evenin's an' see the trains. The sparks doo goo! There!

CLARE. B . . . b . . . w . . . w . . .

MARY LAMB. The boys ought to write.

PATTY. John.

MARY LAMB. I set my brother's coach on fire. He died of fright. The horses dragged him through the town in the burning coach. It set light to the trees and houses. Over the bridge. I watched from my upstairs room. Sparks flying over the water. The coachman jumped. Coat on fire. Splash. Then out of the town. Horses rearing. Screaming. Through the lanes. Over the fields. Till it was all ashes. I said it was the lightning.

NAPOLEON. She tries to impress. Her brother died of drink years ago. I ruled Europe. The pope handed me the crown like a waiter and I put it on my head.

MILTON. Does Mr Clare still write?

MARY LAMB. He did at one time. Hundreds of ballads. Songs. I copied them into a book. His terrible hand! A scribble! No one paid me. You could send me some soap.

PATTY. Well you've got a lot of friends here John. Plenty t'talk about. Mind you share the apple jelly round. On't hog it. (*Slight pause.*) On't better stop. Tire you out. They'll be bringin' your teas round. On't git in people's road when they're workin'. If I can help it.

CLARE. L . . . l . . .

MARY LAMB. You look all right.

PATTY. Yes, well.

CLARE. G . . . g . . .

MARY LAMB. Grey hair.

PATTY. On't git younger. P'raps I'll see you again some time. Never know. Anyone told me last week I'd be here I'd a laughed. Sorry you on't had a proper life. Us hev t'make the most of what there is. On't us, boy? No use lettin' goo. (*Pats his arm.*) Learn some way t'stay on top. I'd be a fool t'cry now. 'Bye, 'bye.

> PATTY *goes through the open door in the windows.*

MILTON. Don't know why I said that about my son. Not true. Does his duty. Means very well. Scrupulous in fact. She's missed the cab.

> MILTON *hurries out through the open door in the window. Silence.* DOCTOR SKRIMSHIRE *runs in.*

DOCTOR. Is that Lord Milton going? How distressing. Clare have
   you made trouble?

> *The* DOCTOR *hurries out through the open door in the windows.*
> *He disappears. His voice is heard immediately.*
> (*Off, calling*). Lord Milton. The tea.

End

CLARE POEMS

CULTURE

All men must answer in their lives
Those questions whose answers are enormous
Because when one man decides how he lives
    He changes all men's lives

There are no small questions for small men
All men are Hamlet on an empty street
Or a windy quay
All men are Lear in the market
    When the tradesmen have gone

No man eats sleeps or loves for himself alone
Harvest and dreams and teaching the young
Don't take place in a small room
    But in the spaces of other men's lives

How we eat decides justice
Our homes measure the perversion of science
Our love controls the meaning of words
And art is whatever looks closely
    In the human face

If there were only irrational ways
To make the world rational
Art would still be reason
    And so our race not left to rot in the madhouse

Reason is the mark of kin
Poetry destroys illusions – it doesn't create them
And hope is a passion that will not let men
    Rest in asylum's peace

DARKIE AND THE MEN HANGED AT ELY

No work
Empty bellies
Wet houses
For charity the cold face of the fen

Duties: step out of the carriageway
Pray on sunday
Wait for a war to be paid to kill yourself

What happens?
Resist not evil?
Even the rat that eats a child's face?
We strike the rat away

For that they hang us
Like meat on a butcher's hook
While the judge chews his toothpick
And soldiers harvest with a footpad's knife
For such men reason is a sense of shame

When the untaught go quietly at the teacher's heels
To the graves
Love does not spring up in the rank shadow of the gallows
To cast out evil

Reason is armed when men cast out reason
For if driven from her home in the human face
She takes up refuge in the human fist

So say the five illiterates hanged at Ely

ON ENTERING PARADISE

If tomorrow the gates of paradise flew open
When you touched them
It would still have cost much blood
    To open them

Look behind you down the long sluice
Of blood and debris of war past time
And remember this when a voice calls
    How shall we open the gates of paradise?

Blood of itself is not enough
Even in the veins to keep men alive
And spilt it will not make history
    That is the work of reason

But whenever the tongue of reason is cut out
Then violence rises like a madwoman over her toys
Reason is not reborn from her own ashes
Prometheus has been saved a thousand times
    By the vulture that tears his liver

Remember this when you stand at the gates of paradise
And a voice calls from the sluice

PATTY'S SPEECH

Small and bent lower
Round shoulders in black
Hands bony and clean
As poorman's knife and fork
Her face blank as a scraped plate
Helped by the neighbours since she is stricken
Sometimes she repays in jam
    From the fruit of the medlar tree

She goes to church to be counted
And never to the pub
And all her talk is cliches
A laugh to the carriage trade
A scandal to the schoolmaster
    Absurd in the theatre

Her words are worn steps outside
Stone offices
For her to be articulate would be
Impertinence to a master so skilled in mastery
He uses words to prove language has no meaning
    So the parson brays and the judge gnaws his lip

As she shuts the gates on the asylum
She doesn't speak of incarceration
Her thoughts are muffled by careful footsteps on the gravel
If asked she would say:
I make do with what I have and go without what I haven't
And no man can snap her

MARY

A dark woman heavy as earth
Or light as shadows blown in wind

Who?

The woman you bought a ticket for on a bus
Or met once at the foot of a bridge
While the water made a hollow sound in its channel
Like a man under an operation

Not seen for twenty years
You are still taut from touching her

Who?

She is the woman you slept with last night
Who eats at your table
The mother in your house
Who welcomes guests at your door

But you and she are deformed
They tell you: this vacuum is cast for you
So fill it – as if the coffin were the human mould

No, all nature abhors what fills their spaces
The law that watches your bed
The butcher who waits at your table
The pedant waylaying your child at the school door

They took your wife
Now they will take your woman
You are a poet and should have known
You must imagine the real and not the illusion

She will age with your wife's silence
And your dreams bare in shrivelled wombs
The imbecile children who play in senile men

Your woman spent her life under your roof
You never met – not once
In the living room or kitchen
Clare, you created illusions
And they destroy poets

AUTOBIOGRAPHY OF A DEAD MAN

Who am I?

I am the play of light
That looks in shadows
Some are as black as crime
In others I see
    The innocent in their cells

I am the comet
That runs over the night
As a madman
Having the shape of fire
    That breaks and creates

I am the light that goes
Through the machine
Till each steel face
And knot of iron
    Shines as the human face

I know Darkness
When black hands cup the flame
And the night wind howls
    To empty the world

I sat in the asylum chewing bread
I sang: The Sun is a Loaf
Outside it got greyer and people hungrier
If you are still alive and eat
    Remember

The starving decide the taste of your bread
Prisoners who is free
And the poor the nature of power

So I learned in my cell
And my dark friend in his
    That one day our bread might taste of reason

The Woman

Scenes of War and Freedom

For Peggy

CAST

The Greeks

ISMENE
HEROS
NESTOR
THERSITES
AJAX
HIGH PRIEST
SECOND PRIEST
CHAPLAIN
CAPTAIN
AIDE
CHIEF ARCHITECT
MAID
CALLIS ⎫
LAKIS ⎬ Soldiers
ARTOS ⎪
CRIOS ⎭
TWO DRUNK SOLDIERS
OTHER SOLDIERS AND OFFICERS, SAILORS,
AIDES, GUARDS

The Trojans

HECUBA
CASSANDRA
SON
ASTYANAX
HIGH PRIEST
SECOND PRIEST
CHAPLAIN
AIDE
THREE WOMEN WITH PLAGUE
MIDDLE CLASS BYSTANDERS

TWO ATTENDANTS TO HECUBA
SOLDIERS
THE POOR

Villagers

PORPOISE, a woman
TEMI, her husband
ROSSA
DEMA ⎫ Young girls
GEMIL ⎭
KALERA
NIMPUS ⎫ Women
FALGAR ⎭
ORVO
HYSPOS ⎫ Young men
DARIO ⎭
OTHER VILLAGERS

THE DARK MAN

Note: Many of the parts can be doubled. The Dark Man must not be doubled. The first production had a cast of forty-three.

LIST OF SCENES

The *Woman* was first performed by the National Theatre Company at the Olivier Theatre, London. The production opened on 10th August 1978 with the following cast:

The Greeks

HEROS	Nicky Henson
ISMENE	Susan Fleetwood
NESTOR	Andrew Cruickshank
THERSITES	James Grant
AJAX	Gawn Grainger
HIGH PRIEST	Brian Kent
CHAPLAIN	Norman Claridge
DEACON	Peter Jolley
CAPTAIN	Peter Needham
AIDE	Ray Edwards
CHIEF ARCHITECT	Brian Kent
MAID	Irene Gorst
CALLIS	Derek Thompson
LAKIS	Michael Beint
ARTOS SOLDIERS	Glyn Grain
CRIOS	Harry Meacher
TWO DRUNK SOLDIERS	Chris Hallam
	Keith Skinner
SAILOR	Richard Perkins

OTHER SOLDIERS AND OFFICERS
Alexander Allenby, Elliot Cooper, Roger Gartland, Peter Jolley, Adam Norton, Richard Perkins

The Trojans

HECUBA	Yvonne Bryceland
SON	Dermot Crowley
CASSANDRA	Dinah Stabb
ASTYANAX	Timothy Norton or
	Grant Warnock

HIGH PRIEST	Anthony Douse
CHAPLAIN	Stanley Lloyd
DEACON	Alexander Allenby
AIDE	Harry Meacher
THREE WOMEN WITH PLAGUE	Margaret Ford
	Marianne Morley
	Tel Stevens

BYSTANDERS
      Norman Claridge, Irene Gorst, Anna Manahan,
          Peggy Marshall, Harry Meacher

HECUBA'S ATTENDANTS	Brenda Dowsett
	Jane Evers

SOLDIERS
      Elliot Cooper, Ray Edwards, Adam Norton,
      Richard Perkins, David Pugh, Keith Skinner

THE POOR
    Alexander Allenby, Michael Beint, Sheraton Blount,
    Anthony Douse, Brenda Dowsett, Jane Evers,
    Margaret Ford, Roger Gartland, Glyn Grain,
    Chris Hallam, Peter Jolley, Brian Kent, Louisa
    Livingstone, Stanley Lloyd, Marianne Morley, Peter
    Needham, Tel Stevens, Derek Thompson

The Villagers

PORPOISE	Anna Manahan
TEMI	Anthony Douse
PATRIARCH	Norman Claridge
MIDWIFE	Marianne Morley
KALERA	Peggy Marshall
HYSPOS'S GRANDFATHER	Stanley Lloyd
HYSPOS'S FATHER	Peter Needham
HYSPOS'S MOTHER	Brenda Dowsett
COXSWAINS	Michael Beint
	Gawn Grainger
	James Grant

CARPENTER	David Pugh
PREGNANT LADY	Tel Stevens
NIMPUS	Irene Gorst
FALGAR	Jane Evers
HYSPOS	Derek Thompson
DARIO	Dermot Crowley
ORVO	Roger Gartland
ALIOS	Keith Skinner
TYROS	Adam Norton
MANOS	Glyn Grain
ROSSA	Margaret Ford
DEMA	Louisa Livingstone
GEMIL	Sheraton Blount
LAPU	Elliot Cooper
THE DARK MAN	Paul Freeman

Directed by Edward Bond
Designed by Hayden Griffin
Costumes by Hayden Griffin and Stephen Skaptason
Lighting by Andy Phillips
Music for the songs by Hans Werner Henze

Part One

ONE

Greek camp. Headquarters.
NESTOR asleep on a stool.

SOLDIERS (*off*). Dead. Dead.
THERSITES (*off*). Priam dead!

    A moment later THERSITES *runs on shouting.*

    Hurrah! (*To* NESTOR.) Priam dead!
SOLDIERS (*off*). Dead. Hurrah.
THERSITES (*running out*). Priam dead!

    THERSITES *runs off.*

SOLDIERS (*off*). Priam dead.

    AJAX *runs on.*

AJAX (*to* NESTOR). Priam's dead!

    AJAX *runs off.*

SOLDIERS (*off*). Dead. Dead.
NESTOR (*waking*). What?
SOLDIERS (*off*). Hurrah.

    THERSITES *and* AJAX *run back. They embrace. Off, cheers and*
    cries of 'Dead' are heard throughout the scene.

THERSITES. The bastard's dead!
AJAX. Rotting!
NESTOR. Who is?
THERSITES. Priam!
SOLDIERS (*off*). Dead. Dead. Dead.

NESTOR. Dead?

AJAX. Yes yes yes!

> HEROS *comes on.*

THERSITES (to HEROS). That's why the city was quiet. He's been dying for weeks.

NESTOR. Priam's dead?

AJAX. The fight'll go out of them now!

THERSITES. Give them a month!

AJAX. They'll all be dead.

NESTOR (*embracing* AJAX *and* THERSITES). My boys! I shall see Greece again!

HEROS. We must hold a council. If we miss this chance we could be here for years.

NESTOR. Stools! Stools!

> An ORDERLY *brings on the officers' stools.*

HEROS. Do we know what he died of?

AJAX. Old age!

NESTOR. Not killed?

THERSITES. Some children came up on the wall playing funerals. We shouted up and they said: the king's dead. Then their guards came back and called them down from inside.

NESTOR. I'm sorry he wasn't killed.

AJAX. We heard priests chanting.

HEROS. Let's sit.

> *They sit.*

AJAX. Hecuba will run Troy now. He chose Hecuba – not his son.

HEROS. We've sat outside Troy for five years. This is our first chance.

NESTOR. I'm surprised he lasted so long. He was old when he married Hecuba. Older than I am now. (*Laughter.*) It's true – long thin man with a white beard and little piggy eyes. Even on a calm day he looked doubled up in the wind.

HEROS. He'd have compromised in the end – Hecuba won't.

THERSITES. Her son might make her.

HEROS. When her husband couldn't?

AJAX. You think they'll –

ISMENE *comes in.*

ISMENE. Is Priam dead?

HEROS. Yes thank God!

NESTOR. No women in council. Bad luck.

THERSITES. Ismene might be able to advise us.

NESTOR. Advise us?

THERSITES. Now Troy's run by a woman.

NESTOR. Well . . .

HEROS. Let Ismene stay. What Thersites says is true.

THERSITES *gives his stool to* ISMENE.

Well.

AJAX. You think they'll fight on?

THERSITES. Won't they just –

HEROS. Let's review the situation. Twenty-five years ago Troy was already a falling city and Athens in the ascent. My father'd won his war for the Eastern mines. He'd captured the statue of the Goddess of Good Fortune and was bringing it to Athens. Hecuba told Priam that if he owned the statue Troy would be saved. He took it – and since then Troy's had nothing but disasters. Why? The statue brings good fortune only to those destined to own her. But how can we win the war and capture the statue of Good Fortune when we haven't got the statue to give us the good fortune to win the war?

AJAX. That's the problem.

HEROS. Well, no man's hand can be more impious than the Trojans': to hold what all men call the supreme goddess against her will! On such men the greatest misfortune must fall. What is their greatest misfortune? That we should win the war. This proves that we must.

NESTOR. In a nutshell.

HEROS. But for that very reason Troy must fight. They fight but can't win – the goddess of Good Fortune will punish them by giving us the victory. I know what's happening in Troy. It's so clear in my head. Listen! – I'll tell you.

A scene inside Troy

PRIAM *on a bier.* HECUBA, CASSANDRA *and the* SON. HECUBA *wears ceremonial mourning. She is made up like an old aristocratic whore. She looks tragic but doesn't cry.* CASSANDRA *has a round face, long fair hair, and is pale and has been crying. The* SON *is a little short and thickset, but he moves simply and is dressed heroically. The scene has an air of theatricality.*

Note: in the first production HECUBA *was played by* NESTOR, CASSANDRA *by* THERSITES *and the* SON *by* AJAX. PRIAM's *body was invisible. There were no* PRIESTS. *The scene is to be imagined as occurring in* HEROS's *head.*

HECUBA. Burn Priam before the war temple and scatter his ashes – (*She turns to the* SON.) – on the battlefield yourself.

SON. Mother! Even my father's funeral – she uses that to put my life in danger.

CASSANDRA. Yes, mother – that's dangerous!

SON. It's only done for heroes who died in battle.

HECUBA. If he was your age he'd have gone on the battlefield and sent the Greeks packing – we'd have celebrated victory long ago!

SON. If you'd let him he'd have given the Greeks everything at the start – lock stock and barrel!

HECUBA. Cover his ears! They say the dead still hear voices from this world for a time. He lies there and can't strike his son while he insults his mother!

SON. You bully people by acting! She treats this city as if it was on a stage.

CASSANDRA (*wearily*). Please.

SON. You worry what he hears when he's dead! She shouted at him every day when he was alive!

HECUBA (*turns away and talks almost to herself*). Who will help me? What can I lean on? – not even this wall. My enemies sit out there and wait for it to crumble. If it was iron they'd wait for it to rust. They have the patience of the damned. I'm shut up with the spiders that will build webs on my tomb.

CASSANDRA. Mother.

HECUBA. No, I won't be comforted. (*She takes the ring from Priam's finger and holds it over her head between finger and thumb.*) Your father made me head of the city. He swore an oath in the temple. Who speaks against his oath? (*No answer. She ceremoniously puts her finger into the ring.*) People, war, armies, cities! I would like to sit at home and hear myself say children, friends, family – the words of my girlhood. If you were a leader, a soldier, I'd be on my knees begging: mercy, don't take such risks, don't go to the wall today. Instead you make me shout like an old hag – and blame me for it! (*Turns away from him.*) When I'm dead the Greeks can come over that wall and cut this city open. Then let them kill and burn and loot! I'll give them nothing.

The SON *goes.* PRIESTS *follow with the bier.*

A sullen child who obeys out of fear. He'll throw his father's ashes as if he was throwing them in my teeth! He understands nothing. At least there should be peace in our homes. Instead – (*She doesn't finish the sentence.*) There! The same words: hate, fear, war, prison.

CASSANDRA. Give the statue to the Greeks. Without father to guide us –

HECUBA. Trust the Greeks? No, I'll never do that. What would the Greeks have to lose once they'd got it? We must hold on to it – that's the only way to save our lives.

HECUBA *and* CASSANDRA *follow the* PRIESTS *out.*

ISMENE. But why d'you say she –

NESTOR. No woman-talk in council! Well now: how long will the war last? Till it ends. When will it end? Hecuba's old – but the Trojans are long-livers. Take Priam!

HEROS. Nestor, go home. You've served Greece long enough. Spend your last years in that nice house by the sea.

NESTOR. I'm not an old dodderer yet! What would my soldiers do if I left? They love their old Nestor.

THERSITES. Send a delegation to Hecuba. Offer to go if she gives us the statue. No plunder, burning, forced labour.

AJAX. After five years? Listen to your men: When we get through those gates – women, loot, drink, arson!

NESTOR. At my age you don't live long enough to enjoy revenge when you've got it. The wine's better on my own hill, and I'm useless to women. But the men want to go home with some silver in their pockets, a piece of material for the wife, and a Trojan helmet to put on and frighten the kiddies.

THERSITES. Tell them they can leave tomorrow – or wait years for a piece of material. They'll get good wages in Athens – building the new city will pay well. Or they could have land –

AJAX. You'll hand over your estates?

THERSITES. In the colonies.

AJAX. That would mean more fighting.

THERSITES. At least it'd be a new war with different scenery.

ISMENE. I think the men would rather –

HEROS. Ismene –

ISMENE. It's obvious! Look how they try to turn their quarters into homes, as if their wives were looking after them! Some of them married girls from the countryside here – they want to take them home to their parents.

HEROS. If we promise the Trojans something we must keep our word. Remember, the goddess sees and judges. It's difficult to control men in the last days of a war. Do we want to leave Troy killing our own men when the Trojans couldn't? Is that what the goddess wants?

NESTOR. We'd have to guarantee – in the eyes of the goddess – to try to restrain them. No one could do more than that.

HEROS. Let's vote.

NESTOR *and* THERSITES *put up their hands.*

AJAX. I'm against! The enemy's lost its leader –

ISMENE. He says the leader was always Hecuba.

AJAX. – so let's wait and see how this affects their morale. This vote can change the whole course of the war. How does our commander vote?

HEROS. There's a lot to be said on both sides. I'm for sending a delegation – on balance.

THERSITES. Three one.

ISMENE. Hecuba will be more likely to listen if your delegation has a woman.

NESTOR. That's too much!

THERSITES. The situation's new. We must adapt to it. I'll go with Ismene and do the talking.

NESTOR. Then go! It's usual to send the oldest – and therefore wisest – member of the council. I give up my place to Thersites!

NESTOR *goes out.*

HEROS. So, Thersites and my wife? (AJAX *and* THERSITES *nod.* HEROS *beckons to* AJAX.) You.

HEROS *and* AJAX *go.*

THERSITES. Why did your husband vote for the compromise? He must destroy Troy – his power in Athens depends on it.

ISMENE. Wishes don't change but the cost of fulfilling them changes all the time. When Miron wanted to make the sculpture of a discus thrower the only man who could hold the pose long enough was a cripple who couldn't move. You fight beside him – what do you think?

THERSITES. You know him better than I do.

TWO

Greek camp – HEROS*'s quarters.*
Night. HEROS *stands before an open window looking across at Troy.*
A MAID *is folding back the bed sheets for the night.* ISMENE *comes in.*
She wears a nightgown.

MAID. Good night sir.

HEROS. Thank you.

MAID. Ma'am.

ISMENE. Good night.

    The MAID *goes.*

ISMENE. You're not angry?

HEROS (*looking round at her*). At what?

ISMENE. Me going to Troy?

HEROS (*turning back*). No.

ISMENE. I wonder what she'll look like.

HEROS. You won't see for paint. (*He goes on looking out.*) Her husband married her when he was old. That's the most ruttish sort of infatuation. My father met her. He understood Priam. All that old man's excesses lie at her door. She pushed him.

ISMENE. I meant the statue.

HEROS. Ah. When I was a child people still called Troy the fabulous city of the East. We played sacking Troy. Now I stand in front of it and it's a closed coffin with someone moving inside.

ISMENE. Will you keep your word? No killing or looting?

HEROS. Athens will want me to pay for the war. Cheap labour would have helped. (*He goes to the desk and prepares to write.*) Who shall *I* trust? God? Ask the soldiers! The government? (*He looks across to the window.*) It's a beautiful night. If I make mistakes I'm punished – by the government or the troops or God. I'm God to my men – obviously I am. Does God cheat? I don't know. (*He starts to write.*) I must tell Athens Priam's dead.

ISMENE *gets into bed.*

(*Writing.*) I was born at a time when I summed up a nation's strength. My father had doubts, my heirs will have weaknesses. Of course I'm only a dummy on Athens's knees: but the voice is clear in me. They say the ewe killed in the compound to celebrate my birth had human milk in the udder. (*He looks up towards the window.*) The stars are very clear tonight. (*He looks down at his hand.*) My fingers look like five white towers. (*He puts down the pen and looks across at* ISMENE.) The death of a king requires a certain prolixity. (*Slight pause.*) When circumstances change, strengths become weaknesses. Let's get home to Athens and build it quickly! – so we're still young when we lead the first kid to the altar. (*Slight pause. He stands.*) I'm going round the lines.

HEROS *goes out.*

THREE

Greek look-out.
Morning. Three private soldiers. LAKIS *stands on duty.* CALLIS *and* ARTOS *lounge on the ground. All three are quiet, relaxed, but watchful. They are armed with long spear poles, narrowed to a simple point at the end.*

CALLIS. Take a good look. You'll miss it when we're gone. (LAKIS *kicks a stone at* CALLIS.) Don't worry, you'll be here longer than that will. You'll be kicking up its dust when you're marching.

LAKIS. Up you get.

CALLIS (*not moving*). Why d'you want to go home anyway? Your old mother thinks she's rid of you. She'll have a nasty turn when she finds you on the doorstep. Then you say: Take my nice little Trojan wife to the kitchen. O, she'll be very pleased.

ARTOS. You taking her back?

LAKIS. Yes.

ARTOS. Will she go?

LAKIS. Yes.

ARTOS. When I ask mine she just laughs. You can't really tell with a Trojan. Her family's shut up in there and I'm out here shovelling earth on top of them. One day she might spit in my face.

LAKIS. You treat her all right.

CALLIS. Sometimes.

ARTOS. I've gone in unexpected and found her crying.

CALLIS. Hey!

LAKIS. What?

CALLIS. Is it still there?

LAKIS. Find out!

> LAKIS *jerks* CALLIS *to his feet.* CALLIS *takes* LAKIS's *place on watch. He picks up a spear.*

ARTOS. Mine!

CALLIS. Sorry. (*He picks up his own spear. Looks at Troy.*) O, it's moved. To the right. I tell a lie – the left. (*The others laugh briefly.*) Like staring at the back of a mirror for five years. You end up forgetting what you look like.

ARTOS. No loss in your case.

CALLIS. That wall's marked you for life. You're its! Even if you got home your girl'd be homesick for that wall. When we're daft old buggers we'll talk about it for hours – as if this was the good time. Hey!

> LAKIS *and* CALLIS *stand and stare off stage.*

LAKIS. What?

CALLIS. Two!

LAKIS. Running?

CALLIS (*suddenly*). There! Three!

ARTOS. What on earth . . .? Women!

CALLIS (*through his teeth*). Weird.

LAKIS (*to* CALLIS). Get the captain.

ARTOS. *Wait . . . !* Women! – we stand to do ourselves all right.

LAKIS. But –

CALLIS. They're running!

ARTOS. Refugees! We're onto a good thing.

CALLIS. What if they're armed?

ARTOS. Women running towards us with open arms and legs!

CALLIS. It's a dream!

The men watch tensely in silence. Three VEILED WOMEN *run on. They stop for a moment and glance at each other. Then they mince towards the* SOLDIERS *with open arms.*

ARTOS. Giving yourselves up!

LAKIS. Wait!

ARTOS. Hello lovely!

The FIRST WOMAN *reaches* CALLIS. *She embraces him wildly, panting.* ARTOS *panics and dodges away from the* SECOND WOMAN.

CALLIS. Let's see what you've got for a – (*He pulls the veil off. Her face is deformed.*) Agh!

The FIRST WOMAN *clings to* CALLIS. *He screams and tries to beat and kick her off.* LAKIS *kills her with his spear. The* SECOND *and* THIRD WOMEN *are chasing* ARTOS.

LAKIS. Plague!

CALLIS. Agh! I touched her!

ARTOS. Plague!

LAKIS *turns on the* SECOND *and* THIRD WOMEN *with his spear. They run out.*

LAKIS (*to* ARTOS). The captain!

ARTOS *runs out.* CALLIS *writhes on the ground to clean himself.*

CALLIS. She spat at me! Here!

LAKIS. Wash! You must wash!

CALLIS. Filth!

> CALLIS *staggers towards* LAKIS. LAKIS *backs, keeping him off with his spear.*

LAKIS. Wash!

> CALLIS *runs out. The* SECOND WOMAN *creeps quickly on behind* LAKIS. *He takes a few steps towards the body of the* FIRST WOMAN *and peers down at her.*

LAKIS. God. Skin like a slug.

> *The* SECOND WOMAN *jumps on* LAKIS's *back. She clings and bites. He struggles, throws her off and spears her. She falls down.* LAKIS *runs out after* CALLIS. *The* SECOND WOMAN *gets to her knees, stretches out her hands towards Troy and creeps a few paces towards it.*

SECOND WOMAN. . . . Troy . . .

> ARTOS *comes on with the* CAPTAIN *and other* SOLDIERS. *They watch the* SECOND WOMAN *a moment as she stretches out her hands and creeps towards Troy. She is too wounded to notice them. The* CAPTAIN *kills her.*

CAPTAIN. Fanatics! Where's the others?

ARTOS. The river! They touched them!

CAPTAIN (*to* FIRST SOLDIER). Keep watch!

> FIRST SOLDIER *takes up sentry post.*

They touched you?

ARTOS. O no.

FIRST SOLDIER (*pointing off*). There's one! And there – another one!

CAPTAIN *and* SOLDIERS (*shouting a warning*). Plague! Plague! Watch your front!

CAPTAIN. They won't get through. A general alert.

FIRST SOLDIER (*looking at the dead* WOMEN). God what a sight!

CAPTAIN. Stay at your post! (*To* ARTOS.) They got them drunk then pushed them out.

AJAX *comes on with an* AIDE. *He goes straight to the dead bodies and looks.*

AJAX (*to* AIDE). All berserkers killed on sight. Dogs, rats, birds and so on. All lines kept lit at night.

AIDE. Sir.

AIDE *goes out.* FIRST SOLDIER *reacts as he watches other* WOMEN *being chased off stage.*

CAPTAIN. More coming across, sir – (*Gestures off stage.*) – but the men know.

AJAX (*to* ARTOS). You were here?

ARTOS. Sir –

AJAX. How did they get so close? Court martial, Captain.

CAPTAIN (*to* SECOND SOLDIER). You.

SECOND SOLDIER *takes charge of* ARTOS.

FIRST SOLDIER (*looking off*). They got one sir! Go on, go on!

AJAX (*to* CAPTAIN, *indicating the bodies*). Get rid of them.

CAPTAIN. Sir.

THERSITES *comes on.*

AJAX (*looks towards the city*). Look – they're burning the bodies!

They all stare silently towards the city.

THERSITES. A pall of black smoke is being slowly lowered over the city as if it was a coffin – and they go on fighting!

HEROS *comes on.*

ARTOS (*to* SECOND SOLDIER). That'll stink . . . Great oily black smuts in your hair and clothes and food . . .

AJAX. Carry on.

> ARTOS *and* SECOND SOLDIER *go out. The* CAPTAIN *posts another sentry and goes out with the rest of the* SOLDIERS. *The* OFFICERS *look towards the city.*

AJAX. I'll move the men back to the ships.

HEROS. Not necessary.

AJAX. Put a cordon between them and the city.

HEROS. That smoke might be a trick. We can't withdraw and leave their way open to the countryside –

THERSITES. But in a plague we always –

HEROS. No. Pay the men a bonus. Gentlemen, if and when we are infected, *then* we'll consider withdrawing.

AJAX. But plague! – they'll feed their dogs on bodies and chase them out to our lines –

HEROS. Surely you see? One loophole – and they'll take the statue out of the city and hide it in the mountains. We'd never find it.

THERSITES (*shrugs*). They probably smuggled it out long ago.

HEROS. No, not till they're desperate. The plague may make them desperate. This is the very worst time to pull back.

THERSITES. Yes – but if we lose our whole army –

HEROS. You speak as if the plague was punishing us! Troy has the plague! Can't you see? – the goddess has taken us one more step closer to victory!

> *They go.*

FOUR

Troy – the palace.
HECUBA *and* CASSANDRA. HECUBA *is a dignified public figure.*

HECUBA. When I married your father houses had been falling

down in the city for years and no one rebuilt them. There was no money, the mines were empty. I was going to wear something bright, but I thought it ought to be mourning. Lend me your belt. (*She puts on* CASSANDRA's *belt.*) Better ... I never saw him when he was young. I thought I'd be able to tell what he'd looked like if I saw him asleep. But he looked even older – as if a mask had been pushed through from underneath.

The SON *comes in with the* TROJAN HIGH PRIEST, *the* SECOND TROJAN PRIEST *and the* TROJAN CHAPLAIN.

SON. Say nothing to the Greeks. Just listen.

HECUBA. I shall do anything I can to save the city – not your honour. (*To the* TROJAN PRIESTS.) The plague?

TROJAN HIGH PRIEST. We're praying. It could be over in a month. It's contagious, not infectious. People must sleep and eat and live apart. Mothers can handle children, but children can't play together. Shops are under guard: everyone gets one food ration to prepare on their own.

HECUBA. Are there many dead?

TROJAN HIGH PRIEST. We don't know. It hasn't spread from the poor quarter. We must take strength from our afflictions.

SON. Amen!

HECUBA (*turning away from the* SON). I've begun to hate you young-old people. I'm tired of listening to you argue with your undertakers about the future. Even victory would now cost us more than defeat at the beginning – and what hope is there of victory?

AIDE *comes in.*

AIDE. The Greeks.

THERSITES *and* ISMENE *come in.*

HECUBA (*formally*). I speak for the Trojans.

THERSITES (*formally*). We speak for the Greeks. During the five years the Athenians have been at Troy children have grown to be intelligent youths, gardens have matured, old people have died and their graves been lost in weeds. Return our goddess and we will go without looting, burning or forced labour.

HECUBA. Whoever trusted the Greeks?

THERSITES. The gods have punished you with the plague – but it could spread to us. We want to go.

HECUBA. We have the statue. You say what luck has it brought us? If we give it up what luck could we hope for? That would be your best reason to break your word and destroy us. Perhaps I shall just destroy the statue. God knows, it's not given us much luck –

SON. We'll send our decision when we've –

HECUBA. But you still might not go. I've had five years to study the Greeks. Only a fool would stay for a statue that didn't exist, but only a fool would have sat out there for five years. Who can trust the Greeks?

THERSITES. We swear on the statue.

HECUBA. I feel as if I was talking to visitors from the past: perhaps all this was decided by Priam long ago.

THERSITES. The plague is in the present.

HECUBA. We have a chance against the plague. What chance would we have against the Greeks if we gave you the statue? Our people's will to resist would go. If you had it, would there be any limit to your ferocity? Why should I trust the Greeks? Let me speak to Ismene alone.

THERSITES. That's impossible.

HECUBA. Perhaps two women could find some way of solving this.

THERSITES. It's not possible.

HECUBA. I see! The Greeks don't trust one another but expect the Trojans to trust them.

THERSITES. Wars aren't decided by women talking!

HECUBA. We're talking of peace! Now I insist!

THERSITES. I refuse!

HECUBA. Then I ask . . . for a small thing when you ask me to risk so much.

ISMENE. I can only say what he can.

HECUBA. My dear, I don't even know what I wanted to talk to you about. I thought I'd try – in every way I can – to find a solution. That's the duty of all of us here.

THERSITES (*looks at the* SON, *then back to* HECUBA). Well – (*Turns to* ISMENE.) – speak to her.

HECUBA. How sensible even the Greeks can be when they want something. (*Nods to the others.*) Go.

   HECUBA *and* ISMENE *are left alone.*

HECUBA. Sit down, my child. (*They both sit.*) Will you take tea?

ISMENE. No thank you.

HECUBA. How long have you been married?

ISMENE. I don't think I quite –

HECUBA. How serious you young people are! Are you always serious?

ISMENE. Seven years. I've laughed in that time.

HECUBA. And no children. Perhaps the goddess of luck would give you children. They say your husband's the most handsome man in the world.

ISMENE. He's often called that.

HECUBA. How nice. Mine was old when I married him. Very old when he died. But we had sons and daughters. I can't imagine what it's like, married to a young man. I'd like to see yours.

ISMENE. I hope you will.

HECUBA. And you miss your mother?

ISMENE. Of course.

HECUBA. There's a good girl! And a lucky one – married to the most handsome man in all the – (*Stops.*) O, I didn't mean – (*She stops again.*) And one day you'll be queen.

ISMENE. Athens is a republic.

HECUBA. Yes, they call you something else. My husband doted on our children. When they went fishing they had to make their rods and lines. And hooks.

ISMENE. How sad that their lives have been wasted.

HECUBA. Tragic. Is that why you asked to come here?

ISMENE. I didn't say I'd asked.

HECUBA. O, your Greek men have sat on my doorstep for five years without having one bright idea. It must have been you.

ISMENE. My husband says Priam stole the statue because you seduced him.

HECUBA. That's not very nice of him.

ISMENE. It wouldn't have been your fault. Leaders should take their own decisions.

HECUBA. O, Priam was a born leader. Cautious – or bold. A good husband. A wise king. But useless. When the old play games they mistake that for youth – it's only senility. Troy is senile. Priam took me to bed . . . to make the city young again. It didn't work. So he stole the statue. That worked for a time. Look how we've resisted you! What other city could have done that? But nothing's changed. Labour for a stillborn child. There . . . I shouldn't have seen you: you've made me tell the truth.

ISMENE. You've been misjudged. But what can I do? Return the statue – then we can leave you in peace.

HECUBA. One good reason?

ISMENE. The plague! Set us free – all of us – and I'll kiss your hand when we go!

HECUBA. Why should I trust your husband?

ISMENE. The Greeks. Athens is a republic.

HECUBA. Your husband.

ISMENE. He's not only handsome – *he's* a born leader. He makes good decisions.

HECUBA. He married you. Though I ask myself why. You're not the most beautiful woman in the world.

ISMENE. No. Now let's talk about what we –

HECUBA. Perhaps you're the wisest? Or the best?

ISMENE. No.

HECUBA. What a pity. At your age I was sensational. A great beauty! I wish you'd seen me. They called me the Venus of Asia. Of course you know that. I can still see it in the glass.

ISMENE. Yes.

HECUBA. As to Athens a republic. Well, your husband's family is the richest in Athens and money buys power. Shall we tell the truth? This is one of those times when a pinch of truth will bring out the full flavour of our lies.

ISMENE. This is too serious to play with words –

HECUBA. Let me show you something. (*She rings a bell.*) If I gave you the statue your husband would still destroy us.

ISMENE. He gives his word.

HECUBA. Yes – and you carry it.

AIDE comes in.

HECUBA. Before the war they answered the moment I touched the bell. The Queen of Athens wishes to see my grandson.

AIDE goes out.

Your husband will burn Troy to the ground.

ISMENE. Not if you give him the statue!

HECUBA. To the ground!

ISMENE. None of this has ever made sense!

HECUBA. Sense! What has this to do with sense? If men were sensible they wouldn't have to go to war! Is it sensible for the handsomest man in the world to marry the ugliest woman? (ISMENE *stands.*) It's certain that when he married a liar like you there'd be only one result: he'd make you the ugliest woman in the world!

The doors open. CASSANDRA *comes in, leading* ASTYANAX *by the hand.*

CASSANDRA. My son's come to say a nice how-d'you-do to the lady.

ISMENE. Excuse me, I must –

HECUBA. Please don't make a scene in front of the child. One shouldn't frighten children.

CASSANDRA. Go on.

ASTAYANAX. Who is she?

HECUBA. The wife of the Greek leader.

ASTAYANAX. Grandma that's naughty.

HECUBA. How my dear?

ASTAYANAX. It's bad to play when you're mourning. My tutor told me.

HECUBA. Play my darling?

ASTAYANAX. You said she was a Greek. The Greeks are ugly. With long tails and hair between their toes. Ugh! And their breath smells and their eyes are all gummy and when they have a cut black oozes out. My tutor's seen it.

CASSANDRA. Darling, don't talk so much.

ASTAYANAX. Perhaps Greek ladies are different from Greek men, mother. But it can't be nice for the Greek ladies. (*To* ISMENE.) Does your husband have hair between his toes? Ugh!

CASSANDRA. Her husband is very handsome.

HECUBA. Kiss me. (ASTAYANAX *kisses her.*) Go back to your lessons.

ASTAYANAX. Yes grandma. (*To* ISMENE.) I can make houses out of paper. Goodbye. You're a sad lady.

CASSANDRA. Hush!

ASTAYANAX. Are you sad because you'll lose the war? When you're in prison I'll come and show you how to make houses out of paper. Can I grandma?

CASSANDRA. I promised your tutor five minutes.

CASSANDRA *takes* ASTAYANAX *out.*

HECUBA. There are thousands of children like my grandson in Troy. Old people like me. Girls like my daughter. In war death's always painful and slow. You wait for it all the time. I give you the statue – my people despair, they already have the plague, and your husband waits at our gates till we give in. Then he enters and butchers!

ISMENE. I give my word!

HECUBA. You know it yet you come here like a pious nun and beg me to set you free – all of us free! Your word? You call me a seducer? You're a whore murdering children to satisfy her clients!

ISMENE. We'll take the statue and go!

HECUBA. Liar!

ISMENE. We will!

HECUBA. Liar! Tell me – under the same roof as that child – your husband will go!

ISMENE. It's easy for you now your husband's dead. Mine's alive. You tell me to make his decisions – but I have no power.

HECUBA. No, I ask you to tell the truth. You could have stayed at home – if someone else's country can be your home – and worried about your dress or the evening meal. I can't make you answer my questions, but I can make you listen to them. If you ignore them you corrupt yourself. We both know the truth: your husband would take the statue and still burn and kill and loot . . . I can't shout any more. My son spends more and more time with the priests. When leaders do that it means you're lost. Shall I give you the statue – so at least some of you go and we can hope to hold out a little longer? Or face the worst now? No, you can take it from our dead hands.

ISMENE. So much trouble will come from this.

HECUBA. I can't see one ray of hope.

ISMENE. I won't go back. Let me stay in Troy.

HECUBA. I haven't asked for that. How will that help us?

ISMENE. I can't go back now we've spoken. Send for Thersites.

HECUBA. I'm sorry – you'll be trapped too.

ISMENE. You must say I'm a hostage. Nothing will be gained if I stay out of shame. Say you'll let me go when they go.

HECUBA. What's the use? They'd come back.

ISMENE. I can't alter everything, but I can do this. Fetch Thersites now – so I can't change my mind. (*She rings.*)

HECUBA. What will your husband do?

ISMENE. I shall see.

AIDE *comes in.*

HECUBA (*nods*). I'm ready.

AIDE *goes out.*

Protest in front of Thersites.

THERSITES, *the* SON, PRIESTS *and* SOLDIERS *come back.*

THERSITES. What have the ladies decided?

HECUBA. I'll give you the statue –

THERSITES. Good!

HECUBA. But there's still one problem: who can trust a Greek? I shall keep Ismene here till you're back in Athens. If you don't go, the priests will cut her throat on the goddess's pedestal – which will be vacant after twenty-five years.

The SON *applauds.*

THERSITES. This is against the laws of war!

ISMENE. It's against all civilized laws.

HECUBA. The goddess sent me these instructions in an oracle. I'm sure your leader will respect that.

THERSITES. I won't leave without Ismene.

HECUBA. You're welcome to our hospitality. I'll send my decision back by runner.

THERSITES. At what stage would you give us the statue?

HECUBA. When you're on your ships.

THERSITES. And Ismene?

HECUBA. I'll keep her till you're back in Athens – or drowned on the way.

THERSITES. Let me speak to Ismene alone.

HECUBA. Certainly.

Everyone except ISMENE *and* THERSITES *leaves.*

THERSITES. Ismene, your husband's position will be very difficult.

ISMENE. So is mine Thersites.

THERSITES. Of course. I meant – Ajax will put pressure – country before self. It's an impossible situation for your husband!

ISMENE. Why? What does the country want? The statue. Now they can have it.

THERSITES. Yes, yes. In politics you always ask for more. If we agree to this, what will they want next? Fools! – why did we let you come? I'll go now and the sooner something can be done. Goodbye.

ISMENE. Goodbye.

THERSITES *goes. A* SOLDIER *comes on and takes* ISMENE *away.*

FIVE

Greek camp – Headquarters.
NESTOR *and* HEROS.

NESTOR. It could still work out for the best: we could get Ismene and the statue.

HEROS. After they've fortified their coast. With a fortified coast they'd be impregnable. And she could still keep Ismene! What sort of welcome would I get in Athens? Come home with a stone and no wife?

NESTOR. The goddess is certainly testing us.

HEROS. Troy, statue, my wife – in her hands! Now she'd like to make her revenge complete. Get rid of us and throw my wife's body after us in the sea! We're at her mercy! Why why why did I let her go? That woman is a – a –! Athens and Troy can never be at peace! Troy must be destroyed. Stone by stone. If we stay but refuse to talk – would they kill her?

NESTOR. I've seen things done in this war I wouldn't think
possible. They're so commonplace we don't notice any more.

HEROS. I can't believe they'd kill her. If they did, I'd kill myself
The moment we had the statue.

NESTOR. Athens will need you even more then. I'd offer my own
life.

HEROS. There are seven wonders of the world. What I'll do to
Troy will be the first of the seven crimes. Call the council
Nestor.

SIX

Troy – the palace.

HECUBA, ISMENE, *the* SON, THERSITES, PRIESTS *and* SOLDIERS

THERSITES. You stole the statue of our goddess. Now you've
stolen our commander's wife! We stay here till we get both
back. All Troy is shamed by this!

HECUBA. My dear child, I'm sorry the Greeks value you less than
I do! (*To* THERSITES.) Well at least we have one thing your
commander wants: the statue.

SON. Cut off her hair and send it back with this man! Why is she
pampered? Let her starve! This woman is a killer of our
children! Sparing her even so long shows more humanity than
the Greeks will ever have! Yes, go back and tell them the
Trojans disagree on some things but agree on this: to use this
woman in any way that helps to destroy you! They think they're
at war? Tell them the war starts now!

ISMENE. The Trojans are great cooks Thersites. When I'm home
in Athens I'll have a Trojan cook in the kitchen. To our taste
the food's exotic – but there are many things we can learn. Eat
with us before you go. How well everything's worked out!
The Trojans will give the Greeks what they want: the statue

And the Greeks will do what the Trojans want: go. And when they do, I'll follow. Why should the Trojans keep me? The Greeks would come back!

THERSITES. The council will do what's best, Ismene.

ISMENE. O, I'm not putting myself before the best interests of Greece. For once reason –

SON. Heros sent his wife here to get peace at home!

ISMENE. For once reason is on both sides. We shouldn't call this statue the goddess of Good Fortune, but the goddess of good sense.

TROJAN HIGH PRIEST. Sacrilege! I object!

SON. It's said we've offended the goddess and the only way to please her is to kill this woman!

TROJAN HIGH PRIEST. On the goddess's feast day, which falls next Wednesday.

SECOND TROJAN PRIEST. The closeness of that day to the day when the woman fell into our hands is providential.

THERSITES. If that's how you decide strategy I see why you'll lose.

ISMENE. O please don't say –

THERSITES (admonishing). Ismene my dear –

ISMENE. I must speak! We're at war so neither side can trust the other. Why shouldn't we give the Trojans a token of our good faith? If it helps, I will! I won't go back to my husband till the Greeks go back to Greece. I don't say this lightly. War breeds fanaticism faster than plague. But I trust Hecuba to protect me.

THERSITES. What if she died of the plague? Who'd protect you then, you silly reckless woman. I demand to speak to Ismene alone!

ISMENE. No! We ask to be trusted – we must do nothing in secret!

THERSITES. I'm to go back and tell our council that!

ISMENE. Why not? The Trojans aren't going to send me back just because the council told you to come here and call them naughty! I'll be kept anyway! I'm helping the council by

making their choice easier: they can now get all they say they
want by being honest! And besides, the Trojan women have a
right to ask me for this!

THERSITES. Ismene!

ISMENE. Yes, a right! The Trojan women *expect* you to break
your word –

THERSITES. What!

ISMENE. Of course you won't! – but they see you as monsters
who've murdered their husbands and fathers! My husband's
love for me – the Greeks' love for me – they fight you with *that*
because they love their own families! That's almost a good war!

HECUBA. Now try our specialities before you go. I'm sure you're
bored with army food.

They all go except the SON *and the* PRIESTS.

TROJAN HIGH PRIEST. Unwise to say so much, sir.

SON. I must speak the truth!

TROJAN HIGH PRIEST. Tchah! Truth's too precious to waste in
an argument. The goddess hides the truth. It has to be divined.
I've hung a pigeon in a cage high over the city where it sees
everything. Tomorrow we'll cut it open and see what it's
recorded.

SON. Well what?

The TROJAN CHAPLAIN *is sent out.*

TROJAN HIGH PRIEST. As my life is so close to the goddess I do
sometimes hear her whisper. But I must open the pigeon to be
sure.

SON. But what?

TROJAN HIGH PRIEST. Doubtless the goddess will say one woman
running the country is enough – and she is the woman. She'll
pronounce on your mother's – if I may say so – obvious senility,
and power will pass to you.

SON. I shall keep the goddess – and her priests. If the Greeks left,
who'd come next? Barbarians, savages. My mother doesn't under-

stand this! She thinks she can seduce Mars! With the goddess we can resist all our enemies! I have faith to inspire the people.

TROJAN HIGH PRIEST. When they see the Greek woman humbled their faith will already be strengthened.

They go.

SEVEN

Troy – a prison.

ISMENE *alone. Her hair is shorn, she is pale and in rags.* HECUBA *comes in.*

HECUBA. I watched our behaviour get worse as this war went on. We'll end as barbarians. D'you get enough food?

ISMENE. Yes.

HECUBA. The priests say my mind's gone. They blame it on the burden of office: they mean I've learned from experience. My son's taken over, we'll keep the statue, and Troy will be destroyed. (*Sits.*) I'm in prison too. I eat, sleep and dress as I like, and that's all.

ISMENE. I knew when I came here my husband had lied, but I pretended I didn't. Now he'll build his great new city – but if I lived in it I'd have to pretend all the time. I can't pretend now: that's why I'm in prison. In prison you're free to tell the truth.

HECUBA. My husband blossomed when he was old. He'd stand in the sun for hours like a youth. A wonderful old man's passion. He was like a frail raft on a great river, it gathers all the force from the water and travels so fast. Won't you go back to your husband at all?

ISMENE. You carry a child inside you but you don't choose when it's born. It may come early – or be dead. It lay under your heart as if that were a gravestone. I've been sitting and thinking. I shall speak to the Greeks myself, and tell them to go.

HECUBA. How they've shorn your hair! . . . It won't do any good. I pleaded with my people, and they locked me up.

ISMENE. I shall try.

EIGHT

Greek camp – Headquarters.
HEROS, NESTOR, THERSITES *and* AJAX *sit on stools in council.*

HEROS. The council has the right to decide war matters, but let me
decide this.

AJAX. It *is* a war matter.

HEROS. I decide not to give way. The moment we left our lines
the Trojans would take the statue up to the mountains. We
must stay put now more than ever.

THERSITES. Say we can't decide. Play for time while the plague
spreads.

HEROS. No, don't give them one ray of hope. I move next business.
Of course my wife's conduct must be kept from the troops.

> *The others nod.* AJAX *goes out and a moment later returns with
> the* TROJAN HIGH PRIEST *and* SECOND TROJAN PRIEST.

TROJAN HIGH PRIEST. Sir, it's now clear beyond a peradventure
that rather than let the goddess pass into your hands Priam's son
will destroy her. His impiety horrifies us! Of course the goddess would reincarnate herself –

AJAX. If he destroys her he'll destroy her guardians. Let's hope
she reincarnates them!

TROJAN HIGH PRIEST (*to* HEROS). Sir, we're not servants of
Troy – or Athens. We serve religion. Let us ask, to whom does
the goddess belong? To the Victor! – him she will have blessed
with fortune! So, to whoever owns Troy!

HEROS. But how to get Troy!

TROJAN HIGH PRIEST. Priam's son rules Troy while it stands.
You can only own its ruins. But when Troy falls – at the
moment power slips from his hands – he will destroy the goddess in his sacrilegious fury!

HEROS. Anticipate it and bring her here.

TROJAN HIGH PRIEST. Our duty is worship.

AJAX. Last time you promised to –

TROJAN HIGH PRIEST. No. We said a decision would be made. The goddess decides.

SECOND TROJAN PRIEST. Though that is loosely put. She decides nothing.

TROJAN HIGH PRIEST. True. Admirable man! It was decided long ago.

SECOND TROJAN PRIEST. The goddess merely *sees*.

AJAX. What does she see?

TROJAN HIGH PRIEST. She hasn't said.

HEROS. Goddam!

TROJAN HIGH PRIEST. You haven't put yourself in the place where her light can fall on you. Just as the humblest suppliant wanting to know when to open his shop or sow his corn must make the right offering – so must the great of this world.

HEROS. What offering?

TROJAN HIGH PRIEST. We slaughtered many pigeons to be sure. The answer is always clear: the ruins of Troy.

HEROS (*sighs, then bursts out angrily*). Troy Troy Troy Troy! I wish I'd never heard the name! Why has my wife refused to come back?

TROJAN HIGH PRIEST. An impious woman, sir – with respect.

THERSITES. Who forced her?

TROJAN HIGH PRIEST. No one.

NESTOR. I don't believe it!

SECOND TROJAN PRIEST. Even peacocks' entrails couldn't explain her.

HEROS. It was Hecuba!

> *The* SECOND TROJAN PRIEST *tugs the* TROJAN HIGH PRIEST's *sleeve.*

TROJAN HIGH PRIEST. We must go while it's dark.

> *The* TROJAN HIGH PRIEST *and the* SECOND TROJAN PRIEST *go out.*

HEROS. When the dust of Troy finally goes up they'll have a moment of power. The statue is in their hands.

NESTOR. My boy, if what those priests say about your wife is true, she's put you in a terrible position. The ancient punishment for treason in time of war is fixed: common women burned and ladies immured. Your wife is in danger of being walled up alive in the ruins of Troy.

Commotion outside.

HEROS. What now?

AIDE *comes in.*

AIDE. Sir –

The GREEK HIGH PRIEST, SECOND GREEK PRIEST *and* GREEK CHAPLAIN *force their way in past him.*

GREEK HIGH PRIEST. Sir, there was no doubt! Trojan priests seen entering and leaving this council. We must ask for an –

HEROS. We're trying to get them to smuggle the statue out.

GREEK HIGH PRIEST. Sir, when the goddess is ours you'll let Trojan priests attend her? Look at the state of Troy! That shows what use they are!

SECOND GREEK PRIEST. Amen!

GREEK HIGH PRIEST. The goddess speaks Greek – in the spiritual sense.

GREEK CHAPLAIN (*low*). The goddess speaks Greek in the spiritual sense.

GREEK HIGH PRIEST. The Greek eternity speaking to the Greek temporality.

GREEK CHAPLAIN (*low*). The Greek eternity speaking to the Greek temporality.

GREEK HIGH PRIEST. Bless you, brother! (*To* HEROS.) The Greek Hierarchy alone –

GREEK CHAPLAIN (*low*). The Greek Hierarchy alone –

GREEK HIGH PRIEST. Yes, yes – thank you, brother! –

GREEK CHAPLAIN. Yes, yes – thank you, brother! –

HEROS. I've no intention of allowing Trojan priests to serve in Athens. They've protected the Trojan theft up to the last. I imagine the Athenian parliament will vote to stone them to death outside the city walls.

GREEK HIGH PRIEST. Ah! But the Trojan priests don't know this.

GREEK CHAPLAIN. – know this.

HEROS. They have a good idea. That's why the negotiations take so long.

GREEK HIGH PRIEST. O Athens will be blessed with this captain at the helm! Brothers let us sweep the temple and give thanks!

SECOND GREEK PRIEST. Amen!

GREEK CHAPLAIN. – give thanks!

GREEK HIGH PRIEST. We tell our soldiers how wisely they're led.

GREEK CHAPLAIN. – they're led.

They all go.

NINE

Battleground in front of the Trojan wall.
ISMENE *comes on, escorted by Trojan soldiers.*

ISMENE. Greek soldiers! Go home! Is there any loot worth the risk of your life? Women? There are women in Greece! The goddess? If the Trojans listened to me they'd throw it out to you over their wall. That's how they'd punish you most! What luck could it give you? You'll go home when you've got it? You can go home now! You're wasting your life making your tombstone! (*She starts to move on.*) No one answers: there *is* no answer.

NESTOR *comes on with an* AIDE *and the* CAPTAIN.

NESTOR. Ismene your husband's at home with the doors and windows bolted. He can't face his shame. He knows you're forced but he commands you to stop whatever the cost. Obey him!

ISMENE. Nestor, you're old enough to set these young men an example. If you don't go soon you'll never see Greece.

NESTOR. I'm not a traitor!

ISMENE. Soldiers I've heard Nestor in council. They say, find out what Nestor thinks and then do the opposite.

NESTOR. Ismene, you're insulting! (*He turns and shouts back to the Greek lines.*) She's off her head!

ISMENE. Soldiers, I speak to you, not your leaders. They have everything at stake here. If they lose Athens will throw them out.

NESTOR. Soldiers, she says these things – these ravings! – to *prove* she's being forced. We understand the code, Ismene! Go on! Very good dear!

ISMENE. Who needs to be led to food? Or warmth? Or shelter? You only need leaders to lead you astray! The good shepherd leads his sheep to the butcher!

NESTOR. Soldiers, I forbid you to listen!

ISMENE. Go home! Then you've won the war!

NESTOR. She's mad! (*To* AIDE *and* CAPTAIN.) Clap! Make a noise! Noise! Noise!

> NESTOR, AIDE *and* CAPTAIN *stamp, clap and beat their weapons.* ISMENE *shouts over them.*

More!

NESTOR, AIDE and CAPTAIN. Hooooo! Hooooo! Hooooo!

ISMENE. What happens when you get to Athens? The shepherd will still fleece his sheep! They're in your hands now. You have weapons. In Athens they'll take your weapons away! (*She moves on.*) Soldiers you'll never get the statue! The Trojans will break it to pieces!

NESTOR (*to* AIDE *and* CAPTAIN). Shut up, shut that row up! (*They are quiet. He shouts to* ISMENE.) We can *prove* that's a lie! Even the Trojans wouldn't destroy that holy statue: their land would be cursed and laid waste!

ISMENE. It's already laid waste!

NESTOR. Noise!

> NESTOR *gestures to the* AIDE *and* CAPTAIN. *All three go off making a noise.* ISMENE *walks on round the walls.*

Priam's city has nothing to give you but a grave and rubble to fill it! Soldiers, nothing but a grave and rubble to fill it! A grave and rubble! Soldiers a grave and rubble!

> ISMENE *and her escort go out.*

TEN

Troy – the palace.
PRIESTS *and* HECUBA.

TROJAN HIGH PRIEST. Ma'am we've been to the Greek leaders.

HECUBA. I wondered when you would.

TROJAN HIGH PRIEST. Hear us, ma'am. At last the viscera are clear. The goddess's time for passing to the Greeks has come. People with plague are wandering about in delirium. The soldiers refuse to cut any more down. The poor are rioting. We can't maintain order in the city or defeat our enemies outside.

HECUBA. You gave my son power.

TROJAN HIGH PRIEST. Cut him down like a dog!

SECOND TROJAN PRIEST. The goddess decrees it!

TROJAN HIGH PRIEST. Sacrilege takes strange forms in the young. Your son wants us to be defeated! – to have the pleasure of attacking the goddess with an axe!

HECUBA. If I take power I shall give the statue to the Greeks. And they may still destroy us.

TROJAN HIGH PRIEST. Not the college of priests. Heros is unsure. He'll protect us – not out of reverence but superstition. We'll make you high priestess.

> *The* SON *enters with* SOLDIERS.

SON. My mother with the traitors.

TROJAN HIGH PRIEST. Sir! We came to beg her to join our prayers for victory!

SON. I've had visitors: the Greek priests.

TROJAN HIGH PRIEST. Sir, the goddess has spoken against you! Submit!

SECOND TROJAN PRIEST. Return the statue –

TROJAN CHAPLAIN. Demand mercy –

SON. Would the Greeks listen? They speak only one language: sword sword sword!

HECUBA. What else can we do?

SON. We can fight and die or surrender and die. All the arguing and scheming was for one thing: how each of us saved his neck. But it's always been clear we won or died together. No exceptions were ever possible. And now I think because we didn't stand close, our chances aren't worth *that*! So let us see. Take those priests out in the street. Now! See what *their* entrails say in the gutter. I am the priest now! I'll come and interpret their offal!

TROJAN PRIESTS. Please! Please! We spoke to the Greeks on the goddess's command! She sent us! To persuade them!

SON. The street!

TROJAN PRIESTS. The negotiations are almost finished! Let us complete it!

> SOLDIERS *take the* TROJAN PRIESTS *out.*

SON. I'm honester than you, mother. You want to take a chance with the Greeks: but you know it doesn't exist. I won't even bother to take it. I'm not your enemy, mother. I'll fight for you and the city. That stone – is only a stone. A goddess wouldn't let those sewer rats pester her! Not if she had the insight of an idiot! I'm so tired today. I prayed and worked for this time – when I threw Troy against Greece. Now it's come when I'm weak. The weight of this war, the plague and the city, crushed me. My life is like a stone I could spit out of my mouth.

HECUBA. I saw this war corrupt almost everyone it touched. It's taken you to the limit of corruption.

HECUBA *starts to go.*

SON. No doubt. I'm off to the temple to weep and wail and inspire the people. I shall be the man who stands on the street corner of history with a rope round his neck and beckons the spectators to come and be hanged.

ELEVEN

Battle ground in front of the Trojan walls.
ISMENE *wanders on with her Trojan escort. She is tired and dirty. From the Greek lines an uproar of rattled spears, shields and tins and rhythmically shouted orders and clapping.*

ISMENE. Soldiers, nothing but a grave and rubble to fill it! Peace! Peace! Peace!

GREEK SOLDIERS (*off*). Traitoress! Traitoress! Traitoress!

ISMENE. You'll be thrown into a grave on top of women and children you killed. Rubble from the ruins you make will be thrown on top of you! Soldiers peace! Peace! Peace!

ISMENE *wanders off with her escort. The uproar dies.*

TWELVE

Troy – temple precinct
A few respectable BYSTANDERS, *sniffing nosegays and stuffed oranges against the plague. The* SON *with a phalanx of* SOLDIERS. *He prepares to enter the temple.*

SOLDIERS. Goddess of Fortune
            Sharpen the sword
            Weight the axe
            Guide the spear
            Deep in the joint
            Of the neck armour

BYSTANDERS (*sniffing nosegays and oranges*). Praise the goddess. May the goddess be praised. Let the goddess bless the people.

SON. Goddess of Fortune
    You took away your blessing
    When false priests served you
    We purify your temple with our tears

BYSTANDERS (*sniffing nosegays and oranges*). Down with the Greeks. Death to Athens. Death to their leaders. The destruction of Athens.

SON (*holding up a blood-stained sword*).
    Goddess of Fortune
    Who punished the false priests with plague
    Accept their blood on this sword
    And give us victory!

BYSTANDERS (*sniffing nosegays and oranges*). Cleanse the water. Heal the sick. Feed the poor. Protect the law. Open the markets.

The SON *begins to mount the steps to the temple. A crowd comes on: the poor, starved, wounded, sick, lame, crazed. Some have early symptoms of plague. They are all filthy and in rags.*

CROWD. Food! Water! Heal us! We're starving! Alms! Bread! My wife's dead! My son! Plague! Money! Help us!

The SON *and the* BYSTANDERS *are forced to back up the temple steps.*

SON (*on the top of the steps*). Trojans! Goddess! Friends!
CROWD. Death!

SON *is stabbed from behind. He falls down the steps. The crowd* *rush into the temple. The* SOLDIERS *and* BYSTANDERS *creep towards the dead* SON.

FIRST BYSTANDER (*peering and sniffing a nosegay*). Us next.
FIRST SOLDIER. Time to run.
SECOND SOLDIER. The only chance.
SECOND and THIRD BYSTANDERS (*to* SOLDIERS). No. No. Help us.
FOURTH BYSTANDER. What good could we do if we stayed?

The SOLDIERS *and* BYSTANDERS *hurry off. The crowd pours* *out of the temple. They carry the statue of the goddess high over* *their heads. A plain, grey, schematized female shape, of worn but* *not smooth stone, about three-quarters life-size, exaggerated in* *length not thickness.*

CROWD. Out! Out! Out! Throw her out! Chuck her out! Get rid of her! Out! Out! Out! Bitch! Bitch! Bitch! No more bitch! Out!

The BEGGARS *spin, stamp, shout, chant, laugh, cry – but above* *all dance and sing. A* BEGGAR *collapses. Some clutch them-* *selves and each other in pain and excitement. Some wave rags* *like flags and handkerchiefs. The figure is jostled along high over* *their heads.*

Wait! Wait! Listen! (*Noise subsides for a moment.*) Let the Greeks have her! They deserve her! To the Greeks! Throw her out! We're throwing the goddess out! No more bitch! Bitch out! Plague out! War out! Famine out! Out! Out! Out! To the Greeks!

The crowd jostle out with the statue. Sick BEGGARS *limp off* *after them. They stumble and fall as they try to catch up.* *Others run into the temple. Others carry the* SON *out, pulling* *at his clothes and giggling. The stage is empty.*

THIRTEEN

Greek camp – Headquarters.
NESTOR, THERSITES, HEROS *and other* OFFICERS *assembling as a court.*

NESTOR. You're tired.
HEROS. I've walked through Troy.
NESTOR. Shall I postpone the hearing?
HEROS. Get it over.
NESTOR. What procedure? The oldest member usually presides.
HEROS. Just as normal.
NESTOR. There's no need for you to take part.
HEROS. I said as normal! (*Calmer.*) I can't break the law and then build a new city of justice!

> AJAX *comes in and reports to* HEROS.

AJAX. The city's ready for tomorrow. There'll be no fighting amongst ourselves – each regiment's got its own area. The palace loot is being shipped out now.
NESTOR. I'd rather have gone away empty-handed than face this.

> NESTOR *and the others sit on their stools.* ISMENE *is brought in by a* GUARD. *She wears dress clothes and jewels.*

NESTOR. Sit down. (*She sits.*) In one way the case against you's clear. The whole Greek army heard you commit treason day after day. What isn't clear, to some, is why. Yet I suppose that's also clear. You were a hostage trying to save her life – right and proper in a woman. The fault lies with some of our council for sending you.
FIRST OFFICER. Do we lead our men to the butchers?
NESTOR (*interrupting*). One moment.
SECOND OFFICER. Favouritism!
FIRST OFFICER. This woman belongs to the highest rank in our society!

SECOND OFFICER. She attacked us in front of our men!

THIRD OFFICER. Ask her what she thinks now!

NESTOR. I run this court and ask the questions! (*To* ISMENE.) Now, isn't what I've said true?

ISMENE. I don't wish to quarrel with my city. But I have only one life – and so there's only one way I can live it. That's why I'm afraid.

AJAX. Answer the question. Do we mislead our men?

ISMENE. I am a Greek –

OFFICERS *applaud ironically.*

ISMENE. – and speak the truth as far as I can –

OFFICERS. Answer! Answer! Answer!

NESTOR. Order!

AJAX. The things you said – were they true?

OFFICERS. Answer!

ISMENE. Soldiers have died who would be living now if –

OFFICERS. Sentence!

NESTOR. I see! You're ashamed you were weak in Troy, so you're brave here. That's easier – you know we're more merciful than those fanatics. Ismene, this is weakness too – you make yourself a traitor twice over. This show of strength comes too late. We'd forget your insults to Greek men. But now you're insulting Greek women! You show the world one of them defying her husband in open court.

ISMENE. Nestor, the world's changed since you learned to talk like that. Your subtlety sounds silly.

OFFICERS. Shame! Sentence!

THERSITES. You say these things because you're safe. The punishment for treason – no one would ask for that barbarous sentence –

ISMENE. No one ask? The Greeks not barbarous? I shall speak the truth!

THERSITES. What truth?

ISMENE. In Troy I saw the people suffer. Young men crippled or killed, their parents in despair and dying of disease. I told them as they were dying – they couldn't hear but I told them because I'm Greek! – I shall do all I can to stop this. No more suffering caused by men! I said that – if the sight of them hadn't made my mouth dry I would have sung it! Yes! And now tomorrow: tomorrow you'll go into the city – the frightened people are spending their last night in their homes – and you schoolboys will prowl through the streets looking for something left to steal or kill. Is that Greek?

NESTOR. They'd do the same to us.

AJAX. Our men are entitled to their day!

OFFICERS. Hear hear!

ISMENE. Entitled?

AJAX. I demand the full sentence on this woman!

OFFICERS. Sentence! Sentence!

ISMENE. Ajax the boy demands! My turn! All of you: me next!

NESTOR. Be quiet! I will not tolerate this!

OFFICERS. Sentence!

> HEROS *stands. The shouting dies down.*

HEROS. You have no doubts?

ISMENE. I have many doubts – I – (*She stops.*) I wanted someone wiser than me to speak.

> *Some* OFFICERS *laugh.*

SECOND OFFICER (*to* THIRD OFFICER). Is your wife wise?

THIRD OFFICER. How could I know?

> *Some* OFFICERS *laugh.*

HEROS. Why did you say you'd have sung those things?

ISMENE. Sung? I don't think I said I'd – (*She stops again.*) I only know what I saw!

HEROS. If you have doubts, why are you so defiant?

ISMENE. I'm not defiant!

HEROS. You're defiant.

ISMENE. But if I say what I saw –

HEROS. And prouder than any soldier. You were the one Greek in Troy. You'd only seen war from a hill top –

ISMENE. O I've known since I married you –

NESTOR. Don't interrupt!

HEROS. You were under great stress. You suffered like someone under torture.

ISMENE. Not as much.

HEROS. I won't quarrel. But you suffered.

ISMENE. Yes.

NESTOR. In that case the court can see its way to –

ISMENE. But I shall suffer more tomorrow!

THERSITES. Ismene, we're trained – we train ourselves – not to suffer in that way. If we did we couldn't do our work.

ISMENE. Precisely!

NESTOR. She says precisely as if something had been cleared up, and she's only made it more muddled.

ISMENE. Tomorrow – tomorrow leave Troy alone. Troy has –

NESTOR. She's started again. Clearly you're still under stress. I hand you over to your husband's keeping. Under his care you'll recover from your ordeal.

ISMENE. Tomorrow – don't go to Troy. They say war turns women into prophets. I will prophesy. You have your goddess of Good Fortune. Let her do her worst! I passed the statue out on the square when I came here. The soldiers had carried her there with blood on their hands. You could see the shape of their hands where they'd held her. I curse every Greek who goes into Troy! I curse him and his house! Young soldiers were sharpening knives and swords on the square. They were pumping the pedals like laughing schoolboys. The great army sandstones whirled round and round. They'd started to drink – at least some of them will be too sick to go! They jumped on the pedals in excitement and the stones screamed like children.

During this speech the OFFICERS *have broken up, talked among*

themselves and played army games. Only NESTOR, THERSITES
and HEROS *have remained in their places.*

HEROS (*calmly*). I ask the court to be allowed to speak to my wife
alone. I want to persuade her to apologise to the court, or at
least be quiet.

NESTOR. Ismene, your husband's a good, wise man. That makes
it even more painful.

The court clears. ISMENE *and* HEROS *are left alone.*

HEROS. One starving child and all your love goes. We don't love
because things go well, we love because everything's against it.
I've seen sights you can't imagine: I won't tell you about them.
If I left Troy tomorrow, Troy would attack us – or someone
else would attack Troy. When will there be peace? When we
honour virtue and are hungry for simplicity. That won't come
overnight. But the new Athens will stand for that. It will
produce its own quarrels and its critics. But when people suffer
they'll remember Athens. It will be the last thing many people
will see before they go mad.

ISMENE. Troy's like a wounded animal. It can't run away. Yet
you'll bend over and watch it while you mutilate it!

HEROS. We've given Troy every reason to hate us. There must be
no more Trojans to carry on this war. Ismene, I've made love to
you but you're still a virgin. If the army raped you on the street
corners of Troy tomorrow, you'd still be a virgin. You receive
nothing – you only give. All women are virgins when they're
faced with murder – perhaps that's why soldiers murder them.
They'll brick you up with three days' food – to give you time
to repent before you meet the judges of the underworld. I'll
see it's poisoned. Eat it as soon as you're walled in. When
Troy's destroyed you'll be in a world where the gods don't
raise their voices. You can look down on us with their dis-
passion.

ISMENE. Many people die saying what I've said. Who are they?
Who killed them? How many more will die – and who'll know?

If I were free tomorrow to curse the Greeks when they went into Troy – then I'd be remembered.

HEROS. You'd be a sideshow. A parody of the real truth.

ISMENE. I'm a virgin? You want to be an innocent murderer! Burn and kill – the victims are dead, the soldiers are too drunk on wine and violence to remember – it will all disappear the next day. No, I shan't kill myself. I'll be alive when you go into Troy. I shall sit in the dark and listen till the last wail. Not to tell tales when I go to heaven, but so that the truth is recorded on earth.

FOURTEEN

The Trojan wall
The wall is ruined – a gap, half-filled with rubble, leads to a road into the city, which is off left. CASSANDRA, ASTYANAX *and* TROJAN WOMEN *sit and lie on the right. Each has a refugee bundle.* ISMENE *is bricked into the wall on the left.* ARTOS, CRIOS *and the* CAPTAIN *guard her.*

FIRST WOMAN. It's still afternoon.

SECOND WOMAN. But late.

FIRST WOMAN. The city's quiet. They're killing the old people.

CASSANDRA (*covering* ASTYANAX's *ears gently*). I must wash your hair.

ARTOS. Tap.

> CRIOS *taps the wall.*

(*To* CRIOS.) Enough jewellery on her to keep me in luxury if I live to be a thousand.

> ASTYANAX *goes to the gap in the wall.*

CASSANDRA. Where are you going?

ASTYANAX. To see the city.

CASSANDRA. Sit down.

ASTYANAX. It'll be gone tomorrow. (*He starts to walk back.*) Will we go on the ship tonight? How long will it take to burn the city?

SECOND WOMAN. Keep your child quiet!

THIRD WOMAN. We want to listen!

ASTYANAX (*whisper*). Where's grandma?

CASSANDRA. She'll be here soon.

ASTYANAX. Will we go in a big ship?

SECOND WOMAN. Please keep your child quiet!

CASSANDRA. I'm sorry. (*To* ASTYANAX.) Try to sleep. (*To* SECOND WOMAN.) The boy's nervous.

ASTYANAX. Don't want to sleep. Have horrid dreams.

CASSANDRA. You must be a good boy tomorrow and help your mother.

HEROS *and* THERSITES *come on.*

HEROS. These woman had water?

CAPTAIN. Mid-day, sir. We searched the bundles, sir.

AJAX, SOLDIERS *and* GREEK PRIESTS *bring the statue through the gap in the wall. It's draped and garlanded. The* GREEK PRIESTS *swing incense and some of them carry loot.*

GREEK HIGH PRIEST. Bow! Bow! Bow!

SOLDIERS. Goddess! Goddess! Goddess!

GREEK HIGH PRIEST. Trojans bow too!

GREEK CHAPLAIN. Bow too!

A TROJAN WOMAN *spits on the ground in front of her.*

AJAX. Let the snake spit!

HEROS. Greeks – honour our goddess for the Victory!

SOLDIERS. Victory! Victory! Victory to Athens! Athens! Athens!

ISMENE (*in the wall*). I heard children running to warn their parents: Greeks! Then soldiers running after them. Racing to get the first child. Seeing who threw him highest. (*General confusion.* CAPTAIN *bangs on the wall.*) Then the soldiers kicked in the doors and threw loot down to the priests from the windows.

GREEK PRIESTS (*angrily to the* SOLDIERS). Chant! Chant! Chant!

SOLDIERS. Goddess of Fortune
      Hail!
      Who sharpened the blade
      And guided the axe through the helmet
      Hail!

    The PRIESTS *go to one side with the statue.*

HEROS. Delirium!

AJAX. O those cunning Trojans! Every house – money under the floors, up the chimneys, in the yard!

    HECUBA *comes through the gap. She has two* WOMEN ATTEN-DANTS *with her.* SOLDIERS *whistle and jeer.*

CASSANDRA. Mother!

HECUBA. I stayed with our people to the end. (CASSANDRA *and her* TWO ATTENDANTS *try to help her over the rubble. She pushes them back.*) I can walk . . . (*Sees* HEROS.) O Heros, I won't shout and curse. You great wise man, let me kneel at your feet and learn.

HEROS. What!

HECUBA. Teach me. Not how to herd women through the streets and goad them with your swords so you can chase them, or how to jeer when the old run and fall down, or how to mock when you lean over them with your sword, or kill a woman and wipe the knife in her husband's grey beard, or throw a man's blood down on his own doorstep – not all these skills of violence –

HEROS. The Trojans owe all this to you.

HECUBA. – but how to tell between right and wrong. You must be wise, to know that. We had a library in Troy but I never found it – and you've burned the library now. Philosophers hunted for centuries – came to us from the whole world – but they couldn't tell me. Now here is the man who can! No one would license so much murder and not know the answer.

HEROS. Troy would have done the same!

HECUBA. Troy would have been wrong! Is that the lesson? No, teach me more! You great destroyer – now be Troy's bene-factor! Teach us the meaning of justice! I've come from the ruins of my city to ask. If you can't teach me the –

HEROS. Your young men were killed in the war. No problem. Middle-aged – men and women – will be shipped to the mines. Unwanted child-bearing women died in today's action. You and your daughter will go to Greece – with your own women. Your conditions will be tolerable. The child must be killed.

CASSANDRA. No.

HEROS. Now. It's better over. (*Motions to the* SOLDIERS.)

CASSANDRA. No. No. Please.

HECUBA. You won't pollute your swords on a child?

HEROS. Throw him off the wall – (*Indicates off-stage to the* SOLDIERS.) where it's high.

CASSANDRA. No. No.

WOMEN. Please.

HEROS. Quickly.

WOMEN (*crying*). Please. No.

HECUBA. No. No. Don't – I shall be blamed. I provoked you. I was wrong. Don't burden me with this! Forgive me! You see the state I'm in. Look – I say please. You've made me humble now. Take him to Greece. Bring him up an Athenian.

ASTYANAX. Grandma!

HEROS (*gestures to the* SOLDIERS. *To the* WOMEN). Let the child go.

HECUBA. Teach him to hate us. Tell him I stole the statue. Say I ruined Troy. Heros think of the ways you can gratify your hate! Teach him I'm a whore!

HEROS. Women give them that child!

WOMEN. No! He's our only child. Our son. The rest are dead. Leave us this child. We're all his mother. Don't kill our son, you'd kill hundreds of children at one blow. Make a hundred women childless!

HECUBA. If the stones could speak!

HEROS (*to* SOLDIERS). Take it!

The WOMEN *cry.*

HECUBA. Think of the cruelty you'll have! Watch him thrown from the wall? Phoosh! – a waste! A sack of rubbish thrown through the air! It's gone! Take him to Athens – teach him to imitate Priam to entertain your friends – teach him to hate me – his mother. When you're old and can't even lift your sword to admire it – he'll stand by your bedside and curse Troy – talk filth about us. Even your old age will be gratified. Your last bed will be a place of lust!

ISMENE (*in the wall*). Heros let the child go!

HECUBA. I have appealed to him in the name of God and the devil! What can I do?

AJAX. She's mad.

ISMENE (*in the wall*). Heros, listen!

HECUBA. What! There! Listen – the ground spoke! Yes – speak – speak!

ISMENE (*in the wall*). Take the child! Make him our son!

HECUBA. There – again! It spoke! (*To* HEROS – *laughing.*) Now you will listen!

The WOMEN *cry.*

THIRD WOMAN. His wife.

HECUBA. What?

SECOND WOMAN. His wife.

THIRD WOMAN. In the wall.

HECUBA. His wife? There? In there! Who is this monster?

HEROS. I will not stop today. In this war there's been death – from every angle! We all saw it! Now you! He'll die and you'll see his body!

HECUBA. Now that is a simple lesson – and I have learned it!

> HECUBA *turns and goes back through the gap with her* TWO
> ATTENDANTS. *The other* WOMEN *weep.*

AJAX. Stop her!

HEROS. Let her go! Find a beam and hang yourself! Did you leave
a beam for her? Be patient? – wait one minute so you have time
to think? I waited five years! She had five years to save him –
and all the rest, all of you had five years! The lives lost here – I
waste them for the sake of one child? That's mercy? Those
soldiers buried in the ground – if the ground could speak it
would use their voice and say No! I sum up this war today. I
won't feel shame for that!

> *During this the* SOLDIERS *have taken* ASTYANAX *out. The*
> WOMEN *screamed and then cried.*

CASSANDRA. Since his father was killed he's often played at
soldiers with his friends. They pretended to die on the wall.
(*She starts to go towards the gap.*) Let me go to him. Please.
My little boy with the strangers. He's not used to being handled
roughly. (*A* SOLDIER *bars her way.*) Let me kiss him once.
While he can see me. Not when he's dead. Let me stroke his
hair. Please. (*She goes back to the* WOMEN *crying.*) This world is
cruel. If the whole sky was a cloth and I wrapped it round my
wound the blood would soak through in one moment. I cannot
bear this. I don't know how.

> *Off,* one scream.

THERSITES. I'll see.

HEROS. Let her hang. Like a criminal on a gibbet. I won't have
her buried.

> *Hecuba's* TWO ATTENDANTS *run on through the gap and sit
> down with the other* WOMEN.

THE TWO ATTENDANTS. The queen . . . The queen . . .

HECUBA *screams, off.*

WOMAN (*off*). The queen! The queen!

HECUBA *comes through the gap. She has blinded herself.*

HECUBA. Where? Where? Where? Show him my face. Women point me out. The man who killed my son. Look. Look.

The WOMEN *groan. More* WOMEN *appear in the gap behind* HECUBA *and watch. The* GREEK PRIESTS *rush out with the statue.*

FIRST ATTENDANT. Our mistress has blinded herself.

HECUBA. Who's there?

ISMENE (*in the wall*). Is Troy burning? I don't understand this sound.

HECUBA (*groping*). Show him my face! Let that man see my face! Where? Where? Fetch that man-child to my feet and make him see my face!

HEROS. Bitch!

HECUBA. What? What is –? I see him in my head! (*She rubs her eyes with her hair.*) Him! Still there! Is there no way to put him out of sight? (*She walks towards* HEROS, *pointing at him.*) He's in my head! There!

HEROS. Bitch!

AJAX. Bitch!

THERSITES. Bitch!

SOLDIERS. Bitch!

The MEN *draw their swords to protect themselves.*

HECUBA (*stops*). It speaks! There! I see! This eye – all of you – (*Pointing.*) There – there! (*Calls to her* ATTENDANTS.) Shallios! Where is my knife! I have one eye! Quickly! My courage will go! I must be blind!

AJAX, THERSITES. Bitch!

HEROS. Take her! Bitch! All of them! The ships! Burn the city! Now! Now! Men to the ships! Burn it!

The SOLDIERS *run the* WOMEN *out – they help some of them with their bundles.* HEROS, AJAX *and* THERSITES *go through the gap towards the city.*

ARTOS (*tense*). Captain?

CAPTAIN (*tense*). You wait till the last ship. Deal with stragglers. Don't worry: there's a nice pile of loot on one side for you lot on duty today.

CRIOS. Good old captain.

The CAPTAIN *goes out through the gap.* NESTOR *comes on through the gap with* TWO SOLDIERS. *All three are drunk, oily, dirty and bloody. They carry bundles of loot.*

NESTOR. Well boys the last city I'll sack! I ran up the streets like a lad, didn't I?

FIRST SOLDIER. You did, sir.

NESTOR. I drank and swore and sang and waved my sword like a lad. I held the girls for the boys. Didn't I?

SECOND SOLDIER. You did old grandad.

NESTOR. And my god if I didn't have loot on my back like a common soldier I'd have had strength for the women too!

FIRST SOLDIER. You would sir!

NESTOR. Ha ha I would!

FIRST SOLDIER. They love a long beard.

NESTOR. I can reek my youth on me now! Snff! I can smell my manhood again. Smell! Smell!

NESTOR *holds out his arm to be smelt.*

FIRST SOLDIER. Like the dustbin of a brothel sir.

NESTOR (*puts on a Trojan helmet and waves his sword*). Rah! Rah! Wasn't I brave lads! I skipped like a goat. Blood on the sword at my age! What? I showed some of my generation to the grave!

SECOND SOLDIER. You're one of us sir.

NESTOR (*looks at the helmet*). Chopped chap's head off – then shook it out the helmet. I've got a thirst on me boys. I could drink the sea and piss out salt!

SECOND SOLDIER (*offers* NESTOR *his wine*). Try some of the best sir! (NESTOR *drinks and dabs his forehead.*) My gods I've been with the greats today! I'll have stories to tell when I've got a beard grandad.

NESTOR. Yes, my boy, we were all with the greats today. With the heroes whose mirror is the sea, and whose hair is the yellow shore. O lads let us remember the solemnity of the world and the awfulness of war.

FIRST and SECOND SOLDIERS. Yes old father.

NESTOR. And that we're mortal.

SECOND SOLDIER. And drunk.

FIRST SOLDIER. In the morning, it's Greece and home and –

NESTOR. No. I sail tonight. At my age the days count. I shall look back at Troy burning – with this wind there'll be a bon-fire! – the sky and the sea red. Then far out – there's a good wind – the fires will die down and the sea turn black. I shall see the stars. In the morning there'll be a smudge of smoke on the horizon. And I'll turn my face to Greece. You smell the olives before you see the land, as if they could root in the water. Now lads, down to the shore – and make our sacrifice.

The TWO SOLDIERS *support* NESTOR *as they go out.* TROY *starts to burn.*

ARTOS. Glad I'm not on board with them tonight.

SECOND SOLDIER. Let me sir. (*Takes* NESTOR'S *bundle.*)

NESTOR. Thank you son. My boy.

NESTOR *and the two* SOLDIERS *go.*

ARTOS. Tap again.

CRIOS (*taps wall. Calls.*) Hey? (*No answer.*)

ARTOS. Go on.

CRIOS *taps again. No answer.*

Part Two

An island. The shore of sand slopes upstage to the sea. Left, a low wooden hut. On the edge of the sea, right, flat rocks and a path to the beach.

ONE

Spring.
Music, off. A crowd of fishing villagers come on. The women carry a few loaves and the men a platter of fish. They place them on the flat rocks. ISMENE *leads* HECUBA *from the hut.* HECUBA *has an eye-plug bound to her head by a band.* TEMI, *the chief villager, and his wife* PORPOISE, *both middle-aged, supervise the festival.*

PORPOISE. Boys here, girls here. (*To* HECUBA *and* ISMENE.) Further back.
BOYS (*sing*).   Fish from the sea
           White bread from the oven
           The green green mountain
           For the hairy goat

           Goat skin on my shoulder
           Fire laughs on the hearth
           Bread smiles in the oven
           God throws his net
           To fish! Fish! Fish!

The GIRLS *dance. From time to time the* BOYS *shout in unison* 'To fish! Fish! Fish!' *The* OLDER VILLAGERS *watch. All the* VILLAGERS *cheer when the dance ends. They laugh at* TWO OLD WOMEN *imitating the girls' dance.*

PORPOISE. The race is ready!

VILLAGERS. The race! The race!
PORPOISE. Here! Here!

> *The boys line up. One is ahead of the others.*

GEMIL (*a young girl*). Orvo cheats!
PORPOISE. To the back! Right back!

> ORVO *goes to the back. The* VILLAGERS *laugh.*

ISMENE. She's sent someone to the back!
PORPOISE. Off!

> *The* BOYS *race off. The* GIRLS *follow. The* OLDER VILLAGERS *gather together.*

OLDER VILLAGERS.   Sun
                    Bright steersman of water
                    Watch the race
                    And the runners' return!

> *The* OLDER VILLAGERS *follow the younger ones out.* HECUBA *and* ISMENE *are alone.* HECUBA *starts to go down to the beach.*

ISMENE (*looking off*). They're running up the hill. In front of the harbour. So steep!
VILLAGERS (*off, in the distance*). Hyspos! Orvo! Alios! Faster! Not so fast! He'll run out of breath! (*Laughter and the shouting of names fades.*)
ISMENE. How did I lose my mind?
HECUBA. I've told you so many times. You can't remember.
ISMENE. Tell me!
HECUBA. You child. The islanders let us live here and give us food. You're my eyes – and I make you eat, and wash, and rock you to sleep when you're afraid.
ISMENE. How have I suffered?
HECUBA. Your husband was at war with –
ISMENE. Why?
HECUBA. – my city. You took pity on us, so he put you in –
ISMENE. A wall. But I didn't die.

HECUBA. No. You'd put on all your jewels. They said you were vain and wanted the dead to honour you in the underworld. O you were clever then! The soldiers waited till their officers had gone. Then they opened your grave. You were sitting up in the dark covered in jewels. They took them and ran away.

ISMENE. They didn't kill me.

HECUBA. Perhaps they were afraid to kill someone they'd found in the tomb.

ISMENE. But I'd lost my mind.

HECUBA. Yes, you were buried for five days. You went into the city and no one recognised you any more. They put us on their ships and sailed for Athens. When the Greeks won the war they thought their troubles were ended. Now they learned they were beginning. The plague came back and spread from ship to ship. The fleet split up. There was a great storm. Many ships sank. I saw the waterspout come out of the grey clouds. It was spinning and shafts of lightning flashed from the sides. It was white and twisting – and ran towards us over the water like a dancer or someone drunk. The sea was flat and white and seething. Then the wall of water hit us. It seized the ship and jerked us inside and half way round the circle and suddenly dropped us out inside, yes, inside the waterspout. It was calm there. The white wall was spinning round us. I looked up and through the top far above I saw the stars. The boat was drifting slowly towards the wall of water on the other side. I don't know how far off it was – yards or miles. When we came near I heard it screaming. I looked over the side of the boat. The sea was flat and smooth, like a sheet pulled down over a bed. As clear as a mirror. I stuck out my hands and saw them chained and roped together in the water. I looked up. The white screaming wall was a foot away. We went into it and shot up to the sky. We came through the top and tobogganed down outside on the slope of water. (*She touches her head in violent pain.*) Ai! This band is tight. The plug's pressing my eye. (*Calm.*) A tree grows, puts out twigs, and people say: See how the tree flourishes! But the twigs grow inside too – and become branches digging deeper and deeper into the soft wood. The tree bears so much fruit it can't all be eaten. Farmers sell it, birds feed their young on it, wasps burrow in it, passers-by sit under the tree and enjoy it. And all the time the branches grow into the tree, and the weight of the arms tightens their roots in the trunk till it's knotted and rimed and the tree stops bearing fruit. Then it's cut down and burned.

ISMENE. How could you see?

HECUBA. I have one eye. But I shall never uncover my eye. Hush! When the storm died down we were wrecked on this island. The fishermen – (*She stops.*)

ISMENE. What is – ?

HECUBA. Sh! A ship!

ISMENE. Hurrah! The merchant – beads and sweets and bright –

HECUBA. No! He comes later! (*Agitated.*) Take me to – (*She starts to walk but stops in agitation.*) No other ship comes to the island!

ISMENE. You frighten me!

HECUBA. No, Ismene, it's nothing. A boat's lost its way.

ISMENE. They're running everywhere!

HECUBA. We've been safe for twelve years. I'd come to rely on it.

GIRLS *run in.*

GEMIL. Ships in the harbour!

ROSSA. Two!

GEMIL. Tied up!

DEMA. No one saw them!

ROSSA. We were all up here!

WOMEN *rush in.*

WOMEN. Stone them!

KALERA (*a woman*). Greeks!

NIMPUS (*a woman*). In the harbour!

WOMEN. Stone them!

NIMPUS. The gods are against them!

GEMIL. Cheats! Cheats!

NIMPUS. And that girl!

KALERA. With our men!

DEMA. Let's stone them!

WOMEN and GIRLS. Stone them!

HECUBA. Be quiet you silly women. The moment something happens you squawk like a gaggle of geese.

DEMA. Stone them!

HECUBA. Who's on the ships? They may be my friends. It'll be nice for you if they come and find my blood on the ground.

KALERA. Throw them in the sea!

ROSSA. Say they died years ago!

NIMPUS. They never came!

HECUBA. And what would your gods do next time the men let down their nets? Wait quietly and see who the strangers are. If they're my enemies they won't harm *you*.

FALGAR (*a woman*). They will!

HECUBA. Bright Apollo
Who travels each day with the sun

Let your light show
Only things fit for the eyes of gods

Let no foulness stain us
As you stand on the sea –

The doorstep of heaven
That gazes up at the house

The WOMEN *and* GIRLS *move to the right.*

ISMENE (*to* HECUBA). Soldiers.

Slight pause. NESTOR *comes on with* SOLDIERS *and* SAILORS *in working dress. The* VILLAGERS *follow them on.*

NESTOR. Hecuba? Don't be alarmed. I am your friend Nestor.

HECUBA. How did you find me?

NESTOR. It took some time! The sea's so big. We asked the merchants who trade between the islands. In the end we heard of you.

HECUBA. What d'you want?

NESTOR. The Athenian government offers you sanctuary.

HECUBA. Can I go home to Troy?

NESTOR (*sighs*). There is no Troy. Athens has put one of its great new houses at your disposal. The garden's superb! What flowers! What scents! Have you heard of the new Athens? On the hill a great –

HECUBA. I'm a politician's widow: I listen to gossip.

As NESTOR *speaks the* BOYS *return from the race in twos and threes. They join the* VILLAGERS.

NESTOR. Painted palaces and mansions, crowded streets, halls of justice. The public gardens are already mature in our kind Athenian climate. Fruit trees, laurels, olives. Fountains in the squares. Troy was nothing in comparison! And our port – the market of the world! They say one day the doors of our poorest people will hang on silver hinges. You'll have such comfort! Luxury! I remember a famous saying (*Kisses his finger tips.*) mm! our cooks *are* Trojan! New Athens offers peace to its greatest enemy. The world is reconciled. Come and uncover your eye, don't sit here in rancour.

HECUBA. You enjoy your old age, Nestor. So do I.

NESTOR (*shrugs*). Well well, I won't try to change you. I know that's not easy.

HECUBA. What other reason made Athens send me so distinguished a visitor? Come to the point.

NESTOR. Time only heals if you let it.

HECUBA. Your beard must be very long.

NESTOR. It is a bit longer.

HECUBA. And as white as a baby.

NESTOR. Yes, but I have rosy cheeks and my eyes are as bright as when I was young! I feel like a boy! These last few years have been the happiest of my life. We worked like miners to build our new city! We wanted to live to enjoy it! If you looked at me you'd see how prosperous Athens is, ma'am. I've come for the statue.

HECUBA (*laughs*). I'd forgotten the statue!

NESTOR. These good people say you're priestess of their shrine Is the statue here?

HECUBA. The island's poor. You work or you don't eat. This is the most I can do. Ismene sweeps and fetches for me.

NESTOR. Is that Ismene? My god I wouldn't have known. (*To* ISMENE.) Strange, strange, strange. The cleverest woman married to the handsomest man, my dear. Not a wise match.

HECUBA. Nestor I can't give you the statue. I can do much better: tell you it's gone.

NESTOR. Gone?

HECUBA. Yes.

NESTOR. Where?

HECUBA (*points*). There.

NESTOR. The sea?

HECUBA. When our boat was floundering in the storm the captain – a Greek – panicked. We shipped water so I told them to throw it overboard.

NESTOR. . . . I'm confused . . .

HECUBA. We survived, but the captain drowned.

NESTOR (*bewildered*). . . . That would be sacrilege . . .

HECUBA (*shrugs*). O it was long ago. And time heals all.

NESTOR. Heros will be angry. We've searched so long! He can be violent you know. It's hidden on the island!

HECUBA. Surely you're too old to worry about his rages!

NESTOR. I was looking forward to taking it home. All that cheering and waving! – I'm out of breath. The climb from the quay.

HECUBA. Carve a fake.

NESTOR (*after a slight pause*). I'd rather not. I'm too old to meddle in sacred things. Doesn't give the gods time to forget it before you meet them. It's gone, he'll have to accept it – he's mortal like the rest of us. (*Sighs.*) I wonder if he'll take away my new house. I planned the garden to catch the sun.

TEMI. Sir will you eat with us in our hall? We have the best fish.

PORPOISE. And good olives and bread.

TEMI. And the merchant buys our wine for the other islands.

NESTOR. Gladly, gladly. In the old days of my father – my brothers and uncles and I, we often sailed round the islands. Fishing, hunting in the mountains. Saw a lion once. There in front of me on the path! Grrrrraaaaahhhhh! I ran – I was a boy. I slept by the fire on the beach many times and woke up to hear the sea. Will you eat with us?

HECUBA. Me? No, you disturb me – bitter words come in my head. I've no wish for revenge. But I don't want to remember. You'll eat well with them.

NESTOR. As you wish. I'll rest my men for a few days. I'll say goodbye before I go.

HECUBA. Say it now. Spare your legs.

NESTOR. True. Goodbye. Strange. (*To* TEMI.) I need food and water for my ships.

TEMI. You can have what we've got.

NESTOR. Don't expect to be overpaid. (*He wags his finger.*) Athens didn't build big houses by throwing money away.

> NESTOR *and the men go.* ISMENE, *the* WOMEN *and* GIRLS *follow them out.* HECUBA *is alone.*

HECUBA. Ah! Ah! I can hear my grandchild's voice. I thought I'd forgotten. Let me die quietly here, in dignity . . . I love to play on the beach, there's nothing to bump into – O not running and horseplay, losing your breath at my age isn't a pleasure – but walk on the sand and let the water-line guide me. I listen to the sea and it washes away all my anger and so I'm at peace. Now there's a storm blowing up. Millions of drops of rain, each one with a human face.

> O Apollo of the bright hair
> No one can watch your journey
> Over the shining water

Or see those eyes that never weep
But you warm us
And we hear the calls of your children
Who play in the sea

TWO

One month later.
A MAN *stands by the rock. He is deformed, short and has dark*
hair and pitted skin. He takes some of the latest offering and eats it
mechanically. He is not hungry. HECUBA *comes from the hut. She*
walks towards the sea, stops, clasps her hands tightly together, and
then walks on.

MAN. Sanctuary.
HECUBA. What?
MAN. I won't hurt you.
HECUBA. Go away! There's no sanctuary on this island. You came
    with the merchant.
MAN. I stowed away!
HECUBA. A criminal!
MAN. No, I ran from the mines. The merchant let me work my
    passage. But he'd hand me over when we came to an island with
    a garrison – for the money.
HECUBA. This is not my island. Speak to the islanders.
MAN. Speak for me. They'd stone me. Let me work here – fetch
    water – I could farm some land – guard this place.
HECUBA. A place doesn't have to be guarded on this island if it's
    holy.
MAN. Everywhere we landed I looked out for somewhere safe.
    Time was running out – we'd get to the big islands soon.
    Then I heard about this: it was as if god had helped me!
    If I must die I'll die here in the sun, not in the mine.

ISMENE *hurries on.*

ISMENE. Guess, guess! They sold things cheap in the end. I carried a lady's parcel home and she gave me some money. Feel! (*She puts a little doll in* HECUBA's *hand.*) Blue eyes! And a little dress! (*Suddenly realising, to the* MAN.) The merchant's gone!

MAN (*pointing off*). Look! Fishermen.

ISMENE (*stares angrily from* HECUBA *to the* MAN. *Then she snatches the doll*). My doll! I carried the lady's parcel. (*Presses the doll to her breast.*) I found it on the quay. I couldn't give it back. The ship had gone.

HECUBA. Sh!

ISMENE. My doll! Mine! Mine!

ISMENE *hurries into the hut.* TEMI *and* PORPOISE *come on with* ORVO *behind them.*

TEMI. D'you know this man?

HECUBA. He says he's –

TEMI. The merchant told us. He's run from the mines.

HECUBA. Yes.

PORPOISE. You think you're safe? (*She shakes her head.*) The Greeks were here not long ago.

MAN. I thought it was safe – (*He stops in bewilderment.*)

PORPOISE. At least he's used to hard work.

MAN. Yes let me work! Up here out of your way –

TEMI. No, that's not seemly. Besides, it's women's work. You can work in the boats.

PORPOISE. He'll wish he was still down the mines.

ORVO *laughs.*

TEMI. Did he threaten you?

HECUBA. No.

TEMI (*to* PORPOISE). See what the village says.

PORPOISE *and* ORVO *take the* MAN *out left.*

Will the Greeks come back?

HECUBA. I don't know.

TEMI. Are we safe?

HECUBA. Yes.

TEMI. Some of them want to get in the boats and sail off. The
sea's big. There are other islands, perhaps better than this.

HECUBA. You'd always be watching the horizon for the Greeks.

TEMI. That's what I said. But now he's here (*He gestures offstage.*)
. . . ? The mines belong to Athens.

HECUBA. If the Athenians come you'll drown him out at sea and
say he's never been here. That's how you get rid of criminals
and unnatural births. He's at risk, not you.

TEMI. True. I'll go down.

TEMI *bows and goes.*

THREE

A month later.
ISMENE *sweeps the rocks. The* MAN *comes in.* ISMENE *stops.*

ISMENE. You're not supposed to be here.

MAN. I waited till the old woman went down on the beach.

ISMENE. The fishermen'll catch you.

MAN. Let me watch.

ISMENE. Watch?

MAN (*points*). I often hide over there and watch you.

ISMENE. Why? I'm not beautiful.

MAN. How d'you know?

ISMENE. The women say.

MAN. Ha! They're jealous. They smell of fish.

ISMENE. Jealous of me? I'm a slave!

MAN. So are they – cook, scrub, make nets, gut fish, bear kids.

ISMENE *goes into the hut. The* MAN *looks round and then starts to follow her.*

ISMENE (*off*). Don't go!

The MAN *stops.* ISMENE *comes out of the hut with the doll.*

ISMENE. There! D'you like it?

MAN. O god you're beautiful.

ISMENE. Well. You've watched. Now go away.

MAN. I want you.

ISMENE. Like the fishermen – they quarrel with their wives and then beckon me with their finger!

MAN (*points off*). Come over there.

ISMENE. No.

MAN. Is it the old woman? Does she spy on you with her eye?

ISMENE (*shocked*). No! Does she?

MAN. At her age they're like children! She'll be dead soon. Then what'll you do?

ISMENE. Take over here.

MAN. The women won't let you.

ISMENE. They will!

MAN. They know about you and their men. That's not how priestesses are trained.

ISMENE. Go away! I work hard – do what I'm told – what more can I do?

MAN. I could look after you when she's dead.

ISMENE. What did you have in your mine?

MAN. Silver.

ISMENE. And what's that dirt in your face?

MAN (*shrugs*). Dust from the rock.

He goes to her and holds her.

ISMENE. I can't.

MAN. The hut. Come on. Please.

They go into the hut. Immediately the door shuts HECUBA
comes on. She gropes to the rocks and sits. She wraps herself in a
shawl. ISMENE *comes out of the hut.*

ISMENE (*flustered*). I was asleep – I swept up and then –

HECUBA. I'd have stayed on the beach but the wind's up. I have
to be careful at my age. Go back to him.

The MAN *comes from the house and starts to leave.*

HECUBA. Is he there? Stay here – I'll go inside.

The MAN *makes a noise of disgust.*

ISMENE. You're jealous!

HECUBA. Ha! At my age your emotions are simpler. And a lot
simpler than wanting to – (*She gestures towards the* MAN.) –
thank god. (*To the* MAN.) You – wherever you are – I don't
spy, with my good eye or the bad one. (*The* MAN *says nothing.*)
The rest was true. If I knew she had a chance to be happy when
I was dead, that would be something – not much, fools will still
burn cities, but I can't change the whole world. (*The* MAN
doesn't move.) So you'll look after my daughter? You can't even
look after yourself. What'll you do when the Athenians come?

MAN. The villagers said they won't!

HECUBA. They'll come.

MAN. Let them! One slave? They won't even notice!

HECUBA. They tell me you're crooked. That'll give you away.

MAN. I'll hide.

HECUBA. Fool! Hide and seek! The fishermen'll drown you the
moment the Greeks come over the horizon. If they didn't kill
you the Athenians would. I'm an authority on Greek justice.
They have big nets to catch little sprats.

MAN. What shall I do?

HECUBA. I'll tell the fishermen to prove their loyalty by handing
you over – and I'll tell the Greeks to let you go. They'll fuss but
agree.

MAN. Why?

HECUBA. They're sentimental under the armour. And besides, they want something from me and they think I can be stubborn. You're all I shall ask in return. (*Shrugs.*) I might as well get something out of them.

MAN (*craftily*). And what d'you want out of me?

HECUBA (*suddenly quietly, fiercely angry*). In your mine you were as safe as a mouse in its hole.

MAN. Ha! You haven't been down there.

HECUBA. O you'd have lived a few more years. Rats don't last long once they scuttle out to the light. You searched all the seas for a safe place: and walked into this trap. I'm the only one who can save your life . . . (*Sneer.*) And you ask what I want in return . . .

MAN (*slight silence*). I – I didn't understand. I'm sorry. (*Silence.*) What can I do? I can take care of your daughter.

HECUBA. Like all men! Reasonable now. When he came: (*Mimics.*) 'Huff, huff! O god you're beautiful!' – I've had sons, some of them almost reached your age. You couldn't have said anything reasonable about the weather!

MAN (*to* ISMENE). I'll come to see you tomorrow. I'll take care of you. I'm not much, with this body. But you don't seem to mind. (*He goes to* HECUBA.) The villagers like me. Between us she'll be safe. Some arrangement can be made.

The MAN *takes* HECUBA'*s hand and then starts to go.*

ISMENE. What's an – an arrangement?

HECUBA. Hush . . .

ISMENE *goes away crying.* HECUBA *is alone.*

FOUR

A month later.
A formal meeting. On the left, facing right, HEROS, AIDES, *the* CHIEF ARCHITECT *and* GUARDS. *On the right, facing left,* HECUBA *and a few paces behind her, as her guide,* ORVO. *The other* VILLAGERS *are upstage, left and left centre. Some of them surround* HECUBA. *All the* GREEKS *wear ceremonial military or professional dress.* HEROS *looks like Michelangelo's Lorenzo de'Medici at the Basilica of San Lorenzo.*

HEROS. Queen Hecuba the Athenian state greets you. You have heard of the New Athens. Of the pax athenaea that covers the world. We have replaced fear with reason, violence with law, chaos with order, plunder with work –

HECUBA. I told Nestor the –

HEROS. New Athens has changed the world! Not made it perfect, but a place where it's wise to hope. One day –

HECUBA. The statue's in the sea.

HEROS. Athens! Even the name's a blessing! Athens of marble and silver! It sparkles in the sun and floats like a ship in the moonlight. The people say that soon the doors of our poorest will hang on silver. The temple is marble. The walls of the inner shrine are covered in silver. The great doors are solid silver. The bowls and knives and chains for the sacrifice are silver. The priests carry silver rods. The centre of the shrine is a floor of beaten silver where the goddess will stand. Her simple stone will remind us that the wise are humble.

HECUBA. What will you put in its place?

HEROS. The goddess will stand there.

HECUBA. It's lost.

HEROS. No, she's in the sea, and we shall find her.

HECUBA. But . . . (*Stops.*) In the sea?

HEROS. Nestor says you know where she is. You gave the order to throw her in.

HECUBA. I can't be exact.

HEROS. The sea's shallow round these islands. The fishermen are good sailors. (*The* FISHERMEN *lower their heads and shuffle their feet.*) They'll drag the bottom with nets.

HECUBA. There was a storm.

HEROS. Don't see the statue as lost. It's hidden! The whole world was upside down. That's why the goddess hid in the sea: it's the safest place. (*To the* FISHERMEN.) We'll divide the sea into squares. You'll drag from square to square till it's found.

A ripple of laughter from the VILLAGERS.

HECUBA. That will take time.

HEROS (*shrugs*). We could find it tomorrow. Or today! Remember the goddess of Good Fortune is on our side! (*To the* CHIEF ARCHITECT.) Make a start.

(*The* CHIEF ARCHITECT *goes. The* SOLDIERS *move in on the* VILLAGERS. *One of the* YOUNG MEN *is pushed – a moment's scuffle. The* SOLDIERS *push the* VILLAGERS *out. An* AIDE *nods to* ORVO *to go.* HEROS *gestures to his* AIDES *to go. He is alone with* HECUBA. *He takes off his helmet.*)

How is your life here?

HECUBA. Nestor said you haven't changed.

HEROS (*studies his face in the side of his helmet*). Not too much. (*He gestures after his* AIDES.) I've sent my staff off to the harbour. Come to Athens. Share our good fortune. You say nothing. Nestor told me Ismene lost her mind.

HECUBA. O, she doesn't dribble.

HEROS. When I thought she'd . . . (*He leaves the sentence unfinished.*) I married again.

HEROS *takes* HECUBA *to the rocks. She sits and he stands in front of her.*

So at last you have me in your hands.

HECUBA. O, I'll tell you where to search.

HEROS. I'd hoped to find you more – at peace –

HECUBA. I am.

HEROS. – reconciled. You're strong. You have nothing and want nothing, so you have nothing to lose. Yet you have what I want. No power on earth can move you. I'm in your power. I've never been in this situation before.

HECUBA (*laughs lightly*). It's easy for me to want nothing. How long will you stay?

HEROS. A month, if I have to. Then I must get back to Athens. The search can go on, of course, till it's found. I ought to get it started. Goodbye.

HEROS *goes out*. ISMENE *comes from the hut*.

ISMENE. Was that my husband?

HECUBA. Yes.

ISMENE (*suddenly angry*). I'm a child! A big stupid animal!

HECUBA. Sh!

ISMENE. Sh! Sh! Hush! Hush! Nothing I say matters! I'm an animal who gets two meals a day for being house trained and taking you round on a lead. Hush! You could help me – if you opened your eye!

HECUBA. Open my eye?

ISMENE. I have to tell you everything I see – but I don't know what I see. And now that man and his soldiers nodding and winking! What does that mean? I'm afraid!

HECUBA. No – I've kept my promise too long. I left the world when my children were killed –

ISMENE. You call me daughter!

HECUBA. My real children! I can't go back to the world when –

ISMENE. But the world comes here! That man! Those soldiers –!

HECUBA. No! Let me sit patiently in my darkness. I've earned this happiness –

ISMENE. When I look at your face I see something new. I look at you and think I'm going to remember. I stare at your face – but it stays blank! If we looked at each other my mind would come back!

HECUBA. I smile – isn't that enough?

ISMENE. No! No! You think you smile like the guardian of this shrine! You look like an old hag grinning at herself in the mirror! You frighten me more than the Greeks! They put me in prison but you're my gaoler!

HECUBA. Take me inside! Gaoler? Oh, you get the best of it, believe me! No, this is stupid – boasting about our sufferings like two old women fighting for fish! If I uncovered my eye – I'd have to keep it uncovered, once I'd seen the light! I won't! The dead are dead, the past is past, my children are gone. Ismene, don't remind me!

ISMENE. You call me daughter. I don't call you mother. Why call me daughter? – doesn't that remind you?

HECUBA (groping towards the hut). I'm really tired.

ISMENE. Don't call me daughter!

HECUBA. Not if it offends! Now you've hooked a man you show your true colours. Not that he's much to boast of.

ISMENE. Bitch!

HECUBA (dismissive). I've been called that before by a Greek.

ISMENE. Bitch!

HECUBA. My little joke. You know your mind's weak, Ismene. You don't understand jokes unless we explain them to –

ISMENE. You bitch!

HECUBA. Perhaps. Am I?

ISMENE. O you are!

HECUBA. We've never quarrelled before. Now we're screaming like fishwives. Once I thought I would open my eye . . . I imagined the scene. Some great occasion. I looked, and recognised a child left on the mountain. Or reconciled two brothers. I'm not a bitch. You mustn't call me a bitch.

ISMENE. I told you I'm afraid. I can't lead you any more.

HECUBA. If I were a priestess a god would come down now and

tell me what to do. Instead, my enemies come – and I must be ready again. Yes, ready for all my old anger to sweep through me, like the fire in Troy. Help me to take it off.

ISMENE. Yes, yes.

ISMENE *helps* HECUBA *to unfasten the bands from the eye-plug.*

HECUBA. Gently.

ISMENE. Gently.

HECUBA. Careful (*The cover is removed.*) I'll keep my eye shut. Shut – then slowly – with my back to the sun! Then cover it!

ISMENE. Gently.

HECUBA. Give me your hand.

HECUBA *holds* ISMENE's *hand in one hand and shades her eyes with the other. Slowly she opens her eye a little.* ISMENE *peers closer.*

ISMENE. O I can see your poor eye . . . A white line under the red – . . .

HECUBA. Ismene . . .

ISMENE. A thin white line . . . like the moon . . . under the red –. What can you see? Look, my hand. (*She holds her hand in front of* HECUBA's *face.*)

HECUBA. Ismene . . . a light.

ISMENE. What?

HECUBA. A light! A light! (ISMENE *steps back.*) The plug! My band!

HECUBA *whimpers, covers her eye with one hand and gropes for the band on the rock with the other.*

Ismene, are you there?

ISMENE (*pushing the band into* HECUBA's *hand*). Yes!

HECUBA (*covering her face*). A light!

ISMENE *runs into the hut.* HECUBA *sits alone on the rock. She tries to calm herself.*

(*Quietly.*) A light . . . Apollo . . .

ISMENE *runs from the house with a light.*

ISMENE. Here!

HECUBA. Is it here?

ISMENE. Yes!

HECUBA (*uncovers her eye*). Where? Where? Is it lit?

ISMENE. Lit. Lit. (*She holds the light closer to* HECUBA's *face.* HECUBA *reaches for it and pulls it closer.*) Too close! What d'you see, my darling?

HECUBA. Nothing.

ISMENE. Look!

HECUBA. I am.

ISMENE. Careful! Too close!

HECUBA. There's nothing.

ISMENE. I'll wash it! (*She turns to go.*) Water!

HECUBA. Nothing!

ISMENE. There will be. It's dirt. (*She wipes at* HECUBA's *eye with the binding.*) Close it!

HECUBA. I'm blind!

ISMENE. In time – in time –

HECUBA. There's nothing!

ISMENE. There must be!

HECUBA. No light. Not even a shadow. Nothing!

ISMENE. O Hecuba we uncovered it too quickly. Stupid, stupid. We've lost your sight. We should have done it in the house.

HECUBA. No, nothing. No glimmer – not even a moment. It was covered so long – injured, diseased – the sight went long ago. I've been blind for years and didn't know it. I thought I could choose! O Ismene that day has come back! (*She stops.*) My child, my child – you? You saw my eye. Did you remember?

ISMENE. No.

HECUBA. Nothing? Nothing for both of us?

ISMENE. We couldn't look at each other.

HECUBA. No. (*Slight pause.*) I wounded myself too deeply.

jabbed round with the knife. I had no chance. But you – perhaps you'll start to remember.

ISMENE. I don't know.

HECUBA. I'll never be angry with you again Ismene. Perhaps you shall understand. Oh my child, my child – the child I haven't lost. You love me. And look, a blind old woman covered in tears because she loves her daughter.

ISMENE *leads* HECUBA *into the house.*

FIVE

A month later.
HECUBA *and the* MAN.

MAN. They catch netfulls of fish and tip them back in the sea. If fish could think they'd say men were mad. How long will he search?

HECUBA. Sh . . .

MAN. He promised a lot of money to the crew that found it. The fishermen were excited – now they don't care. They grin at each other while they work. He puts soldiers into every boat to make sure they work properly. What do soldiers know about fishing? They keep shouting orders that don't mean anything. The nets aren't even tight. If it *was* there he couldn't find it!

HECUBA (*sits on the bench in front of the house*). The villagers are afraid. They go through the movements pretending to fish, like mad people working with nothing.

HEROS *comes on from the beach, upstage. He wears a short tunic but no helmet or armour. He carries a sword in a scabbard at his belt. The* MAN *moves away downstage left.*

HEROS. I walked on the beach. I haven't been so alone for years. In Athens I move in procession. Bump into guards. I'd like to stay.

HECUBA. The month's gone.

HEROS. A few more days. A week. A thought keeps coming in my head. It's so clear. Perhaps we've already found it – on the first day – one of our nets scraped it up from the bottom – and then it slipped back. I see it so clearly: falling back in the water. Then slowly rocking, backwards and forwards. (*Calmly and thoughtfully.*) Perhaps we shouldn't move on to new areas. Go back over the old ones. (*Sits on the ground.*) Is this your runaway?

HECUBA. Yes.

HEROS. The law is: you're taken back to the mine and killed under ground in front of your fellows. No exceptions. But I've been asked for mercy, and as this island is half outside the world, I allow it. Keep out of the soldiers' way.

The MAN *falls to the ground. He cries.*

HEROS (*looks round*). Quiet as sleep. They call you the bitch of Asia – a whole continent trails after your name like a comet. I have only a city. But a great one.

HECUBA. The currents may have carried it away.

HEROS. Not far. Too heavy. The fishermen know where to look.

HECUBA. Sand's drifted over it.

HEROS. The bottom's quite firm.

HECUBA. If it's heavy, it fell down a crevasse. What will you do if you can't find it?

HEROS. One day I'll look over the side of the boat and see it smiling up at me from the bottom.

HECUBA. But if you don't?

HEROS. It's not to make me famous. It's a millstone round my neck. God rot it. I must close the past! Say: finished. Not all that rational. But you cover your eye. That's not rational. I look at the face that Priam kissed – and it's a mask. If I could see your eye I'd know if you lied.

HECUBA. No, you'd search for some other sign.

HEROS. I questioned the sailors who were in the boat with you. One even helped to throw her out. Imagine! – she was in the hands of that little wizened man. You're the only one who took a bearing on the rocks. (*He sits by* HECUBA *on the bench.*) Have you told me the truth, Hecuba?

HECUBA. Yes.

HEROS. But why? I'm your enemy. I killed your family, destroyed your home –. Of course I was raving with war-madness, but I did it.

HECUBA. There are some things I thank you for. You got rid of the statue.

HEROS. No, you still have it. Out in the sea. You sit here and listen to the water. All day. Does it tell you what we do? Laugh at us? Quietly tell you where the goddess is?

HECUBA (*stands*). Well, I've done what I can to help.

HEROS. One day they'll bring her out in a net. The net will be full of slippery seaweed and fish threshing for life. It'll stretch and bulge as if she was alive inside. Then – I reach out and help her to step from the net. Is my wife in there? (*He points to the hut.*) I want to speak to her.

HECUBA. She may not want to speak to you.

HEROS. I'll tell her about the past. That could cure her.

MAN (*to* HECUBA). It'll make her worse.

HECUBA. Hush! Who said you could interrupt? (*Thinks, then speaks to* HEROS.) Yes. But be careful.

HEROS. O, I'll handle it.

HECUBA (*to the* MAN). Fetch her out.

HEROS. No, let him take you down to the beach.

The MAN *starts to lead* HECUBA *out.*

HECUBA. If she remembers . . . be patient.

HEROS. I'll shout when I'm finished.

The MAN *and* HECUBA *go out upstage right.* HEROS *waits till they've gone. Then he taps on the door and steps back. After a moment* ISMENE *comes out.*

ISMENE. O. You want the old lady? She's on the –
HEROS. Who am I?
ISMENE. A Greek.
HEROS. A rich man. What shall I give you?
ISMENE. O . . . you Greeks are silly.
HEROS. Are we?
ISMENE. Looking for a stone in the sea! You won't find it.
HEROS. Why not?
ISMENE. Even if you looked the day after it was lost, it would have been swept away.
HEROS. You were in the boat when it was lost. You remember the storm?
ISMENE. There're always storms.
HEROS. Troy? You went round and round the walls shouting peace!
ISMENE (*indifferently*). I don't remember.
HEROS. Shut your eyes.
ISMENE. Have you brought me something?
HEROS. Hm-hmm.
ISMENE. No, I'm not a child today.
HEROS. Shut your eyes.
ISMENE. O! But be quick!

> ISMENE *squeezes her eyes shut.* HEROS *puts his hand on her breast. She opens her eyes and runs upstage.*

HEROS. Stop!
ISMENE (*faces him*). What d'you want?
HEROS. Where's the statue? Tell me! *Please!*
ISMENE. I told you I can't!
HEROS. Try!

> ISMENE *saunters away, stops, then faces him again.*

ISMENE. I know you're my husband, you know.

HEROS. You remember?

ISMENE. I peeped the first time you came and asked Hecuba.

HEROS. Sleep with me tonight.

ISMENE. Tch tch tch.

HEROS. I'm said to be handsome.

ISMENE. Beauty doesn't attract me any more. That went too.

HEROS (*takes out coins*). I'll pay.

ISMENE. For a doll? They cost a lot!

HEROS (*suddenly quietly very angry*). Ismene, in war the good hides behind the bad. You're the only one I've seen stay innocent through a war: I had to stop that – the bad was hiding behind the good. I raised my sword. But there was no malice. It was for Athens. Will you forgive me?

ISMENE (*sits and plays in the sand, running it through her fingers*). I do.

HEROS (*still seething with quiet anger*). A leader really needs only one virtue – restraint – but many vices. A good ruler knows how to hate. He even knows the limits of restraint. From time to time he surrenders it to anger. How else can he make the people afraid?

ISMENE (*building a sand castle*). Here's the drawbridge.

HEROS. From time to time the people must be afraid – not of him but of each other – or the city falls apart. Fear is like a seed which he plants at the top of the tree.

ISMENE. Here's the door.

HEROS. I'm taking you back to Athens.

ISMENE. No! No!

HEROS. Don't be afraid.

ISMENE. I am! I am!

HEROS. Of me?

ISMENE. Of *me*! I won't go! I can't behave – look at me now! (*She throws down the sand.*) They'd lock me away in a city!

HEROS. My child, Athens can give you a prison bigger than the whole of this island! We're that rich!

ISMENE. But the sea's not a wall!

HEROS. Then think of what I've said. If I can't find the statue I must prove – to the citizens of Athens – that I made every effort to find it. In effect that would mean the painful destruction of these islanders and the razing of their village. I have a duty to Athens not to let chance make me a laughing stock. I take a duty to Athens very seriously: it is the home of freedom. I put myself in this worst possible light so you understand my position. I shall plant the seed on top of the tree. Unless you remember.

ISMENE. These people aren't to blame!

HEROS. I've always wanted peace, and everyone to be happy when they can. Yet they'll be killed to satisfy people who don't even know their names.

ISMENE. Don't hurt them! Please!

HEROS. When the wind blows the apples fall – or the tree gets too heavy and the wind blows that down.

ISMENE. Yes – now – I remember –

HEROS. What?

ISMENE. The war – and the storm – at sea – that was terrible! – and – where the ship was sunk?

HEROS. I tried to help.

ISMENE. I do remember! Round and round the wall shouting peace!

HEROS. Liar.

ISMENE. I do! I do! She tells the truth anyway! Why don't you believe her? (*Cries.*) Don't hurt them!

HEROS. You mustn't cry. (*He gives her the coins.*) There. You've been very good.

ISMENE. Really?

HEROS. Yes. No tears. (*He goes upstage and calls.*) Hecuba! (*He comes back to* ISMENE.) Excuse me. I must go.

HEROS *goes out.* ISMENE *goes upstage and meets the* MAN *coming on.*

MAN. You've been crying! You remembered!

ISMENE. No. Nothing. He said –

MAN. Then you can stay? Yow-eee! (*He tickles her.*) What an idiot! Typical woman! Mind like a hole with a gap in it! No manners! Can't behave!

ISMENE (*laughing and struggling*). Who can't walk straight? Who's got a dirty face!

MAN (*tickling her*). Say sorry!

ISMENE (*laughing*). I'm not! I'm not! I'm not!

MAN (*tickling her*). I'll give you something to be sorry for.

HECUBA *is coming slowly on stage.*

ISMENE. Make him stop!

HECUBA. What's he doing?

ISMENE. Hurting me! (*Laughing.*) I'm sorry!

MAN (*tickling her*). Not enough!

ISMENE. O stop! Stop! Stop!

HECUBA. Hush! Children! Behave yourselves! We'll scandalize the village –! (*The* MAN *starts tickling her.*) Stop it! (*She laughs.*) Ismene make him stop! O dear. (*Laughs.*) We'll scandalize the –

ISMENE. I'm not sorry! I'm not sorry!

The MAN *chases* ISMENE.

Pig!

HECUBA. Stop it! The pair of you!

MAN. Mind like the handle of a bucket and nothing underneath!

They calm down.

HECUBA. Tickling a woman of my age! Well – you didn't remember! What did he say?

ISMENE. I've forgotten that too! It's his fault!

MAN *and* HECUBA *laugh.*

MAN. Did he scare you?

ISMENE. I forget!

They laugh.

HECUBA. Well – go indoors.

ISMENE. You see! She treats me like a child.

HECUBA. I want to *talk* to him – not listen to your chatter. (*To the* MAN.) Tell her. She might listen to you.

ISMENE. If he's staying I'm going anyway.

ISMENE *goes into the house.*

HECUBA. He won't find his stone. So he'll kill the islanders for a vote in Athens.

MAN. I ran over half a continent to get here. I won't sit down while he sharpens his knives.

HECUBA. Sh! It was clear when that smiling old man came and said 'statue' that one day this island would be pulled out of the sea by its roots and the people on it shaken down like ants. He should be killed. But if the islanders kill him to save their lives, his soldiers will kill them. Absurd! He must be killed! I've walked on the beach and daydreamed of killing him myself. Sheer fantasy! I'm blind and I haven't strength to scratch him with a pin. He'd chop *you* down like a stick. Yet he must be killed!

MAN. I'll take my chance.

HECUBA. Huh! We need more than that. Tell me about your mine.

TWO SOLDIERS *and a* SERGEANT *come on.*

MAN. Soldiers.

SERGEANT. Don't be alarmed.

HECUBA. What d'you want?

SERGEANT. Protect you from the villagers.

HECUBA. The pax Athenaea has reached the island.

HECUBA *stands and the* MAN *leads her towards the hut.*

(*To the* MAN.) Come in.

SIX

Three months later.
Day, overcast. NESTOR *stands by the hut.* HECUBA *is inside. The*
door is open. The MAN *sits and watches the beach.* TWO SOLDIERS
lounge upstage – only one of them has been seen at the end of Scene
Five.

NESTOR. The storm season's started. If he doesn't leave now the
  journey will be dangerous. He took up power – and uses it to
  sit on an island and look for a pin in the ocean! Ha! A soldier's
  place is his post. Waiting on the wind and sea – that's not the
  soldiering I understand.

HECUBA (*off*). He sat outside Troy for five years.

NESTOR. The Athenians don't even want his statue. O, they'd
  call it a sign from heaven – but they've ignored plenty of *them*
  in the past!

HECUBA (*off*). He's still on the beach?

MAN. Yes.

NESTOR (*goes to look*). Up and down, staring at the sea. I'd better
  get it over. (*He calls and waves.*) Yoo-hoooooo!

MAN. He's running.

HECUBA (off). He thinks you've found it. But he won't run too
  fast. Then he needn't feel ashamed if he has to hide his
  disappointment.

NESTOR. He could sit on this island for the rest of his life. Talk
  and drink, not bother to wash his beard for weeks on end. I've
  seen it happen. Go out with one fisherman and a boat now and
  then. Study the currents so he thinks he only needs to go out
  one day a year as long as it's the right one. And when he's old
  someone will take him to Athens and he won't recognise the
  place he built! Then come back here for the last time and fish
  for it with a rod and bent pin.

HECUBA (*off*). But before he becomes a quiet little man peacefully angling in a boat, he'll turn the world upside down with an axe.

NESTOR (*quietly to himself, as he watches* HEROS *on the beach*). My poor boy, I wish I brought you good news!

> HEROS *comes on.* NESTOR *goes towards him with open arms – but* HEROS *stops some way off.*

NESTOR (*expansively*). My boy . . .

HEROS. Nestor, what are you doing here?

NESTOR. The council sent me.

HEROS (*coming downstage. Trying to control his breath*). Phew! Watching the sea change colour. Doesn't sparkle this time of year. Grey. Like dirty windows. (*To* NESTOR, *pointing down at the ground.*) I meant *here*! (*To the* SOLDIERS.) Your orders were: let no one come.

FIRST SOLDIER. Sir . . .

HEROS. No one!

NESTOR. O, they know me of old – I'm an officer –

HEROS. I said no one, Nestor.

NESTOR. Then make your orders clear. So we know where we stand.

HEROS. I was clear: no one.

NESTOR. My mistake.

HEROS. Report to your officer after duty.

FIRST and SECOND SOLDIERS. Sir.

HEROS (*to* NESTOR). You think I'm unreasonable. This place is almost part of the sea. We *feel* it. All except you. Would you rush into a temple and yoo-hoo? I risk the welfare of Athens being here. It's our duty to take absolute care. We owe it to Athens. Yoo-hooo! (*Distant roll of thunder.*) It's a matter of military discipline. (*Flatly.*) Now thunder.

NESTOR. I'm surprised I'm not accused of farting.

HEROS. Nestor. Keep the circus for your soldiers. Look, I explain this not to justify myself but out of respect for your age.

NESTOR. The matter's closed. I'm not offended, my boy.

> *A distant roll of thunder.*

HEROS (*quietly, angrily*). Yoo-hoo. (*Calmer.*) Welcome to the island, Nestor. This storm will hold up the search. A day lost now – (*He stops in frustration. Calmer again.*) How is Athens?

NESTOR. Not well. Rebuilding the city has broken down the old ways. Our property – even our lives – need protecting. Ajax and Thersites quarrel through every council. It's embarrassing. They hold meetings behind everyone's back. We need you, my son, not the statue.

HECUBA (*off*). An empty temple would have great dignity. We should worship the force, not the image.

HEROS. I've seen cats piddling against empty temples.

NESTOR. The council orders you to sail within a week. They give clear orders too.

HECUBA (*off*). I'll fetch a bowl of water from the sea. Place that in the temple. The Athenians would understand that.

HEROS. Yet it might be tomorrow. Even while we're talking they may have found it. (*A distant roll of thunder.*) It may be standing on the quay. Unless the fishermen have hidden it to extort more money.

NESTOR. The winter storms are starting. We must get away.

HEROS. I'll search the village. If I put them under canvas they'll be easier to watch. To go away now! We might have stopped within an inch – one inch of sand – and tomorrow it would have been ours! I won't stop now!

HECUBA *comes from the hut.*

HECUBA. No. I've had a dream for five nights: so I must believe it. Not in the early morning, like other dreams, but in the middle of the night – as if it came from under the sea.

HEROS. What dream?

HECUBA. The goddess. She tells me she's ready to leave the sea.

HEROS. Yes.

HECUBA. She'll send a sign to the man who will find her. This time the sign will be clear. The man will win a race.

HEROS. An ordinary race?

HECUBA. A foot race round the island.

HEROS. I challenge any man to this race! Greek or Islander!

HECUBA. The goddess has chosen the runners. There are two.

HEROS. I'm one?

HECUBA. Yes.

HEROS. Who's the other?

HECUBA (*gestures around for the* MAN. *He limps to her.*) Him.

HEROS. He's crippled.

HECUBA. You needn't run.

NESTOR. I'm against this. This search for holiness is impious!
Do what you have to do and let others judge! Call god when
you finish – not when you start!

HECUBA. I dreamed five times.

HEROS. And I'll get the statue? (*No answer.*) It's a trick.

NESTOR. Good! Now we'll get on our ships and go. We have
homes, families, money, work. Why why why d'you want more?

The stage is lit by a flash of lightning.

HEROS. She's trying to tell me something. I can't understand.
To win I'd risk everything – gladly! But race with a cripple –
what do I *risk*? I'm tripped? Lose my way?

A roll of thunder, a little closer.

HECUBA. You can see the whole coast path from the hill in the
middle of the island. (*Shrugs.*) You can't lose your way.

HEROS. I'll break my leg!

HECUBA. The path's smooth.

HEROS. No! No! I won't do it!

HECUBA. There is one condition.

HEROS. What?

HECUBA. A prize for the loser. The loser is killed. That's the risk.

NESTOR. I forbid this race. I'll arrest you as mad, Heros!
(*To the* SOLDIERS – *indicating the* MAN.) Take him! (*The*
SOLDIERS *take hold of the* MAN.)

HEROS. Wait! I begin to see!

HECUBA. You've been given so much: armies, victories, a city, your looks. Now you're offered the greatest gift. But to get that you must hold on to nothing. Be willing to lose – and be content. A small risk. She'll share the small risk with you. If you don't take it – perhaps you'll lose everything.

The MAN *stands between the* TWO SOLDIERS. HEROS *looks at him.*

HEROS. Who are you?

MAN (*shrugs*). I've never been asked before. I don't know. I was born in the mine. In the compound on top. Most are born under. I've heard my mother was a cook. I suppose my father was a guard.

HEROS. That's why the goddess made me save your life: for this!

MAN. When you built your new city our hell grew with it. It's not true the guilty go to hell: only the weak.

HEROS. Enemies of the state or criminals!

MAN (*shakes his head*). I was born there. Why d'you cover your new city in silver? Your mud bricks, the soles of your shoes, are worth more than silver. I know what value is. I made your statues in Athens. You think I'm the broken bits that were chipped away! No – I made their smile.

HEROS. I see why the goddess challenged you! Will you take the risk?

MAN. The work's shaped round our lives as naturally as the seasons. At five I dragged baskets of rock through the tunnels. The rope round my waist cut a groove in my flesh. I was glad when the groove was cut. I was a machine with a gulley – here – for the rope. *That* pain would be kept *there*. An iron cable and a a pulley are oiled where they rub together. The gulley in the flesh can't be oiled. The flesh would go soft. The rope would tear it. It must be two stones. Rubbing together. The flesh of a child. Each day. All day! When the child – with his nipped-in waist like an ant – can lift an axe – he's sent to the face. First we break it with fire. Then we crawl in while it's hot – Athens is built fast! Our hands and knees are hoofs! We don't dig in a straight line. We follow the bend of the seams. They're put there by the devil. Our bodies are twisted round his finger in the dark. Like string. When we're too old to dig we go to the top – corpses surfacing! Old men and women – the difference went long ago, their sex is small knots on the skin – empty the children's baskets and crouch by the trough, sorting and sorting, their hands going up and down, sorting, like the legs of a beetle turned on its back.

HEROS. I didn't make the world.

MAN. Only Athens!

HEROS. Things change. Step by step. Let them out, they'd starve!

MAN. You don't want them to dirty your new streets!

HEROS (*offers his hand*). If I win this race – and every chance says I'll win – then I'll do what I can to help those people.

MAN (*refusing his hand*). You'll go away and forget. Every second of my life – till I ran – was watched by people like you – holding a whip with a silver handle. If you could count our crumbs, you would.

HECUBA. Tomorrow is the feast day. Nestor, you judge the winner. No swords, the day is holy and must not be polluted. (*A distant roll of thunder.*) For this, since it's the last day of the war that destroyed my city, I'll uncover my eye and watch the race from the hill. Go and prepare for tomorrow. Nothing can be done till then.

They go.

SEVEN

The same night.
A violent storm approaches from the sea. The edge of the rain clouds has already reached the island : a few heavy raindrops. Out at sea, lightning and the roar of wind, water, thunder and rain. The MAN *sits motionless, facing the sea.* HECUBA *comes from the hut.*

HECUBA. What can you see?

MAN. The storm hasn't reached us yet.

HECUBA (*comes closer to him*). Be my eyes.

MAN. The sea's rising. The water's black. Tomorrow.

HECUBA. Is there a moon?

MAN. Yes.

HECUBA. And fast clouds!

MAN. Tomorrow!

HECUBA. It's a mad woman with a lamp. Running from window to window.

MAN. I can't run like him.

HECUBA. Run as fast as you can. Then walk straight home and get your sword. Tell me. The lightning!

MAN. Showers of sparks where it hits the water. It lights up the whole sea.

HECUBA (*holds him*). And the serpents?

MAN. There are no serpents.

HECUBA. Yes, yes, where the wind lifts the water in coils.

MAN. Hecuba, go indoors.

HECUBA. Not real serpents, you silly man! Is there a spout?

MAN. What?

HECUBA. A waterspout?

MAN. No.

HECUBA. Ah! But there will be. Tomorrow. Soon. It comes over the edge of the horizon like the finger of a giant. Hauling him-self on to the earth. Don't be afraid! When it's gone you see: it's only a bunch of grey hairs in a comb. (*She holds him and strokes his hair.*) I wish you were my grandson.

MAN. Will I die tomorrow?

HECUBA. The spout won't hit us. It crosses down on the rocks. But the whole earth shakes.

MAN. Go into the house.

> HECUBA *walks away from him. The storm is closer.*

(*Calls.*) Ismene!

> ISMENE *comes from the hut.*

ISMENE. Come inside.

MAN. Hecuba's on the beach!

> *The storm hits the island.*

(*Calls.*) Hecuba! Ismene, we must get her!

ISMENE. She goes out in the storm! She hides in the rocks! She knows where!

MAN. Is she safe?

ISMENE. Quickly!

> ISMENE *and the* MAN *go into the hut.*

EIGHT

The next day.
Afternoon. Still overcast. A bench has been put upstage for NESTOR. *He sits on it with his lap covered by a blanket.* SOLDIERS. GIRLS *and* OLDER VILLAGERS – *they shout encouragement to runners off stage.*

OLDER VILLAGERS and GIRLS. Yes! Yes! Orvo! Dario! Faster! Look out! He's catching up! Hyspos! Orvo my love!

The YOUNG MEN *run on to the stage in a close finish.* HYSPOS *wins.*

Hyspos!

The GIRLS *garland all the* BOYS. HYSPOS's *family gather round him.*

HYSPOS's MOTHER. All the women will envy me in the market!
HYSPOS's GRANDFATHER. So fast!
HYSPOS (*embracing his grandfather*). It's easy just from the harbour!
HYSPOS's FATHER. See how well our boy treats the old people!
ALIOS. Let's go up the hill and watch the big race!
GIRLS. No! Our turn! Dance!

The GIRLS *dance, imitating the wind.*

GIRLS. Wheeeeeeeeee!
BOYS (*imitating thunder*).

> Boom! Boom! Boom!
> Sea rocks the boat
> Big man's cradle

GIRLS. Wheeeeeeeeee!
BOYS (*sing*). Boom! Boom! Boom!

> Wind blows wheeeee!
> God panting on his woman
>
> Crack bang! Crack bang!
> Old man thunder
> Broke his walking stick
> And fell down in the sea!

GIRLS. Wheeeeeeeee!

The dance ends. The MAN *has come on.*

NESTOR. Well, here's one fool given up.
ROSSA. Towel and water in the hut.

The MAN *goes into the hut.* SOLDIERS *follow and guard the door.*

NESTOR. Interesting that – the girls' dance. Brr! Hope this farce ends soon. (*Claps his hands.*) Dance! I'm cold!

ORVO (*explaining*). The dance is over for the year. We can't dance it twice.

NESTOR. Dance something else!

ALIOS. That's the winter dance!

ORVO. If we danced something else we wouldn't catch fish!

HYSPOS'S GRANDFATHER. And the moon would stay on her back.

The GIRLS *laugh.*

NESTOR. Peasants . . . ! And me! I sit here and wait for a runner to win a race he's already won because I've disqualified the only other runner. Greek wisdom. (*To* SOLDIERS.) You men take your orders from me today. When our commander gets back he'll be – winded. I'll manage this. (*The* SOLDIERS *look at each other uneasily. To the* FIRST OFFICER.) Don't just stand there! See what's happening!

The FIRST OFFICER *goes to the side of the stage, peers off, then walks off.*

(*To the* SECOND OFFICER.) You! Go and tell my cook. Get my dinner on. And make sure we're ready to go.

The SECOND OFFICER *goes out. The* FIRST OFFICER *comes back.*

FIRST OFFICER. The old woman's coming down the hill.

NESTOR (*holds out his hand*). Rain. A few drops. Huh! I said when I got up: feast day – rain. (*He shouts to* VILLAGERS.) You start working for your living tomorrow! No more playing silly buggers and getting paid fortunes. You women back to gutting the fish! Up to your titties in salt! (*To himself.*) Athens! How I long for my city! I shan't leave again. Past soldiering!

HEROS *dashes in. He collapses, exhausted.* NESTOR *leads the* SOLDIERS *in cheering.*

NESTOR and SOLDIERS. Rah rah hoorah! Rah rah hoorah! Rah rah hoorah!

HEROS. Done! Nestor the statue's ours. Put out – one boat! My god I think she'll walk out – of the sea to us.

NESTOR. The cripple gave up.

HEROS. Where is he?

NESTOR (*points*). Hanging himself in the hut.

The SOLDIERS *guarding the hut, and some* FISHERMEN, *go inside.*

HEROS. Give me that. (*He takes* NESTOR's *blanket and covers himself.*)

NESTOR (*rubbing his hands for warmth*). Have they remembered to pick my olives? I left instructions.

HEROS. I'll stop shivering now. If he had a wife or child – I'd take them in care.

The MAN *comes out of the hut. The group of* SOLDIERS *and* FISHERMEN *follows him. He wears clean clothes and a sword hung in a scabbard.*

HEROS. You'll be killed quickly and given proper burial.

MAN. I won.

HEROS. You're claiming you won?

MAN. I was here first.

JEROS. But you didn't run the race!

MAN. The race was seen.

HEROS. If anyone says you ran the race and were here before me –

NESTOR. Tchaw! Disqualified!

HEROS. – then I was tricked.

NESTOR. Let's end this farce. There's no joy in executions once you're past sixty. Last one I went to caught a cold. But this runaway slave – this public nuisance – should be executed. Here. Now.

HEROS. No – I shan't be tricked into cheating! Is that the catch?
I cheat and I'm disqualified? Let's see – we don't know she's in
this. If this is a conspiracy, who will it take in? It took me an
hour to get round this island. He'd hardly get past the harbour
by then!

NESTOR. I've given you so much good advice. What good does it
do you? I follow you like a faithful mongrel and bark. I should
run away. That's what the good people did in the old days –
ran away from the lost! (*He draws his sword.*) How ridiculous!
An old man waving his sword! Tangled up in my beard! What
else can I do?

HEROS. Put that away!

NESTOR. No! No! No! No! No!

HEROS. We'll lose everything! (*He struggles with* NESTOR *for the
sword.*) By god put it away! (*He gets the sword and throws it
away upstage, onto the beach.*) All of you – no swords! I've
come so far I won't be stopped now! I order you! (*To the
SOLDIERS, indicating* NESTOR.) Arrest him! (*The* SOLDIERS
guard NESTOR.) I'm on the edge of everything I asked for. I
will not have my way barred by your swords. Throw them
away! All of you! Down on the beach! (*The* SOLDIERS *throw
their swords away upstage.* HEROS *points at the* MAN.) Him too!
(*A* SOLDIER *takes the* MAN's *sword and throws it down on the
beach. Calls.*) Hecuba! Hecuba! Hecuba! (*To the others.*) We
shall tell the truth now. I feel it. At this moment – at last – for
once – I cannot lose. The truth speaks for me. Hecuba! I don't
administer justice now. It shouts my name!

NESTOR *sits on the bench, guarded by* SOLDIERS, *and cries.*

NESTOR. My son, to whistle up the curs that will devour you.

HECUBA *comes on with* ISMENE. HECUBA's *eyes are uncovered.*
ISMENE *stops and lets* HECUBA *walk forward alone.*

HECUBA. Still impatient. I heard you calling. I didn't hurry.
How I enjoy these trees! And the clouds. I'd forgotten how

strange! The sea's lost – so far out there . . . Look, a ladybird. (*She examines her hand.*) Nine beauty spots. Hard little wings. Scissors! My hand smells. How bitter! A prison. (*She blows the ladybird away.*)

> Fly away fly away fly away home
> Your coat is on fire
> Fly home soon.

HEROS. Did you watch the race while you were admiring the wonders of the world?

HECUBA. Why sneer? There are many beautiful things. I'm sorry I've seen so little of them.

HEROS. You saw the race?

HECUBA. I saw two runners start, and I saw the crippled one win.

HEROS. So you're going to cheat.

HECUBA. Your statue decided this race. Not me.

HEROS. You still go on with it?

HECUBA. I saw you sitting under a tree and smile.

HEROS. Liar! I ran the race! I said you don't have to show who runs the fastest! Walk over the island! But I ran the race! For the goddess's sake! (*He points at* HECUBA.) I trusted this bitch!

HECUBA. You sat under a tree and smiled.

HEROS. Liar!

HECUBA. You stopped. I walked down the hill. You were sitting under the tree like a schoolboy. I stood in front of you and stared at your face. You smiled. You didn't blink. A fly walked across your mouth and over your teeth. The goddess had trapped you under the tree. I shuddered. If I could run I'd have run up the hill. When I got to the top Ismene was still asleep. I'd come from one child to another. I looked back and saw you jump up and run on. You knew nothing of what had happened to you.

HEROS. Good! There was a time when you were not on top of the mountain? Who saw that? Nestor?

NESTOR. My eyes . . .

HEROS (*to* VILLAGERS). You?

PORPOISE. The boys race . . .

TEMI. We were watching . . .

HEROS (*to* HYSPOS'S GRANDFATHER). You?

HYSPOS'S GRANDFATHER. . . . . Our grandson won . . .

HEROS (*to* SOLDIERS). You? (*The* SOLDIERS *stare uneasily at* NESTOR.) How – how – tell me how this lame man could run round this island in half an hour?

HECUBA. How could you sit and smile under a tree while your life was thrown away? I can't answer your questions. Ask your goddess.

HEROS. I would! Everything! But she's not in my hands! I'd ask the sea if I could!

HECUBA (*to the* MAN). This is your only chance.

MAN. I take it!

   The MAN *takes a sword from* HECUBA *and hits* HEROS.

HEROS. Ah no! (*He falls dead.*)

NESTOR. Swords!

HECUBA. Wait! Nestor! Remember Troy! (*General hesitation.*) The cost! I told him: Go! You told him! We begged! Nothing could move him! What did he want? Look! (*She points to the sea. They all turn to face it.*) A little stone in the sea . . . Is it a wonder he's dead?

   They turn to face HECUBA.

NESTOR. Did you have that dream?

HECUBA. Yes! A thousand times. Did I invent it? I don't know. Her voice was like the buzzing of thousands of flies. I saw him once giving orders by a heap of bodies outside Troy. Flies buzzed round his mouth. Or perhaps I fell asleep on the hill this afternoon and a fly walked over my nose – and I dreamed it all before I woke up. We drop off all the time at our age, Nestor. Ismene. (ISMENE *covers Hecuba's eyes.*) Now, you want my life? It matters less than nothing to me.

NESTOR. You, no. (*He points to the* MAN.) But him – he walked across this island and brazenly lied to my face!

HECUBA. There was one winner and one loser. One is dead. Don't disturb it.

NESTOR. But I say to myself, shouldn't I ask what is justice? There's too much truth in this story. I can't find the loose ends.

HECUBA. That should only worry the hangman. Take him to the beach and burn him quickly. The storm's coming up. Nestor, get home before the bad weather sets in. You know how to explain this to the Greeks. They'll soon forget him.

SOLDIERS *take* HERO's *body out upstage while* HECUBA *talks to the* VILLAGERS.

HECUBA. You fishermen work hard and build up your stocks. It'll be a lean winter.

TEMI. We can't! Our nets were torn on the bottom!

PORPOISE (*pointing to* HEROS's *body*). He promised us new nets!

NESTOR. Not one penny! That I refuse! (*He sneezes. Rubs his hands.*) Brr. I'll go and warm my hands by his fire.

A distant roll of thunder.

HECUBA. You women will have to work hard to make new ones. Start while it's light.

The VILLAGERS *hurry away and* NESTOR *hurries after the bier.*

NINE

Next morning.
Calm and clear. ISMENE *stands by the hut and watches* FISHERMEN *bring* HECUBA's *body up from the beach on a wooden trestle covered with sailcloth. The* MAN *walks ahead. The* FISHERMEN *stop but hold the trestle while they speak.*

MAN (*to* ISMENE). We found Hecuba's body on the beach.

TEMI (*to* MAN). We told the Greeks the storm blew itself out last night.

ORVO. They're shipping anchor fast so they catch the lull.

TEMI. We had a meeting. The old people wanted to send you off with the Greeks. But the young men came – they're not part of the meeting, they pushed in – and spoke against it. The Greeks are everywhere. We could all end up in the mines. We may have to take to the sea for a time. We'll burn her on the quay.

The FISHERMEN *take* HECUBA *out.* ISMENE *and the* MAN *are alone.*

ISMENE. The old Greek caught a fever last night. They say he shivered so hard the ship creaked. They're going fast – to see if they can get him home to die in Greece. Where did you find her?

MAN. The waterspout picked her up from the beach and carried her into the fields. She was caught in a fence like a piece of sheep's wool. When the spout passed over her it ripped out her hair and her eyes. Her tits were sticking up like knives. Her face was screwed up and her tongue – a long thin tongue – was poking out.

ISMENE. Since you've loved me my mind's begun to clear. Even yesterday I was calm.

MAN. I may disgust you.

ISMENE. No, never.

Off, one distant shout of the young men's voices.

ISMENE. What is that?

MAN. The funeral games. The young men starting the race. They have to be quick, to go out in the boats.

Poems, Stories and Essays for *The Woman*

A SOCIALIST RHAPSODY

Socialism is a new understanding of the world. All explanations (even in the time of Derrida) rely on a theory of the working of cause-and-effect. The traditional cause-and-effect of literature no longer explains us or our society. The old ways of describing events no longer tell the truth. We do not make society decent by gaining emotional insight into ourselves because this does not give us insight into the working of society. 'To thine own self be true and . . . thou canst not then be false to any man.' This avoids the problem. How can you understand yourself? By discovering the social nature of individuality. The belief that there is some other way in which you can be 'true' to yourself depends on a destructive idea of what people and society are.

Perhaps our economics, biology and history have taught us more than we can yet creatively express. We have not yet achieved a practical creative vision. Shakespeare saw history as the expression of the human soul. He could use a king or prince as the spokesman of history. But as we don't believe history to be the expression of the individual it's harder for us to create individuals who can give history expression: individual self-expression and history are not one in Shakespeare's sense. Hamlet says 'Do as I do', and we believe him if we believe the self-poetry in which he says it. But a writer has to prove each detail of his story – and that is a difficult way to tell it because the point of the story and the reason for telling it are then easily lost. To tell the story well we need to create a 'world poetry' which will express the individual as a force of history – and self-poetry would be part of this. We would then have the practical vision of socialism.

The Woman is one temporary solution to the problem. It ignores facts of the story in order to clarify the story's point and to make clear why the story is being told. The brutality and reaction of our present society will not be defeated by the alliance between one wise woman and one hardened miner. Many things are necessary: organising, thinking, teaching, struggle, knocking at doors, waiting in cells, the courage of great moments and the stamina of ordinary endurance. In *The Woman* I ignore many things because I wish to make clear both the point of the story (that history is a moral force, that morality gets its meaning from human beings and that our actions can have morally good results) and my reason for telling it (to celebrate the world and people of which these things are true). But I also wish to make it clear that the woman and the miner are not superhuman archetypes. They are shown as individuals struggling to take decisions, who are no wiser, stronger or persistent than others may be. Society can be changed only because there are many people like them – and that is the only way in which they can represent large forces working through centuries: they are ordinary people who change the world. If socialist writers can't create characters who are agents of history but who ring true as individuals, then perhaps there could be no fully socialist literature: we should not be able to portray the weapons of history and the tools of reason. Ironically socialist literature would then be tragic literature: the record of individuals as pawns of blind historical forces; and comedy would be reduced to its tragic form – the Absurd, the debasement of both comedy and tragedy.

This play is a story showing in the characters and actions of its protagonists the cause-and-effect of change – especially the stupidity of reaction and the strength of the understanding that opposes it. It celebrates the change and those who make it. That is what makes the play a socialist rhapsody.

HISTORY

The architect knows that a roof is supported by the building's foundations. Gilding the steeple doesn't strengthen foundations. Putting turrets and steeples on the roof will not make the building safer.

We know that our bodies, also, are subject to the physical laws of nature. We cannot *will* to have twenty fingers or jump twenty feet. Yet we think we can run our societies on such chicanery.

Because we have will and consciousness we think we can handle human affairs in a different way. This is as much as to say that if we *wish* the roof to be firm or are dazzled by the steeple in the sky then the building will hold together as if spellbound. Clearly our understanding of history is still only an alchemy and we live on philosopher's gold.

Societies, too, are subject to physical laws of nature. History teaches a truth that cannot be opposed by *will* any more than a madman who thinks he's Napoleon could conquer Europe. Yet in society whole classes make similar mistakes about their identity.

Why are our days crumbling and our times violent? Because we gild steeples. But in history truth – like the physical laws of nature – comes from the foundations. True culture is created there, not at the top.

I wish I could show some of you how to understand this. But some of you build your steeples high till their tops are lost in the clouds. Perhaps now you have nothing to do but fall. If so, take comfort in this: your debris will then join the foundations.

A STORY

In the mine there was a rumour that the mine owner had built himself a white palace next to the sun. This caused great confusion to the miners. They could imagine what a palace looked like. It would be like the holes they cut in the rock. But the holes would be bigger and even longer. (It was said that a man might stand upright in some of them.) But what was sun? And what was white? The miners had never seen white. Nor had their families who lived at the bottom of the shaft below the mine owner who lived near the top.

And one day a young miner decided to go to see the palace and come back to the miners and tell them what sort of thing white was. After his shift he started to climb up the shaft. It was a hard climb. Whenever he tired he slept in a crack in the side of the shaft. Sometimes there was a low roaring below him as a cage loaded with ore came up. At such times he hid in the side. At other times he heard a gentle sighing above him as an empty cage came down. Then he had to move very quickly to reach a hole. His shoulders and elbows were scraped raw by descending cages because he couldn't move quickly enough.

No one searched for him. In the weeks before he left he had hollowed out the roof of his tunnel. On the last day he had knocked it down. The charge hands had assumed he was buried under the fall of rock. One of them had marked the fallen rock with a piece of iron. The piece of iron meant that other miners should not be sent into this tunnel. Charge hands were punished (deprivation of food or, in the case of joking with miners, demotion to the job of miner) if they lost miners through unnatural causes. Natural death in the mine was through routine work. Accidents were not only against nature but even against regulations.

After a few days of climbing, the miner realised he could drop on to one of the roaring cages going up and in this way be carried to the top. He thought about it for a time. Four cages passed him before he risked jumping on to the next.

At the top he found the mine owner. The mine owner was paying his six-monthly visit to the mine. The mine owner threw a rock at the miner. He knew what a miner looked like because his father had insisted he learn the job from the bottom and so he had once been shown a drawing of a miner.

For some reason the miner knew he must be the mine owner. He said, 'I have come to see your palace. And please sir what is white?'

The mine owner smiled. Here was a good fellow, he thought, and he remembered how his father had told him to think favourably of miners. 'Well . . .' he said, looking at the sooty miner. 'White? . . .' he mused for a moment and then smiled and pointed to his head. 'My face,' he said, 'is white.'

With a whoop of joy the miner reached out, cut it off and dropped it down the shaft to the miners.

It would be better for them if those who know what white is also knew what black is.

A DARK MAN

Deep below mountains and cities and forests
In darkness he dug
Ore to give brightness
  But for him only a whip

Centuries later the tunnels were higher
Instead of the whip he was paid
Pieces of silver
  (Judas paid Christ)

In time he works on the top
They try to delude him with myths
'He lives in a world too dark for his simple mind
But his master will lead him'
  Yes, you can be sure
  When he got to the top
  They'd use the daylight to blind him!

The past is full of their crimes
No one will live in peace
Till the last of their crimes
Are known and condemned
   That is the purpose of history
   And why it is called just

ASTYANAX

When the child is taken the women wail
And stare in terror at the sky

Soldiers go among them as if
Under their steel there was only
Iron and wood

And so as not to frighten the child
We began to rehearse with a cardboard box

The women who were to protect him
Could only hold him with tenderness
Or the box would be crushed

So the child is taken

   How can we change the world
   With tenderness?

IN PRAISE OF BAD TIMES

At the start of things the creator put two men into the world. To
one he gave a carrot and some string and a stick so that he could
ride on the other's back. The other carried him and spent his
days reaching for the carrot dangled before his face.

The man on his back was pleased at the secret understanding he had of their situation. He smiled as he rode through the world and said, 'What it is to have knowledge!'

But the man who rode on the other's back was greedy. (In fairness it should be said that hunger would have had the same effect: history is implacable.) And one night he ate the carrot. In the morning he climbed on to the other man's back as usual. He dangled the empty string before his face. The man did not move forward. Instead he looked up and down and then to the sides. He was looking for his carrot.

The man on his back became angry. He raised his stick and brought it down sharply on the side of the other man's leg. The man shot forward. The man on his back was pleased again. That day they travelled farther than they'd ever done before in one day. Later in the year he even discovered how he could loop the string through the other man's mouth and efficiently point him in the direction he wanted to take. This also meant he didn't have to shout so often.

It might seem that the condition of the man on the other's back was now much improved. This would be an illusion. It was the condition of the man who carried him that was improved. It is far better to know the real taste of the whip than hanker after the illusory taste of the carrot. Such a man may be said to be wise.

But there are other men who could learn from the donkey.

ON THE RED FLOOR COVERING

H. covered the great stage
With a red floor cloth
That looked like the tongue
In an open mouth

On it the actors move
To speak their truth

In the world the great
Also walk before us
On a red carpet

But what do they speak?

ANOTHER STORY

A man lost on a journey halted to ask a woman directions. She asked his destination. He told her. She knew it. She gave him directions. The directions were right.

The man followed them. Yet he did not reach his destination. When he was old he abandoned his journey and took refuge in a hostel. One afternoon he lay in his bed staring through the window and fingering his unshaven chin. Through the window he saw the woman. He shouted after her 'Why did you send me on the wrong way?'

She stopped, said she was sorry to see him in this state, that the directions she'd given him had been right, but that when she'd asked him where he was he must have lied. Naturally she had given him the right directions from the place where he'd said he was.

No one should set out on a journey till they know where they are starting. Indeed you may not know – perhaps *never* know – your destination: but you must know where you start. How else can you do anything or go anywhere?

It follows that hope is not faith in the future but knowledge of the past. This hope is not an idle fiction but the surest of facts. It is a promise kept even before it's made.

But for those who hope falsely . . . well, their condition is hopeless.

POMPEI

People who lived on the slope
Went to market each day
Met on street corners
Saw death in the arena
And passed by the sluices that carried water to wash out the blood
Took pains to bring up their children
Bought houses and saved against age
While over the city the mountain smoked

It's said that in those days of imperial violence
Men lived in a dream
Learned how to live with danger
And energy gave way to frantic fever

How far is the missile site from your house?

A STAGE DIRECTION

I put between brackets
The direction *has plague*
For a play

Then I was asked by the make-up technician
To look at the book of skin diseases

If god told me of sin on the last day
I would open this book and show him creation

Those who complain of science
Suffer from a disease

We hope science
Will cure it

A WOMAN

On a mountain I saw in the distance
Leaping and twisting
And lifting her arms as if stumbling
Or reaching for branches
A woman

I came close to see this wonder of nature
She was a smiling serious woman
On her path were such fissures and cracks
That leaping made her journey a dance

Strange dancing that twists yet goes forwards!
But also the arrow
The emblem of straightness
Has for its head
A corner

BLACK ANIMAL

In the ancient world there were silver mines. Few miners escaped
from them. Of those that did only very few survived. The others
soon died. They were not used to living above ground. And
anyway most of them were caught and killed. They were easily
recognised. Their bodies were crippled from working narrow
seams. Their skin was dark and pitted. People who found them
and took them back to the mine were rewarded. If it came out
that someone had seen an escaped miner and not reported it then
he was made to kneel beside the miner and be killed with him.
First the miner was killed. Then the sword – wet with the miner's
blood – was used to kill the other man. Such was the law.

   This is a story about a miner who escaped. He knew he had to
get far away from the mine very quickly. If he were seen near it

he would certainly be taken. He travelled by night. During the day he slept in a hole or a ditch. He ate wild fruit and stolen vegetables and eggs. He drank from streams and puddles.

During the day he slept deeply and didn't dream. He cursed himself because this was dangerous. It would be safer to sleep as lightly as an animal. Then he would be alert the moment there was a risk. But his exhaustion overcame him and there was nothing he could do about it.

One morning he was walking along a path between dark bushes. It was already light and the sun had begun to rise over the horizon. He was anxious. Usually he was under cover by this time. But today he was unlucky. There was no undergrowth and though the bushes were dark the light would filter through them when the sun was higher. There were no ditches or rocks. He started to run. Suddenly the path turned and he found himself out in the open just as if he had been shaken from a box. All the countryside in front of him had been cleared for fields. In the distance there was a small group of houses. Far away a dog yelped. Then there was silence. He felt his heart beating.

Suddenly a flash of light. He made a small noise in his throat. A quarter of a mile away two men stood watching him. The light flashed again. One of the men held a sickle. They were harvesting.

The three stood stock still and stared at each other. The miner wanted to run back to the bushes. Hide. Dig himself into the ground. But he knew he must do nothing to rouse more suspicion. He started to walk round the edge of the field. As the distance between him and the men grew his terror grew so that he wanted to shout. He could tell the men were talking about him to one another. Then the shorter man started to walk towards him. The miner pretended not to see him and went on round the field at the same pace. Out of the corner of his eye he saw the man begin to hurry. He shouted. The miner turned and saw he was a boy. He stopped. The boy came towards him and stopped some way off. The miner said 'What?'

The boy turned and pointed to the other man 'My father . . .'

The man in the distance called 'Hey!'

The boy beckoned the miner with a swing of his arm. He started to walk back to his father. The miner followed slowly. It seemed to take a long time. The gap where the path entered the hedge got smaller. The miner's heart was quieter now. His breath passed in and out of his nose with a little whisper. The man stared at him all the time. The boy hurried and the gap between him and the miner grew as if he was setting the miner free. He went on at his slow pace and tried to hide his limp a little. His dirty black hair fell across his face but he didn't brush it away.

The boy reached the man and stood with his back to the miner. He could see the man talking to him and pausing to let him reply. The boy turned to face him and stepped back and to the side of his father. The miner could see the man's face clearly. It was round and stupid. The eyes were shrewd. The mouth was as tense as the mouth of someone silently totting up figures. The sickle hung from his left hand in the shadow.

The miner stopped. He was close enough now for the man to speak to him. The man said nothing. He seemed to be waiting for the miner to come closer. The miner stayed still. The man sauntered a few paces towards him. The boy didn't move. The man smiled slightly and then nodded in greeting. The miner gave a little nod back, almost a flinch.

'Going far?'

The man smiled again. The miner saw how intently he watched him. The blade of the sickle curled in the shadow as the man changed his grip.

The miner said 'Lost'.

'Ah. Stay here a few days. My older boy's ill. Help me with the harvest.'

The miner nodded.

'Get that coat off your back.' He turned to his son. 'Run to the house. Fetch your brother's sickle. Hurry.'

The boy started to run towards the houses a mile or so away.

They were silent and blue in the thin mist. The miner was filled with despair as the boy ran farther and farther away. To end like this. . .!

'Is that water?'

The man stared at the miner and then nodded. The miner limped to the pitcher lying a few yards to the side. He picked it up and a large stone that weighed down a folded cloth. He threw the pitcher. The man easily side-stepped. As he did so the miner threw the stone. It struck the side of his head with a thud. The man yelled. The miner ran at him, jerked the sickle from his waving arm and struck him three times in the head, chest and stomach. He had to pull the end free. The man sat down and tried to turn away. The miner swung at his throat. The man fell sideways. The miner turned towards the boy. He was running to the village so fast he could not scream. The miner turned back to the hedge. The boy saw a small dark figure on the left. A woman going towards the houses. She carried a basket on her head. Her back was towards them. The boy changed his direction and ran towards her. This took him closer to the miner. The miner ran forward. For a moment he was running towards a point ahead of the boy. As he got nearer the boy passed the point and the miner was running after him. The gap closed. The boy turned to look. He was trying to scream. He had so little breath the sound came out as a groan. The miner could see the dirty soles and the chicken bones of the ankles and the flailing elbows. His breath made an animal roar. He reached the boy and swung at his back with the sickle. He missed. The force of the blow turned him aside. The gap between him and the boy widened. He ran. The gap closed. His breath screamed. He hacked at the boy's hip. The boy staggered to the side. He screamed. The miner killed him.

The woman had turned. She had lifted the basket from her head and was crouching to lower it to the ground. She dropped it. She stood still with her hand to her mouth. She ran a few yards towards the houses, stopped, walked a few paces towards the dead boy and then turned and ran screaming towards the houses.

The miner lurched back to the hedge. He passed the dead man. Blood was smeared on the stubble and there was a dark puddle in the furrows. He ran into the bushes.

The woman reached the houses. Children and other women ran out to meet her. A boy was sent to fetch the men from the fields. Some of the women went out to the dead bodies. At first they were afraid to go too close to them. Then a middle-aged woman went to the boy and began to wail. Other women went to the dead man.

The woman sat against the wall of the house. A little circle of grannies stood round her. They rubbed her wrists and forced water between her teeth. She was still crying and shuddering when the men arrived. The head man sent some of the men to fetch the bodies. The woman told her story over and over again.

'An animal. A black animal. At first I thought it was a great bird with a broken wing. Trying to fly over the field and dragging its broken wing along the ground. But it was an animal. Black.' The woman couldn't say any more. She repeated over and over 'An animal. Black. Black.'

The men formed into a hunting party and set out. The miner ran along the path till it was dark. Then he hid under a fallen tree.

TORTURER'S LAMENT

It's a hard life on duty all hours
Patrolling barracks
Guarding the depot

If there's an exercise it's bound to be hot
Or it never stops raining
It's church parade on the day of rest
And as if fighting wasn't enough
They bounce you out of bed
For fire drill

My wife nags
The canteen girls promise a bit on the side
Then let you down
They can't cook either

The sergeant's a swine to his own
The snotty little puke of a second lieutenant
Is so pig-scared of his men
His hand shakes when he salutes

Then you hear on the news
The investigations have got to stop
They take away the one chance you get to relax
The one bright spot in the grind
Is it decent?

You go in that little room
Dark like the pictures
That's where the action is
A chance to be your own boss
Use your imagination
Watch someone else crawl for a change

Now they want to take that away!
I ask: Is it fair?
They've got no idea
Let them come out here and try this life for a change

POEMS FROM A NOTEBOOK FOR *THE WOMAN*

1.

Who is this mad woman beating with her fists against heaven
As if the sky were a door to be opened to her?
Who? Who? Who? cries the prophetess when they come for an
  answer!
I Hecuba!
Bloody Hecuba with the lion's maul
And the coat matted with male lion's blood!

2.

Kill the little boy
His unripe body has organs
For seed

And if barren
His hands could hold a sword

His eyes playing like water
Wild in the sunlight now
Would narrow with purpose

3.

The plague in the poor quarter
Has started to spread to the rich quarter

Save our city!

4.

The emperor in his new clothes
Is preceded by a flag pole
On which flutters
A piece of the same material

5.

They danced
Later the invader came
And they saw they'd stamped out
Their graves

6.

Not trees in fog
The wet grass and mists
Of the north

Burning brick and stone
Marble and shadow
Men swift as snakes
Bloodier than tigers
And each instant clearly photographed
Evidence for the victim's family

NOTES ON ACTING *THE WOMAN*

The stage design is very simple. A few simple objects and even
these are simplified. They are not stylized. For example, the
temple steps are not made out of glass cubes. We want the audience
to think about the Trojans and not the temple steps. So we make
the steps suggest reality. When you stylize you may escape from

reality into fantasy. Our production is real. It has its feet on the
ground. It is not over-realistic (as some Chekhov productions are)
for a particular reason: we want to tell a story or analyse the
truth. We don't want to record things but to show the connection
between things, to show how one thing leads to another, how
things go wrong and how they could be made to go well.

An actor should use each scene to prepare for the next. We
must not become bogged down in each scene, weighed down with
emotion, trapped in too much detail. We must reach forward to
the next scene. We should be like a parliamentary candidate
touring his constituency before an election. In every speech and
at every doorstep call he makes he must be clear and truthful.
But the election day is coming and if he is to do well on that day
he must move on to the next speech or call. This doesn't mean he
must gabble. He needs a practised, skilful way of telling the truth.
The play comes to a halt if we play each scene with the emotional
urgency we would use to tell someone their house was on fire.
Perhaps we should say that most of the emotion occurs between
the scenes and that the scenes show the consequences of these
emotions. You can make a distinction between a blow and the
consequences of a blow. Very few blows should be struck in the
play because when they are struck they should be a knockout. So
most of the blows occur before the scenes. The scene itself is the
reeling effect of the blow.

This is very simple. It is what happens in human affairs. Most
of our lives are spent reacting to events. For example, people who
were not born at the time are still reacting to the effects of the
world wars. This doesn't mean that we are spectators. We are
struggling in a current, not hesitating on the bank or arguing
whether to jump in.

We could make a crude distinction between the plays of Chekhov
and the sort of play I write – the 'story play' or the 'theatre of
history'. Of course it is also bad taste to overact in Chekhov. But
many of Chekhov's characters are on the side-lines. They exist
between the important events of history and so they have very

little else apart from their emotional life. *We* must be caught up in the events of history. But we must also be in control. We must analyse these events, not merely reproduce them.

If we try to act this play in a Chekhovian way we get bad Chekhovian acting because the play is always struggling against our performance. We have to release the play into its natural freedom. That means that each character in the play wants to tell us his story. He does not want to relive it.

Imagine you are in a waiting-room – perhaps at a surgery or a government office. There is someone who wants to tell you their story – why they need money, housing or attention. Their mind, their words, their gesture, their 'performance' will concentrate on their need rather than the cause or condition of their need. They will not indulge their descriptions because it would not help them to do so. Only a con or liar indulges himself in this way. The others want the facts to be clear – and then you will *know* how they suffered. They will often say 'You see?' or 'You understand?' or 'That is so, isn't it?'. Only the obsessive is so involved in his story that he re-lives it. But he is unable to analyse or say what his need is. People who surrender themselves to obsessions go to madhouses. Our acting must not be an obsession with the past. It is directed to the future.

We must give emotion its proper place. But we must not imagine that it is a revelation of the whole truth.

We are acting the play on a large stage. This large stage is well suited to the play. It creates opportunities which we should use. We can think of the play as a story. The actors then become the illustrations of the story as well as the speakers of the text. When you are on the stage you should have a graphic sense. Use your acting as illustration. The artist emphasises salient features. So must the actor. Don't let emotion dictate the gesture. Find the gesture through emotion in rehearsal. But then work on the gesture. Find what is significant in it and use this. Omit everything superfluous. When the Trojan priests gasp 'Sacrilege' it is confusing if at the same time they bang their rods. Either of these is effective and can be made more effective by study. Another example: Ismene's mindlessness: is a smile more effective than giggling, or could giggling be broken up in such a way that it underlines a smile? Find the gestures which sum up a moment or character and work on these.

We find that on the large stage the relation between language and emotion is very important. We no longer hug the emotions to ourselves. But can we control the language even further? Suppose we think of ourselves as figures in a silent film onto which we dub our voices. This would free our voices from the dictates of the body. More of our emotion would then be transferred to energy and precision. We would use ourselves and not be used by our emotions. Artists should not prostitute themselves to their emotions any more than they should indulge the audience's emotions. Instead we need energy to polish, release and discipline our acting. Energy occurs when an emotion is transformed into an idea.

Emotion by itself is not truth. But when emotion shapes and demands ideas and actions that express it, then it begins to tell the truth. Emotion, once it is experienced and located in rehearsals, has to be converted into energy.

We don't want the abstract energy of American musicals. In these energy has no goal and without the music (which takes the place of analysis) they are boring. Nor do we want the frenetic energy of method acting. This also is based on emotion and not energy.

In acting for television we refine and make our acting appropriate to the small scale. Oddly enough, in our large theatre we must also refine. We don't adopt the bombast of the old actors (which incidentally was probably not as hammy as we think: bad acting has always been bad acting and good acting has always had something good in it). Nor do we adopt the medical twitch of method acting. We are not swept by emotion (as in ham acting) or glued to the emotional base (as in method acting). Our acting does not recreate. It recollects. Its energy is intellectual. It makes the particular general and the general particular. It finds the law in the incidental. Thus it restores moral importance to human behaviour.

(*These are some rough notes made during rehearsals of the first production of* The Woman.)

HANDS

The Woman: Part One Scene Twelve

The hands tell this story

The hands of the bystanders are clean
They make curving gestures
When they threaten the enemy their fingers close
Like rodents' teeth

The hands of the poor when they enter the scene
Beg
As flat and open as empty plates

When they reach the steps and see their enemies
They are united by need and hunger
Their hands become fists
That rise in a chorus of gestures
They change into weapons
They menace and flail

At first the hands of the son hold high
The red sword
In the military rite at the temple
When he backs from the crowd to the top of the steps
One flat palm is raised to push them away
He turns to beseech the goddess
They clasp in pleading
He turns to the crowd
Two flat palms pushing against the air

The hands of the soldiers
Primeval creatures armoured in steel
A bystander touches her ear
The earring's still there!

The assassin holds the son with one hand
The other pushes the knife in his back
The son falls like meat off a butcher's hook
We see the assassin's hand holding the knife
He is still
Like the butcher he waits
Till the meat comes to rest on the scales

Now the son's hands are feeble and old
They wander like dying mice
Over the steps

The crowd roars: The goddess!
Their hands wave like branches and clothes
In a storm
A voice: To the Greeks!
The hands swing in one common direction
Then waving and pushing
With gestures of hate and rejoicing
They take their curse to the shore

THE APPLE

Look the apple
Born in a cold spring
Becomes gold

Yet there is the glory of men
And the beauty of women
Made ugly by class

So winter come!
That we may see summer
Before we are old

HEROS: NO REASON

A little meteor fell on the earth
Like a straw in the proverb
So that it dropped from its course
To the arms of another sun
And swung in the spheres of a new world

Beauty and silver-wealth
And power that sways states
Have no reason
They fail like snow in the sun

It is said Canute laughed at his court on the sand
But the Leader waits for the tide
He claims he can walk on water
When the lie is big the Leader believes it
He says: I am the voice of the people!
But the people speak to each other

Reason and truth are the force
That changes the world
The Leader is crouched in his dark corner
An imbecile child in rags
Playing with reason and lies
And the bones of his army

For weeks the sun shone on the snow
Then the snow melted
The leaves fall in winter
And later the tree

THE ORCHARD

Still night
Bright stars over the orchard
I must answer the questions
Knotted even in the grass

That half the world are poor
That children die as if they were born long ago
Not in our time

In summer when these trees bear fruit
The children will be dead

COLD SPRING

This April is cold
Leaves smaller than babies' fists
The starling sits in a hole
Like an old woman looking out of her door
Waiting for rain to go
Factories turn upside down in the streets
To gaze at the sky

Who would not love virtue
To help the weak
Comfort the old
And instruct youth in the books of wisdom?

Each man's hand holds the same within ounces
Each man's hand is a signpost
The finger pointing to hell or freedom
Each man's hands are the scales of justice
He is weighed in the balance

Hands that would hold must strike
Our feet are as weary as Atlas's hands
  You who love virtue
  Love this cold spring too

SCENES OF WAR AND FREEDOM: A SHORT ESSAY

War and peace are taken to be mutually exclusive. But perhaps what we call peace has really always been a part of war. I do not mean that peace has been a time when men trained and armed for war. Certainly this is true. But I mean something else.

Perhaps war and peace have been phases in one total form of behaviour, one total form of society. If this is so, war would have to be seen not as the breaking down of peace but as its culmination. And then it would be an illusion to talk of a war to end war since there could be no peace able to protect itself.

An irrational society such as ours is divided into classes. This institutionalizes injustice. Injustice is not a passive state but one of increasing conflict. Why?

Firstly, an irrational society justifies its irrationality with myths. It teaches distorted beliefs: that the world is a jungle, men are animals, some men are more animal than others, all men are born to sin or with the need to be violent, only the hard prosper, most men wish to be led, happily others are born to be their leaders, and all this is either chosen by god or ordained by evolution. As we are still ignorant of many other things important to our welfare even these distortions might not be all that serious. But they also distort each man's view of himself. No man can accept that he is irrational and inferior and then behave rationally. A man's view of himself becomes part of his behaviour. It licenses it.

Secondly, and even more seriously, men's intellectual cast of mind has emotional consequences. They are born with the biological expectation that they have a right to live. When a child reaches consciousness this expectation leads into the conviction that he has a right to his humanity. In politics this becomes the desire for justice. How else could human beings be born into the world? How could evolution produce a consciousness of inferiority, an individual's natural conviction that he deserved to be punished, humiliated or deprived? A foetus burdened with this innate knowledge would shrivel in the womb. And if a man is taught these things, if society destroys his sense of dignity – and it is a matter of common fact that it very often does – then this social evaluation conflicts with an innate value. The emotional conflicts that follow, the way in which our need to love others is turned into a hatred of ourselves and others – these are the subjects of a socialist psychology. I want to point out here that these conflicts have political consequences. This is the way in which human character and judgement are distorted to produce fascism, crime, needless aggression, vandalism, social irresponsibility and the other evils which are said to be innate in man.

But there are other people who are told they have a natural superiority and a natural right to privilege and power. How can they have an innate conviction of this? Their reason cannot correspond with their emotion. Again emotional conflicts follow – with the same political consequences. These people act from fear. They are belligerent and reactionary. And their condition is exacerbated by the conflicts injustice produces in the other members of society.

One of the most degrading parts of this debasement of our species is racism. Racism is a human form of the behaviour of more primitive animals who, when they are humiliated or threatened, displace their anger and fear on those even more vulnerable than themselves. In the end injustice and intellectual distortion can so coarsen a society that its members despise out of indifference and kill out of boredom.

These are the ways in which men, who are not born to sin or with an innate need to be violent, become the makers of H-bombs and the organisers of death camps. In politics myths may invent reality.

A society both highly technological and irrational will inevitably lead to fascism and world war. An irrational society cannot devise a way to end war any more than a madman can devise reason. If a society is irrational enough to make H-bombs it must be so irrational that only chance can prevent it from using them. To make prevention sure society would have to be radically changed. It would have to be made rational.

Some actions are so horrendous that there is no moral justification for them. Obvious instances of this are wanton cruelty, genocide and the destruction of the world. Yet of two men facing each other with drawn knives one may be acting badly and the other well. Men are unique in their ability to reason and their actions should not be judged good because of the goodness of their motive: 'I meant it for the best.' Their motive must be based on a rational understanding of the world. We have a moral obligation to understand. At least this is true when we act as citizens, teachers, fathers, mothers and other representatives of society – when our actions have political consequences. The rational interpretation and understanding of men, society and history is socialism. It is a philosophy that has a rational explanation of irrational human behaviour. It is a guide to the practical action of making society rational. This cannot be done without difficulty and setbacks. It is hard to change the world, to escape from the old irrationalism. But these difficulties and setbacks can be explained by socialism. It is a philosophy which gives meaning to all significant action.

In our present time of great change we should not tell people to reform themselves by finding their soul, or to satisfy their desire for reason with inner peace. This is not a dark age when men can peacefully retire to monasteries. It is an age of darkness and of encroaching light. To retreat into inner peace in a world that makes H-bombs is a sign of despair. It is decadent to teach or counsel such a thing.

War and peace are the products of irrational society. They are siamese twins trying to strangle one another. There has to be a new conflict between war and freedom. This is the struggle for socialism. It will be won when society relates men to the world and each other in a rational way, a way without the distortions I have described.

It will be said that this is utopian. No. It is not a *wish*, it is derived from a rational analysis of our situation. Human nature, in its important aspects, is made by society. Our species makes itself through work and culture. We are not born good or evil but with the potential to be either. What we become is largely the consequence of our society and our experience in it. H-bombs and death camps cannot be blamed on human nature. They are the consequences of social organisation. It follows that war is not a consequence of human nature but of society. So a society without war is possible.

Such a society would be rational and have achieved freedom. The alternative is not an irrational society. Our species can no longer live with the irrational. Technology closes some of the doors of history as it opens others. The alternative is the destruction of earth and the life on it. This is the most important argument for socialism – not that it provides work, food and care but that without it irrationalism will bear its final fruit: the destruction of our species. Capitalism cannot avoid this catastrophe.

Perhaps the world will always be a place of some difficulty and often of hardship and loss. This does not mean that it will destroy us or that we must destroy it and ourselves. Freedom is possible.

THE TABLE

The four windows of this stone house face west
My long table stands before the one in the living room
On it are books of plays and poems
A dictionary and a guide to birds
Envelopes and carbons
A bowl of white narcissi
And a bowl of crocuses not yet open
What colour will they be?

The notebook bound in leather
From which this sheet was taken
Looks as solemn as a bible
But the metal clasps in the spine are open
And the sheets can be used

And lately I have eaten at this table
Two times a day I clear a place for the plate
The glass and knife and fork
To eat among the books and see through the window
Birds foraging in the garden

The keys of my typewriter
The crumbs and plans for work ahead
Bring me peace

Soldiers before battle who sit on the grass outside their tents
With fragments of food on their knife
May well feel this

FREE MAN
(For Paul)

In the ancient world there were silver mines. They were dug into the hillside or straight down in the ground. The tunnels were dark and narrow. They were lit by wicks floating in little jars of oil. The miners were men, women and children. They did not belong to families. They were black with filth. Their hair was matted. Their skin was calloused. They crouched and moved awkwardly. They looked like misshapen animals. Animals have grace. Even when they're dying – unless they fall into hunters' hands – their bodies often have dignity. But the miners were neither animals nor humans. They seem to have been invented by madmen. Overseers terrorized them with whips and sticks. The owner owned not only the miners and the mines but also the world above. Miners were not allowed to go into that world till they were dead. Then they were taken up and burned.

Once three young miners made a pact to run away. They'd make it look as if the roof of their tunnel had fallen in. No one would try to dig them out of the rubble. In time the tunnel would be cleared. But when their bones weren't found it would be too late to send out a hunting party.

They were expert at mining rock. They undermined the roof of their tunnel so that the roof held together and could be released with a few final blows. They also meant to save food. But they were not able to do this. And when they knocked the roof in it buried one of them. But the other two made their way to the bottom of the shaft. All the miners looked alike. No one questioned them. They hid in a hole below the shaft. They waited till a miner was tangled up in the wheels of a cart. In the brief commotion they got into the shaft and began to climb to the top.

Their bodies were contorted by crawling and were not useful for climbing. It took them three days to reach the top. When cages passed they hid in the fissures riddling the shaft walls. Far above they saw the little dot of light. They hadn't seen daylight before. If they'd gone straight into it it would have blinded them. But after three days they were already used to it. At the top they waited for night. Then they climbed out and ran away.

They slept in a wood. They stayed in the wood the next day. They ate berries and grass seeds. They sat in the bushes and talked. They had decided they must not stay together. If they went alone the chance that at least one of them would get away would be greater. They smiled at each other – but their lips grimaced with nervousness and fear. When it was dark one of the miners said 'Goodbye'. The other grunted. They left the wood in separate ways.

The miner knew he had to get as far from the mine as possible. Even in another country he would be in danger. His deformity would give him away. No miner was allowed to go free. Someone would take him prisoner and send him back to the mine. There would be a reward.

He walked at night and slept by day. He stole some of his food. The rest was wild. At first he thought about only a few things. How to get away, hide, eat. People were dangerous. He hid from them. But after some months he began to think of more things. First he noticed that the world was colder than the mine. Because he was tired he slept as soon as he lay down. But one night he woke up shivering. Next he found he need not be afraid of everyone. Some people ignored him. They looked up from the fields as he passed and then stooped back to their work. And perhaps only a few of them were happy. He saw hungry children crouching in dirt. They were too weak to play. Once a blind woman poked out her thin hand at him for alms. He saw pieces of men nailed to a gibbet. Another time he saw a group of men laughing and shouting orders in front of a house. They chased the family into the road. The son had to carry the old father in his arms as if he were the child. The men set fire to the house. The women sat on the ground and cried.

There was much beauty. The sky had as many expressions as a human face. Leaves were as restless as children's hands. The faces and bodies and gestures of women filled him with an unfathomable desire. He felt ugly when he watched them. But he tried to walk straighter and his feet felt lighter. At night he thought about the women he had seen that day. Then even the earth was good to lie against.

He was careful. He walked by day but hid when he saw anyone on a horse. He hurried past the big houses. He kept away from the roads and stayed on the paths. He knew that if he were taken back to the mine he'd be killed. Even if they put him back to work he'd soon die. He thought of his time in the mine as a grey corpse from which he'd crawled. Now his life had one purpose: not to go back. That was all. Everything else mattered very little to him. But at night he sometimes thought of the cruelty he'd seen in the world. People could not run away from that.

One day he came out of a wood. A girl ran towards him on a path across the field. A man with a stick chased her. He caught her and knocked her down. He beat her. The miner dropped back into the wood. Fortunately the man hadn't seen him. He hurried into the deepest part of the wood. He'd work his way round and come out beyond the path across the field. The wood was very thick. Thorns stuck into his arms and legs and sides. A swinging branch beat his back. His sweat brought mosquitoes. They stung his face. He heard the girl screaming. He turned and started to run back. He fought his way through the branches and undergrowth. Thorns tore his face. Suddenly he tasted blood. He lost his way. Then he was on the edge of the forest.

The girl lay across the path. From time to time her body jerked. The man crouched at the side of the field. He held his bowed head in his hands. He tore at his thick black hair. The stick was beside him where he'd thrown it on the path. Suddenly he stood up, took the stick and began to beat the girl. She screamed. The man struck her three times. His back was towards the miner. The miner came out of the wood and hurried towards him. He picked up a large stone. He was close to the man. The girl was on her back. She did not defend herself. Her body jerked. She made short gasping sounds like a madwoman. The man struck again, swinging his back, raising the stick high and bringing it down with the whole force of his body. The girl didn't react to the blow. Her body went on jerking in the same rhythm as before. She didn't scream as the stick struck her. Just went on gasping. Her open mouth was filled with a black shadow.

The man said 'You – you –'. He waved the stick in the air. The miner hit him on the head with the stone. He fell down across the girl. He didn't shout. He was unconscious. The woman opened her eyes. She was dazed and couldn't understand what had happened. She staggered to her feet. She looked at the man and then suddenly saw the miner. She stepped back, still gasping. She turned and ran away down the path. The miner watched her lurching and slipping. She fell down, crawled forward a little, got to her feet and looked back in panic. Then she ran on. The miner gasped noisily for breath. He looked at the man. His cheek was squashed against the path like the cheek of a sleeping child. His hand was open. The stick lay beside him. There was no blood.

The miner ran towards the wood. Suddenly he thought of the stick. He ran back, picked it up and ran into the forest. He hurried the rest of that day and all the night. For hours he said 'Fool. Fool. The risk!' at first aloud and then to himself. He ran to the rhythm of the words. It began to get light. He looked for a place to spend the day. The path crossed a wooded slope. He turned off and found a grassy dip. On one side a small boulder. He sat on it. The lush, thick grass was cool against his feet and ankles. He took the stopper from his water bottle and drank two big mouthfuls. He leant forward with his head bowed. He was tired but he did not fall asleep. He whispered to himself 'Fool. Fool. The danger!' He was bowed in thought for a long while, staring at his feet and the grass but not seeing them. 'Why?' he whispered. He let the question, spoken with his voice, sound in his head. 'Why?' His mind went back to the wood where he'd hidden with the miner. He remembered how they'd tried to smile at each other.

He thought of the man lying across the path. Perhaps the woman deserved to be beaten. No, she was in rags. Pale skin. Famished. He shrugged.

He slept half the day. Then he started to walk. For months he'd been able to walk faster. He still limped but he was not so crouched. Today he felt stronger, as if he'd learned something but didn't quite know what.

It was a mild day. Towards evening he stopped to watch a man unyoking his oxen. They walked wearily but quickly into their stall, looking for food.

During the next few weeks it became clearer to him. The mine was hell. But why had he run? It would have been easier to kill himself. He ran for the same reason that he'd helped the unknown girl. He learned why he was alive.

To take such risks! He laughed to himself. He would walk to a distant country. Perhaps cross the seas. In time he'd find work in a village and live in a house with friends. When he died they would bury him.

ODE

The world was old before it bore men
Its young passion was spent
Rocks were grey
Rivers had scoured the hills with wounds
And water healed them

The earth was not naked when we were born
Our cradle was green
Covered with bright flowers

We did not come as monsters half drowned in swamp
Or bone birds shrieking on windy shores
Our hands were already tools not weapons

Men were born to a wise old mother
Surely with such inheritance
We will love peace

Stone

A Short Play

Stone

Men are not asked who they are but ordered to be
Cut to the shape of a square world
And the head bound as surely as Old China
Bound women's feet

Why this unreason?
The tool-user makes tools for his purpose
They work? — no questions!
They break? — new ones!

Just make enough noise to drown your voice
Turn on enough light to blind you
Block out the windows with light
Run long enough to learn how to sleep on the run
This is the first obligation on all tools:
Don't know your own function

So what weight presses you to the ground?
Why does the young hand shake with the palsy of age?

What is the definition of a tool?
A space that exactly fills its prison

Author's Note

The author wrote *Stone* when Gay Sweatshop asked him for a play. He wrote the following programme note for the first production.

To support an injustice to anyone else damages your own life. It involves you in physical repression and violence which can in extreme cases cost you your life (in wars, in hooliganism created by urban decay, in racial violence, and so on). It also involves you in mental and emotional distortions. To justify injustice reality is replaced with myths — for example, that people are born evil, blacks are bad, the tory party is the party of born leaders, strikers want to smash the country. This distortion trivializes human relationships; and as it prevents the rational solution of problems, it produces hysteria and violence.
All major repressions — Nazi anti-semitism, black slavery, the persecution of homosexuals — are signs of the injustice of the whole of the society in which they occur.

Most societies are led by those who profit from injustice. There is a vested interest in injustice (and therefore in irrationality). So, it used to be said that male homosexuals were effeminate and this endangered the empire. No emancipation for homosexuals was possible until imperialism began to crack. Anyone fighting for the freedom and self-respect of colonialised Africans and Asians — or, for that matter, of colonialised factory workers in Europe — is fighting for the freedom and self-respect of homosexuals everywhere; anyone fighting *against* colonial freedom and the emancipation of the working class is just as surely fighting for the repression of homosexuals. To give another example: until more money and effort are spent on a good, universal education for all children — without a money-right to opt into privileged elites — then (at the poor end of society) city roughs will go on queer-bashing sprees, and (at the rich end) public schools will teach scorn and fear of homosexuality. Privilege creates violence as much as deprivation.

You cannot have your freedom at anyone else's expense. Freedom is indivisible. From time to time the struggle for it is waged on different fronts, on those where the next victories seem most possible or most needed. But the struggle is a general one. Homosexual emancipation is not possible without economic and political reforms in other parts of society: in schools, factories, hospitals, legislatures. Unless they support these reforms homosexuals are aiding in their own repression.

I believe it was Einstein who said a society's level of civilization could be judged by its attitude to anti-semitism. Later this was said about capital punishment. We could now say it about homosexuality — except that there are so many things it could also be said about.

Stone was first presented by Gay Sweatshop at the I.C.A. Theatre, London, on 8 June 1976. The cast was as follow:

MAN	Kevin Elyot
MASON/JUDGE	Tony Douse
TRAMP/POLICEMAN/BOY	Antony Sher
GIRL/WASHERWOMAN	Anna Nygh

Directed by Gerald Chapman
Designed by Mary Moore
Music by Robert Campbell
Choreography by Liebe Klug

Scene One

Road. Empty stage. A young MAN comes on. He is eager and relaxed. A middle-aged man comes on. He is quiet and efficient and wears a business suit. He is a MASON.

MASON. Where are you off to?

MAN (*half smiles*). Why?

MASON. You're not lost?

MAN. No, I'm going to find a job and make my place in the world.

MASON. Good luck.

MAN. Thanks. (*Smiles.*) I left home this morning. My father and mother can't keep me now.

MASON. What work d'you want?

MAN. I could learn to do almost anything.

MASON. What did your parents give you to take out in the world?

MAN (*touches his pocket. Half smiles*). Something.

MASON. Generous!

MAN. They didn't have much but they wouldn't let me go empty handed.

MASON. How much?

MAN (*cunning*). Ha-ha.

MASON. Do I look like a thief?

MAN. You might be a clever thief.

MASON. I'm weaker than you. You could knock me down.

MAN. That's true.

MASON. But you wouldn't.

MAN. Why not?

MASON. I'm very rich. But I don't carry money on me. So I

agree: it's not worth knocking me down. Congratulations on changing your mind.

MAN. I didn't change my mind! I never meant to knock you down.

MASON. No? You'll find — out in the world — it's better to expect the worst. (*Takes out a pistol.*) Like this.

MAN (*shortly*). O.

MASON. How much?

MAN. Not much.

MASON. How much?

MAN. Seven gold talents.

MASON (*blandly*). Seven. (*Jerks the pistol.*) Show me.

    The MAN *takes out seven gold coins.*

MASON. Pockets out.

    The MAN *pulls out his pockets. They are empty.*

MASON. Hand it over. (*He names each coin as it is put into his hands.*) Prudence, soberness, courage, justice, honesty, love — (*The* MAN *drops a coin.*) Pick it up. (*The* MAN *picks it up and gives it to the* MASON.) Hope. Now what will you do?

MAN. I won't go home.

MASON. They can't afford to take you back.

MAN. I'd be ashamed to ask them. I wasted their money. They worked so hard for it.

MASON. They should have warned you about thieves.

MAN. They did. But the sun was shining and I thought no one would spoil a day like this by stealing. I shall go to the police.

MASON. Then I shall have to shoot you. You're spoiling my day too!

MAN (*annoyed with himself*). Blast.

MASON. You'll really have to control your tongue. (*Sighs. Shakes his head.*) Shooting people works out expensive. Fortunately I don't have to shoot you. The police are far too busy to worry about your seven talents!

    MASON *gives the money back to the* MAN.

MAN. O. (*Puts the money in his pocket grumpily.*) Thanks.

MASON. Let me give you a job.

MAN. Don't pull my leg.

MASON. What?

MAN. You won't give me a job.

MASON. Why not?

MAN. You wouldn't trust me. You made me look a fool. I didn't show much sense did I?

MASON (*nodding*). Yes, you'll suit me very well.

MAN. It must be such hard work you can't get anyone else to do it.

MASON. No, it's the sort of job people queue up for.

MAN. What's the catch?

MASON. Can't someone just want to help you?

MAN. No.

MASON. Your parents did.

MAN. That's different.

MASON. You bring out my paternal instinct.

MAN. What job is it?

MASON (*takes a stone from his pocket*). Here's a stone. No more than a pebble really. Take it to my house.

MAN. That stone?

MASON. My house is along the road.

MAN. Why don't you take it?

MASON. My business takes me the other way.

MAN. Let me look. (*The MASON holds the stone on the flat of his palm.*) Is it an ordinary stone?

MASON. It's just as you see it.

MAN. Why d'you want it?

MASON. I'm a stone mason. No doubt I see more in it than you do.

MAN (*takes the stone*). It looks ordinary.

MASON. I told you.

MAN. How far is your house?

MASON. Quite a way. You'll come to it. Tell them I sent you.

MAN. Why an ordinary stone?

MASON. It could be the ordinariness that interests me.

MAN. And wages?

MASON. You're paid when you deliver the goods.

MAN. How much?

MASON. That depends how quickly you deliver them.

MAN (*returns the stone*). That's the catch.

MASON (*shrugs*). I don't pay in advance.

MAN. I don't work till I'm paid.

MASON. You won't find an easier job.

MAN. I don't trust you.

MASON. I want to help you. But I won't give money away. That ruins people, especially the young. Encourages scrounging. Deliver this stone — that's not much to ask. I could have robbed you. Instead I offer you an easy job — and you say you don't trust me! I'll be on my way. (*Starts to go.*)

MAN. Well — (*Stops short.*)

MASON (*turning round*). Yes?

MAN. How will I know your house?

MASON. It's by a stone-yard.

MAN. Suppose someone offers me a better job?

MASON. They'll offer to carry *you*?

MAN. I might get lost or fed up.

MASON. Now you see the place of trust. I have to trust you. You could throw my stone away anytime. But I trust you. Within reason. That's why I don't pay till you deliver the goods.

MAN. I see.

MASON. And you have to trust me. Within reason. I say wait to be paid — but I ask so little. If I'd said murder your grandmother — I'd have asked too much. You'd expect to be paid first. Rightly. Or if I'd said sell your soul. Kill your brothers. Swallow the ocean. Then you wouldn't want to be paid at all! — because you're a good lad and you'd rather live by your talents. While they last. So I ask little: carry a stone. And I only ask that because it's the easiest way I can help you without offending my principles. It would be very odd if you said no.

MAN. Yes, I see.

MASON. So you enter my employ?

MAN. Er yes.

MASON (*raised finger*). Call me sir now you're one of mine.

MAN. Yes sir.

MASON (*gives the stone to the* MAN). Excellent.

MAN. I'll take it to your house as quickly as I can.

MASON. Mind you do boy. Good day.

MAN. Yes sir.

> The MASON *goes out.*

MAN. As he said: if I get tired or find something better I can throw it away. It can't do any harm till then.

David and Goliath, or Song of False Optimism

Goliath was bigger than a mountain
David killed him with a stone
Goliath fell down like a landslide
David was light on his feet
He saw the shadow fall over him
And stepped aside just in time

David knelt to thank the lord
Goliath in the kicks of death
Raised his fist — it came down like a bomb
David had good hearing
He heard the mighty rushing of wind
And stepped aside just in time

David sang a victory song
Out of the hole in Goliath's head
An evil gas poured over the world
David had a good sense of smell
He smelt the air turning septic
And got out of that just in time

David danced a dance of praise
When Goliath was struck his spear had spun
High in the air — it came down like a bomb
David had a good sense of touch
He felt the tip scratch the top of his skull
And stepped aside just in time

The MAN *goes.*

Scene Two

Road. Empty stage. An Irish TRAMP *comes on. He is ill, shivering and exhausted. He mutters darkly to himself.*

TRAMP. God damn and blast this blidy earth . . . the creatures in it . . . and the sky that covers it. (*Takes out a bottle. Swigs.*) Ah. (*The 'ah' is perfunctorily routine.*) Curse the day he made it. (*Sits on the ground and weeps quietly.*) Was he like a man tryin on a pair of new shoes? (*Small swig.*) 'I'll try them for size. Hang on now, it don't fit. Pinches me toe. Don't think much of the colour of the welt. Have you anthin more in the fashion?' Tosses us aside in the dark and we've been festerin on a dump site ever since. (*Examines his shoe. Flaps the sole.*) Piss swamp. I was a scholar. We had books in the family. I've been drunk so many years I don't know if I've forgotten how to read or I just see the words double.

The MAN *comes in. He is tired. The* TRAMP *hides his bottle.*

MAN. Are you all right?

TRAMP. Do I look all right?

MAN. No.

TRAMP. At least one of us sees straight.

MAN. What's the matter?

TRAMP. I have this terrible pain.

MAN. Where?

TRAMP. All over. Have you anythin to drink?

MAN. No.

TRAMP. Or eat? (*The* MAN *shakes his head.*) Well don't stand there! I'm not a blidy peep-show.

MAN. I wanted to help.

TRAMP. You're a decent lad. Sorry. I suppose you haven't any money?

MAN. A bit.

TRAMP. Ouch. O dear. What a terrible stab of pain.

MAN. Where?

TRAMP. I wouldn't have believed it could have got that worse if me mother had swore it on the day she died with one hand on the bible and the other on me father's grave — I'm an orphan you understand.

MAN. I'm sorry.

TRAMP. A sorrow shared is a sorrow halved. Give us a hand now.

MAN. Right. (*Helps the* TRAMP *to stand.*)

TRAMP. Fine, fine. (*On his feet.*) Let go and watch. (MAN *lets him go. He staggers.*) There now, see that? Brain damage.

MAN. How?

TRAMP. Will you stop interruptin. These are probably the last words of a dyin man — it'd be a mortal sin if you stopped me gettin me message to the world. I'll sit down and save strength. (*Sits.*) You were sent to me by god. I bet you didn't know that.

MAN. No.

TRAMP. Ho-ho god moves in a mysterious way. He's called people far worse than yourself. O dear here comes the pain again — not that it went away. I'll take a drop of this to keep me goin till me mortal work is done. (*Swigs.*) Now what would your job be? Don't tell me, let me guess. A clever lad like you, you'll be in a well-paid line of trade. You're a doctor.

MAN (*smiles*). No!

TRAMP. You're not? I could have sworn. *Now* I have you! A fine lookin lad like you — you're an actor.

MAN. No.

TRAMP. This is difficult. Good with your hands I bet. I have it, I have it, I have it! Civil Engineer.

MAN. No.

TRAMP. You play the violin.

MAN. No.

TRAMP. Then I'm beat. I'm afraid you'll have to tell me how you earned your money.

MAN. I didn't.

TRAMP. The man's a riddle.

MAN. My parents gave it to me.

TRAMP. He's a blidy heir!

MAN. No — I've just come out in the world.

TRAMP. Well where the blidy hell had you been before? A joke! O it takes me back. Many years ago — not all that many — I was just as strong and handsome as yourself. To look at you I'd say you came from a good family, but — don't be offended, in my eyes it's a compliment — poor.

MAN. That's right.

TRAMP. I could see there was no taint of luxury in you. (*Sighs*.) If they were poor they couldn't have give you much. No, I won't be told! I'll guess. Jassus-christ if I don't guess somethin right I'll lose me self-respect. You don't want that! Half a talent.

MAN. No.

TRAMP. Never a whole talent?

MAN. No.

TRAMP. It couldn't be more? I don't believe it. A talent and a half?

MAN. No.

TRAMP. Och you're talkin of copper. That could never be gold.

MAN. Gold.

TRAMP. Glory be! What a wonderful upbringin you'd get from

people like that. You must have the manners of a saint. So it's
three talents!

MAN. No.

TRAMP. Tch tch tch, to think of them poor people slavin
away for the sake of their lad. Four?

MAN. No.

TRAMP. Wearin their fingers to the bone. Their hair turnin
grey before its time. All so they could see their lad go out and
make the world a better place. (*Sighs.*) You'll have to tell me
son. Sorry to let you down but with parents like that how
could I tell what they'd do? I see the world's not all bad. I'll
die happy with the amount of their goodness ringin in my
ears. How much was it — the excitement's killin me.

MAN. Seven.

TRAMP (*swigs*). I don't believe that.

MAN. It's true.

TRAMP. It's blidy not. Was I born yesterday? Aren't you
'ashamed, lyin and blackguardin your family's name after all
they've done for you?

The MAN *takes out the seven coins.*

TRAMP. Glory be. The fella's a walkin miracle. And there's me
callin him scoundrel.

MAN (*showing the coins*). Prudence, soberness, courage, justice,
honesty, love —

He drops a coin. The TRAMP *picks it up.*

TRAMP (*reads the coin*). Hope. Glory be. Before I hand this coin
back I'll tell you a story. It has a moral and it's true. Twenty
years ago I stepped into the world just like yourself, smilin
and bellowin top of the mornin till people thought I was
mad. And now? (*Sighs.*) How did I get this way you ask? One
mornin an old fella came towards me on this road, on this
very spot — for I've gone round in circles ever since. He was
dirty and stinkin and broken. He held out his hand — so.
Nothing was said. I had gold — it chinked in my pocket as I
crossed over and passed by. I wasn't rich like you — me
mother was a widow — but I had enough t' make me hard.
That night I sat under a hedge and counted me coins. Every

night I ran them through me fingers. This night, back of the
hedge — robbers. Out they hops. Thwack the head-lad thumps
me cross the head with his stick. Me brain was damaged. And
I've been the wreck you see ever since. (*Flips the coin and
catches it.*) Now if I'd given me money to the old fella I'd be
a man still — and richer than I was then. I had a dream. The
lord sent you. Let me save your soul. (*Holds out his hand.*)

The MAN *drops another coin in the* TRAMP's *hand, walks
away, and turns round to face him.*

MAN. I don't believe a word.

TRAMP. Hahaa—hahaa, the lord says it doesn't matter if it never
happened to me! It could happen to you.

MAN. I'll have to take my chance like anyone else.

TRAMP (*lies on the ground and cries*). I let that poor fella die on
the road. Now I'm losing this young one. How can I save his
soul? It's terrible!

MAN. You've got two coins. No more.

TRAMP (*howls*). How can I make him see? How? (*Beats the
ground in despair.*) I'm not after your money! (*Kneels and
clasps hands in prayer.*) God inspire me! Don't let me lose
another sheep! (*Sudden inspiration.*) Ah! Yes! Thankyou
god. (*Turns solemnly to face the* MAN. *Slowly takes a knife
from inside his coat. Holds it out.*)

MAN. I'll kill you first.

The MAN *takes the stone from his pocket. It is recognisably
the same stone but it has grown to the size of a brick.*

TRAMP. God didn't say I was to kill you. He said I was to kill
meself. (*He holds the point of the knife against his own
throat.*)

MAN. You won't.

TRAMP. Ah I will. What d'you know of me? I sleep in the road.
Filthy, stinkin, drunk, out all weathers. Two talents — I'll
drink it away! I'd be better off with nothin. Seven talents —
I could start again. Get warm and clean and decent. Find a
dry place to live. (*Jerks dagger at his throat.*) I'm on me last
legs. You're young. Your life's to come. Why did your people
give you money? To grow fat? Or make the world — god
forgive me for a blasphemous⎟ swine for saying so — a better

place? (*Throws the two coins on the ground, but not too far.*) There's your money with the blood on it!

MAN. You won't.

TRAMP. You haven't seen your man die yet. You think they only stink when they're dead. No, dyin has its own smell. An acidy stink — suddenly in the air — worse than decay. And its sounds. You never hear them somewhere else. Heels drummin as if you're marching downhill. A matchbox rattlin in the throat. O not loud. You could still sip your tea through it if you'd been well brought up. The sound furniture makes in a doll's house when children are playin. Nothin matters more than a game, and nothin's more quickly forgotten when it's over. That's life my boyo! My death will be the end of the game. Watch me play! Snip you're dead!

The MAN *comes back to the* TRAMP. *Suddenly he dives for the coins. The* TRAMP *moves violently — still with the knife at his throat. They each get one.*

MAN. I'll buy the knife.

TRAMP. Seven talents.

MAN (*drops a coin*). Two.

TRAMP. Seven. Hurry. It's nearly time, the whistle'll blow.

MAN. Three. No more.

TRAMP. Four more. Four! By god this is a moment I'd choose to die in! All or nothin! The lot staked! Seven. Coin of the realm.

MAN (*drops four more coins*). That's all. I shall hold on to this one.

TRAMP. Yes . . . well . . . six. But I've been cheated. (*Bites a coin.*) It it good money? Yes, gold — you swindler . . .

MAN. Give me the knife.

TRAMP. That cost *seven* talents! O I won't pig-stick meself. The knife act is over, the cabaret's finished. I'll take me death off your conscience for six talents. But I'll keep the knife. One day you might get it in the back.

They start to go in opposite directions.

MAN (*out front*). Every evening I measure this stone and it's

bigger. The mason is up to something. Something good will
happen to me when I deliver it. Some special reward. (*Looks
at his coin.*) Hope. I'm glad I gave the rest of my money to
him. My kindness will make the world a better place. I'll
cling to my stone! The world is full of surprises.

Merlin and Arthur

Merlin was a great wizard
He took eggs from the air
He took a loaf from a beggar's sleeve
He even made a corpse smile
By letting it smell his fingers

TRAMP (*out front. Counts the coins*). Glory be. (*Shakes his
head.*) The man's dangerous. He shouldn't be allowed out on
the road.

King Arthur was a jealous king
He took the loaf and eggs
The dead man had been his worst enemy
He'd killed him in battle
So he hanged Merlin for treason.

Scene Three

An Inn. Empty stage — perhaps an inn sign. GIRL enters.

GIRL. This inn's called 'The Dance of the Seven Deadly Veils'.
I run it on my own. Not easy! I ought to marry. There's a lot
of men I'd like to share my bed — no problem, as long as they
know a thing or two — but no one I'd like to share my profits
— the problem there is they know too much! There's a lot of
men I'd trust with another woman — frankly I'm not bothered!
— but no one I'd trust with my till! I've got a good business.
Customers come miles to see my famous dance. But I could do
better. A weak woman gets put upon.

Song of the Seven Deadly Veils

How is society organised?
For the happiness of the people?
Or so that profit can be drawn
At as many points as possible?
What do you want from the cow?

Milk or blood?
Then stop sticking your knife in
All over its hide

The governor begging at the widow's door
The soldier as protector of the poor
The strongman waiting humbly for the weak
The spokesman who gives up his turn to speak
When things like this are seen
The world will be a better place
Than it has been

> Evil creates its own remedy!
> Till then we stagger round and lose our breath
> In that old Side Show called The Dance of Death
>
> In the famous dance of the seven deadly veils
> Bad turns to good
> Homes turn to jails
> Can turns to should
> A corkscrew is straight
> Saints turn to whores
> But don't send to ask who's head is on the plate:
> It's yours!

The priest and teacher whisper together
Mankind is a tragic animal
Destined by nature to fight forever
Man against man with tooth and claw
But our pyramids!
Will this brawling pack ever get them built?
Call in the overseer!

The workingman who gets some time for thought
The thinker who's conclusions can't be bought
The office-seeker who can use a spade
The specialist who cures before he's paid
When things like this are seen
The world will be a better place
Than it has been

> Evil creates its own remedy!
> Till then we stagger round and lose our breath
> In that old Side Show called The Dance of Death
>
> In the famous dance of the seven deadly veils
> Bad turns to good

Homes turn to jails
Can turns to should
A corkscrew is straight
Saints turn to whores
But don't send to ask whose head is on the plate:
It's yours!

All men must work or scheme to get money
To buy food and shelter for their families
The Greatest Profit is king of this jungle
That's how vices become virtues!
What follows?
When the judge's throat is cut
It's done by his own law!

The scientist who builds his life on truth
The judge who convicts only after proof
The son who never bore his father's curse
The king who doesn't ride behind a hearse.
When things like this are seen
The world will be a better place
Than it has been

Evil creates its own remedy!
Till then we stagger round and lose our breath
In that old Side Show called The Dance of Death

In the famous dance of the seven deadly veils
Bad turns to good
Homes turn to jails
Can turns to should
A corkscrew is straight
Saints turn to whores
But don't send to ask whose head is on the plate:
It's yours!

The MAN *enters. He is much older — tired, filthy and
exhausted. The stone has become a large rock. He carries it on
his shoulders. It doubles him up and makes him stagger.*

MAN. Let me stay at your inn.

GIRL. Any money?

MAN. No.

GIRL. Move on.

MAN. A cup of water.

GIRL. What're you carrying?

MAN. Give me some bread.

GIRL. What's that?

MAN. A stone.

GIRL. Where're you taking it?

MAN. The stone mason's house.

GIRL. How much does he pay you?

MAN. I won't know till I get there.

GIRL. Have you carried it far?

MAN. O yes. I keep asking people where he lives and they just point on and say further. I'm tired and hungry and cold and the stone gets heavier everyday. But I can't give up now. All my sufferings would be wasted.

GIRL. Put it down.

MAN. No! This is a pub. People keep coming and going. It might be stolen. (*Groans.*) The nights are terrible! Once I could sleep with it on my chest. Now I have to lie on it.

GIRL. What loyalty! (*Aside.*) This is the idiot I'm looking for. Carried that all this way for nothing! — He won't have his hand in the till the moment my back's turned. (*To the* MAN:) Put it down. It's all right, it's gone closing time.

MAN. Thank you.

The GIRL *helps him to put the stone on the ground. He sits on it and sings.*

The Cliffs, or Bad Dream

The white cliffs that stand by the sea
Every night the black water stirs itself
And leaves its bed
And seizes the cliffs
And takes them down to a hole
Under the sea
And in the dark like a blind torturer
It tortures them with pain and supplice
And before there is light it sends them back
To the edge of the sea

And they stand and stare at the black water
Stirring listlessly in its sleep
All day

GIRL. The mason used to be my customer. He's dead. Sorry to
bring bad news.

MAN. What shall I do? He can't be dead!

GIRL. We need disaster to kick us up the arse now and then or
we'd never move. You know what they say, a diamond's only
granite that's had more to bear. I need a chucker out. There's
a man in the back — he's been boozing and stuffing for twelve
months! Make him cough up and chuck him out. Then you can
wash the dishes. The roof needs mending. And the garden
wouldn't know what a spade was if it saw one. A few rows of
peas and potatoes. I've nothing against home-grown produce.
You get one good meal a day and your drink — but I limit the
drink, publicans should abstain. And you can watch me
dance — you'd never afford the prices! (*Feels his arm.*) Right
little porter. Feed you up and who knows, I could be very
friendly. (*Calls.*) Pig! Out! The trotter man's here! (*Off,
grunting and grumbling.*) Hear it? (*Calls.*) Pig, the pork
butcher's come with his knife!

TRAMP (*off*). Who's blidy drunk my drink while I was asleep?

Noises. The TRAMP *comes on.*

TRAMP. Who're you callin pig you blidy sow? This blidy run-
down sty! Give us a drink. (*Sees the* MAN.) Who — (*Recognises
him.*) Ho ho. The late Mr Money! Are you sniffin round that
she-animal? She only does it for money and believe me laddie
you'd get better satisfaction puttin your little penny in the
slot of a china piggy bank.

GIRL (*gives the* TRAMP *a bill*). Six month's lodgings and good
living. Pay up.

TRAMP. No!

GIRL (*to the* MAN:) Do him.

TRAMP. Mr Rockerfella? He won't throw his pal out on the
streets! He'd step aside to let a fly pass.

GIRL. Then he won't stand idle while I'm robbed. (*Shows her
wrist to the* MAN.) See that mark? Him, the swine.

TRAMP. The only way to get sense into her is hammer it in.

The MAN *hits him.*

TRAMP (*blinks. Turns to the* GIRL). Has your booze suddenly
   got better or did he hit me?

The MAN *hits him. The* TRAMP *takes out his knife.*

TRAMP (*through his teeth*): You little swine now.

A fight. They roll on the floor. The TRAMP *flails with the
knife. They go into a clinch. The* MAN *tries to break the*
TRAMP's *neck by forcing his chin back. The* GIRL *speaks in
the silence.*

GIRL. You say do as you would be done by
   But you don't know what you do
   So you do as you are done by
   That's all you are able to do

The TRAMP *bites the man. The* MAN *gouges the* TRAMP's *eyes.
They both dive for the knife. The* TRAMP *gets it. He lashes out.
The knife sticks in the floor. The* MAN *knocks the* TRAMP *out.
The* TRAMP *is still. The* MAN *doubles over gasping for breath.
He rips open the* TRAMP's *pockets. He takes out the coins.*

GIRL. At last! Money.

MAN (*turns away gasping*). Mine.

GIRL. . . . All right lovie. Lug him out the back. I'll see you're all
   right.

The MAN, *still gasping for breath, drags out the* TRAMP. *The*
GIRL *prepares for the dance. She brings food, drink, a pillow
and seven white sheets. She goes out again. The* MAN *returns.*

MAN (*counting his money*). One, two . . . . six. (*He takes the coin
from his pocket.*) Seven. (*He sees the food and goes to it.*)

GIRL (*off, harshly*): Wait!

MAN. I'll pay for —

GIRL (*off, harshly*): Sit!

The MAN *sits. The* GIRL *comes on naked.*

GIRL. This is my famous dance of the seven deadly veils.

INSTRUCTIONS FOR THE DANCE:

The GIRL *begins by dancing wildly. She stops seven times.
Each time she stops she asks the* MAN *for a coin, he gives it to*

*her, and she covers herself with a white sheet. Each time she
dances a little more slowly. After the first coin she gives the
MAN the food and drink and the pillow to sit on. After each
coin he eats and drinks a little more slowly. The dance ends
with the MAN crawling back to his stone to sleep and the
GIRL stumbling to a standstill. She is shrouded from head to
foot and cries quietly under her shrouds. These are the lines
she uses to ask for the seven coins:*

First coin for the meat.
Second coin for the plate.
Third coin for the wine.
Fourth coin for the cup.
Fifth coin for the bread.
Sixth coin for the roof over your head.
Seventh coin for the dance.

MAN. Okay grub. Didn't think much of the dance.

GIRL (*crying quietly*). So naked. So naked. Cover me.

The MAN has gone to sleep. A POLICEMAN enters.

POLICEMAN. What's going on then? (*Sees the* GIRL.)
Disgusting! (*Slaps her face under the shrouds. She starts to
come round. He kicks the* MAN.) Don't sit on the ground, it's
an offence to drop litter.

MAN (*wakes*). What?

POLICEMAN. No doubt you've had a nasty dream so you won't
be at all surprised when I tell you there's a corpse on the front
doorstep and I'm arresting you for murder.

MAN. I didn't do it!

POLICEMAN (*picks up the knife*). Doesn't look like it. (*To the*
GIRL:) I arrest you for performing in an indecent show.

GIRL. I'm an artist!

POLICEMAN. Twist the judge's balls and he may believe you.
(*Points to the props.*) Pick them up.

*The MAN and the GIRL collect the props. The MAN carries
the stone and the GIRL the other things. They leave with the
POLICEMAN.*

Scene Four

Court. The JUDGE *brings his chair on. Sits. The* POLICEMAN
comes on.

JUDGE. Let's start.

POLICEMAN (*calls off*). This way!

> *The* MAN *and the* GIRL *come in. The* MAN *is without the
> stone.*

GIRL (*recognizes the* JUDGE). My landlord.

POLICEMAN. Silence!

JUDGE. Another word and I'll charge you with contempt.
  Constable?

POLICEMAN. I was proceeding down Bartholomew Street in the
  course of my duty when I chanced upon a male figure alyin
  recumbent in the gutter. I disturbed it with my toe but
  achieved no response. I noticed that it had a three-day's
  growth of beard and concluded it was an Irishman. I took the
  fact that it was in the gutter at eleven in the forenoon as
  corroboratory evidence. Naturally, therefore, the man was
  drunk or asleep or both. Having already elicited no response
  with the end of my toe – the little one, sir – I concluded he
  was asleep. I thereupon lent forward to examine the breath.
  Imagine the surprise with which I discovered that although a
  stale smell of beer did indeed linger round his mouth it was –
  if I may use the image – a smell such as you get outside the
  door of a pub when it's locked at closing time. I.e. the man
  was dead. He lay outside a house of ill-repute –

GIRL. I object –

POLICEMAN. – known as 'The Inn of the Seven Deadly Veils',
  which establishment I've long had my eye on. I entered. I
  found the female accused in the last stages of a most lascivious
  performance –

GIRL. Liar!

POLICEMAN. – which, I see from her statement, she calls a
  dance.

GIRL. I'm an artist!

POLICEMAN. The male accused was recumbent upon the floor in a lethargic condition. I concluded this was the result of him just having finished killing the body on the doorstep.

GIRL. I demand a retrial!

JUDGE. The inn in question is an old established business. The account books show that all taxes, dues and rents are paid up to date. We've had no complaints in the past — not to speak of. I conclude — without at all doubting your word officer —

POLICEMAN. Thankyou sir.

JUDGE. — or the obscenity it was your misfortune to observe —

POLICEMAN. That night when I looked down at the curly heads of my little tots sleeping so innocently in their beds I was overwhelmed with fury that these things can be.

JUDGE. — that we may nevertheless not yet have the whole story. Madam, this court offers you its protection. Any threats that have been made to you can be dealt with. Help the court!

GIRL. Ah your honour. Well. That man — I should say monster — broke into my home, killed my best friend — just after he'd asked for my hand in marriage and offered me his protection in business affairs (the damages are going to be enormous!) — stole food and drink and forced me to perform a disgusting obscenity the memory of which will make me blush with shame to the roots of my hair even when as a result of this it goes prematurely grey.

JUDGE. Tch tch. (*To the* MAN:) I presume you throw yourself on the mercy of the court?

MAN. I didn't do it! I hit him but not that hard! I'm a respectable citizen.

JUDGE. Look at your clothes.

MAN. I got like this carrying a stone.

JUDGE. What stone?

MAN. A man asked me to carry it.

JUDGE. Why?

MAN. I don't know.

JUDGE. But you said yes?

MAN. It was a small stone then. It grew.

JUDGE. Don't feign madness here.

MAN. It grew!

JUDGE. If you're resolved to fritter away the court's goodwill on —

MAN. I paid for what I got. With good money. She's still got it.

JUDGE. Madam?

GIRL. Well.

JUDGE. Am I to be disappointed in everyone? Constable!

The POLICEMAN *takes the seven coins from the* GIRL.

JUDGE. Is this your money?

MAN. Yes.

JUDGE. What's their value Constable?

POLICEMAN (*reads the coins*): Pride. Greed. Lust. Envy —

MAN. That's not my money!

JUDGE. You said it was!

POLICEMAN (*reads*): Gluttony. Anger. Sloth.

GIRL. No wonder he smiled when he paid. He's a swindler! Paying with bad coin!

MAN. It's changed.

JUDGE. And the stone grew and the Irishman died of cold.

MAN (*points to the* POLICEMAN). He did it! He must have! He thought he was drunk. Gave him a kick — with his little toe! — and killed him! I'm taking the rap!

JUDGE. Tch tch.

POLICEMAN. Do I have to answer the wild accusations flung at my head sir?

JUDGE. I think you should. This is a court of justice before it's a court of law. The accused is allowed his say. Of course you may preserve a dignified — under the circumstances, even pained — silence and allow the court to draw a conclusion based on the contrast between your calm stoical demeanour and the violent hysteria of the accused and the coincidence that blue is its favourite colour.

MAN. He killed him!

POLICEMAN. I elect to defend myself because I consider it the duty of every good citizen to co-operate fully with the police which happens to be myself.

JUDGE. If only more thought so.

POLICEMAN. I've been kicking people all my life. I've kicked them in all postures from every conceivable angle at every time of the day and night in all seasons of the year. I'm a skilled kicker by profession and a cognoscente of kicking by inclination. I think I may say — with my reputation for expert kicking hanging in the balance — that my kick is controlled. Now if the accused is suggesting that I kicked a man and accidentally killed him, that suggestion is palpably ludicrous.

MAN. He killed him on purpose!

JUDGE. Pride, greed, lust, envy, gluttony, anger, sloth.

MAN. I'm not a murderer!

JUDGE. Constable?

POLICEMAN. I'm not vindictive. The accusations hurled at me today — I don't usually indulge in language but I think the word is appropriate — come in the course of duty. I brush them aside. But. We have to protect the innocent public.

GIRL. Right!

POLICEMAN. For their sake I demand the utmost severity. Thankyou.

JUDGE. Young man?

MAN. I didn't do it!

JUDGE. But offer no proof. (*Chinks the coins patiently.*)

Poem of Naivety

MAN (*recites*):
When I left home my parents
Gave me seven coins for the journey
They said if the journey is long
And these coins don't reach
Look in your soul
There you will find
All that is needful

To thine ownself be true
The rest will follow

JUDGE (*leans forward and picks something from the* MAN). You
haven't got a soul. You can't carry a stone *and* a soul. A soul is
the heaviest thing in the world. When you took up the stone
your soul fell out of the bottom of your trousers. (*Cracks his
fingers.*) You have only a louse — which *is* an anagram of soul
if you add an E. But the E is silent! (*Formally.*) The sentence!
I am a philanthropic nature. You strayed from the narrow
way. It's not my intention to chase you off it altogether. I
shall guide you back to it — set your nose to the grindstone,
your feet on the path of duty to your master —

MAN. She said he was dead!

GIRL. Liar!

JUDGE. I order that the stone which you have carried till now
shall in future be chained to you —

MAN. No!

JUDGE. — and removed only at the mason's house. That will
certainly stop you straying far from the narrow way.

MAN. No!

POLICEMAN. When you're chained you won't have the strength
to argue.

The POLICEMAN *takes the* MAN *out.*

GIRL. I turn my back on life. I'll go in a nunnery.

JUDGE. Impossible. It's your duty to run your inn and dance for
the public.

GIRL. If that's the court's ruling.

JUDGE. But I'll have to raise the rent.

GIRL. Do what!

JUDGE. Double it. I must ensure that only a good class of person
can afford to get in. No more hooliganism.

GIRL. I can't pay anymore! We're screwing the customers now!

JUDGE. Think about it. And the alternative.

GIRL (*spits*). A fly in my mouth.

The JUDGE *and the* GIRL *leave.*

Scene Five

Road. Empty stage. The MAN *enters. He is old and broken. The stone is very big. It's chained to his back. He staggers forwards in sudden lurches.*

MAN. I came to a river. I stepped in the ferryboat. My stone was heavy. The boat sank. The ferryman beat me with his pole. I climbed far up in the mountain. I dragged the stone after me. Yes. Inch by inch. Year after year. At the top I came to the source of the river. The land was spread before me. In the distance a white cloud came up from the earth: steam or smoke. Then I knew: dust! The quarry! I started to hurry down. O the idiocy of it! The journey up was light, light, light to the journey down! The stone dragged me after it as if it was alive. The mountain was steep. I fought all the way. Year after year. At nights I propped it on a ledge and slept. An animal under its stone. Often it rolled away. I woke up. Dragged down in the dark by my chain. I cry at the stupidity of my life. Wasted on dragging a stone to somewhere I don't know for a reason I don't understand.

    BOY *comes in.*

MAN. Help me put this down.

BOY. Who are you? (*Helps the* MAN *lower the stone to the ground.*) Why did they do this to you?

MAN. I'm looking for the mason's house.

BOY. You're almost there.

MAN. Almost — ? You know it? Where? Where?

BOY. Follow the road over the field. It's down in the lane on the other side.

MAN. His house is here? I've reached his house?

BOY (*points*). In five minutes.

MAN. The end . . . The end . . . Sometimes I thought I was lost. Taken the wrong road. I'd never get there. But after a few months I saw the cloud. Far in the distance. For an hour or more. Sometimes even at night in the full moon. I knew one day I'd be here, at the last steps . . .

BOY. Shall I help?

MAN. No — it's easy.

The BOY *goes out.*

MAN.

Help, or Song of Experience

You come smiling to offer service
You bring two good hands to help
Your face is open and guileless

But you find you are too weak to help
The grain you wanted to take to the farmers
Is in a tower — with guards at the door

You haven't even got the things that are yours
To get them you have to fight
The steps of your journey measure out a duel
And the weapons are chosen by your enemy

He goes.

Scene Six

Outside the MASON's *House. Empty stage. An old*
WASHERWOMAN *comes on with a washtub and washboard. She
wears a floral apron. She washes white sheets.*

The MAN *comes in.*

MAN. Is this the mason's house?

WOMAN. Yes.

MAN. Is the mason in?

WOMAN. He expecting you?

MAN. He told me to bring this stone.

WOMAN. Put it down.

MAN (*puts the stone down*). Call him.

WOMAN. He won't come out. You'll have to go in. (*Points to the
stone.*) And leave that there. He won't have any work in the
house. (*She takes a key from her apron pocket and throws it at*

him.) Catch.

MAN (*unfastens his chain*). There.

WOMAN. Now wash your face and hands. He won't have
  any dirt in the house. Says there's enough muck in the yard.
  The windows are always covered. Keeps the dust out.
  Curtains never drawn. The yard's a muck hole. Dirt hangs in
  the air. (*She brushes his coat. He washes in the tub.*) I do all
  the washing. They get black working in the yard. And he —
  (*Gestures to the house.*) — gets worse on the roads. (*Hands
  him the towel.*) It's a lot of work.

MAN (*dries himself and hands the towel back*). Thank you.

WOMAN (*looks at him*). Much better. Something else he's fussy
  about — I have to ask everyone — any money?

MAN. Yes.

WOMAN. Fetch it out.

MAN (*takes the seven coins*). That's all.

WOMAN. See? — covered in muck. Can't see what they are.
  Greasy dirty things. In the tub. (*She washes the coins.*)

MAN. What's the machine in the yard? A huge concrete
  rhinoceros with great steel paws.

WOMAN. Look, like new! (*Dries the coins.*) What have we got?
  You're well off. (*Reads the coins:*) Prudence, soberness,
  courage, justice, love — (*Drops a coin.*) Butterfingers. (*Fishes
  it out.*) Hope. Mint condition! Well the mason will be glad. I
  expect he'll ask you to stay. In you go. Can't stop and chatter.
  Work to do. All this to hang up yet. And wipe your feet.

The WOMAN *goes out with the tub and board. The* MAN *waits
till she's gone. He fastens the chain round him as if it was
locked. He picks up the stone and goes.*

Scene Seven

The MASON's *House. It is dark. The* MASON *is much older. He
kneels by a bucket and a small heap of stones.*

MASON (*mumbling to himself*). Dirt on the tables. In the clocks.

Damn woman cheats. I shut the doors. Block up the keyholes —

A knock.

MASON. Come. Quickly.

The MAN *comes in. He carries the stone.*

MASON. Take that out! I won't have that in here! Out! (*Calls.*) Woman! (*To* MAN:) Who are you! What d'you — ?

MAN. You told me to come.

MASON. Take that out!

MAN. Long ago.

MASON. Long ago?

MAN. You gave me a stone. I had seven coins.

MASON (*yells*). Woman! (*To* MAN:) Seven coins? Gold. Yes, perhaps. Long ago. You were a boy. (*Calls.*) Woman! (*To* MAN:) You've taken your time.

MAN. The stone was heavy.

MASON. But you brought it. I remember now. Good family background. Thrifty people. They gave you the right start. Well — have you still got it?

MAN. Yes.

MASON. Washed?

MAN. Yes.

MASON. Show me, show me.

The MAN *takes out the seven gold coins.*

MASON. Yes, sparkling! Gold. New after all these years! Prudence, soberness, courage, justice, honesty, love — and what was the other one? Hope. Now you shall be rewarded. I'll make you a servant in my house.

MAN. Why did the coins change?

MASON. But I don't know why she didn't unfasten your stone. She's got the key. Silly woman!

MAN. Why did the stone grow?

MASON (*blandly*). We get older. We carry the weight of the world on our shoulders. We make heavy weather. (*He picks up*

*a stone from the pile, holds it over the bucket, squeezes, and
the blood trickles down. Calls:)* Woman!

MAN. Why did the coins change?

MASON. Change?

MAN. From justice to anger, from hope to pride?

MASON. They didn't change.

MAN. From temperance to greed, from love to envy?

MASON. You got confused. Easiest thing. I told you — they
make heavy weather.

MAN. They changed.

MASON. You couldn't tell what they were. Under that dirt?
Look at them now. Prudence, soberness. Look! Justice,
honesty —

MAN. They changed.

MASON *(takes a stone and starts to squeeze it. Blood drips).*
Servants don't argue. *(Stops squeezing.)* I remember you were
a bit difficult.

MAN. I tell you they changed.

MASON. You say that like an idiot! *(Squeezes again. More
blood.)* I'm afraid I can't let you work in my house after all.
You'll have to work in the yard.

MAN. Why was the stone so heavy?

MASON. I see you're a trouble maker. No wonder she didn't
unchain you. She knew what she was doing. *(Calls:)* Woman!

MAN. Why did I waste my life carrying your load?

MASON *(squeezing stones).* You've ruined your only chance. I
wash my hands of you. You're just more dirt that's got in
through the door. You've lived with dirt so long you're as full
of it as the worm under its stone. Fool, arguing! I can get
blood out of a stone — and you stand there questioning me?

MAN. Why did the stone grow?

MASON. A servant bringing dirt in my house. My house is a
palace. Making me shout when I reverence silence. What? Why?
Who? In my yard there's a machine. You saw it? Huge. With a
beak. People bring their stones to my yard all day. The .

machine crushes them down to *this* — heart-size to fit in the hand. But it can't get the blood. They're passed to me. The master-craftsman. And so —. (*He squeezes a stone. It trickles.*) What else? What's at the end of the road? The hole in the road. Why does it take so long? You march till you die! Why are you chained? Because I don't trust you! —

The MAN *leaves the stone and comes to the* MASON.

MAN. Look! Envy — greed — !

MASON. What — ! (*Calls:*) Woman! Foreman!

The MAN *grabs the* MASON *and shows him the coins.*

MAN. Sloth — gluttony —

MASON. Help! Help!

MAN (*holds the coins in front of the* MASON's *face*). Look! Look! Lust!

MASON. No!

MAN. Pride! Anger! (*Drops the coins.*) And now I shall kill you.

MASON. You won't. No. There's no reason. (*Calls:*) Help! Talk. Discuss. You're right. You must be. If it means so much. Tell me. Go to the window. Look. I'm rich. (*Calmer.*) Yes how natural. You envy my quarry, my yard. (*Still more calm.*) I'll make you a partner. It's time I had new blood — (*Quickly.*) new — the enterprise needs new management. You're our sort. (*Wheedling.*) I applaud all this. Initiative. It's time for a change. The new men are —

The MAN *kills the* MASON *by crushing him with the stone. He stares at the body for a moment. He looks up.*

MAN (*calls calmly*): Woman! Call the men to break the machine in the yard.

MAN (*off*). Do you want water to wash your hands?

s *calmly*): No need. They are clean.